Problematizing the Profession of Teaching From an Existential Perspective

D1521747

Studies in the Philosophy of Education

Series Editor

John E. Petrovic
The University of Alabama

Problematizing the Profession of Teaching From an Existential Perspective (2022)
edited by Aaron S. Zimmerman

Love in Education & the Art of Living (2020)
edited by Becky L. Noël Smith and Randy Hewitt

Blame Teachers: The Emotional Reasons for Educational Reform (2015)
by Steven P. Jones

Technologies of Government: Politics and Power in the "Information Age" (2014)
by Benjamin Baez

Dystopia & Education: Insights into Theory, Praxis, and Policy in an Age of Utopia-Gone-Wrong (2013)
edited by Jessica A. Heybach and Eric C. Sheffield

Problematizing the Profession of Teaching From an Existential Perspective

Editor

Aaron S. Zimmerman
Texas Tech University

INFORMATION AGE PUBLISHING, INC.
Charlotte, NC • www.infoagepub.com

Library of Congress Cataloging-in-Publication Data

CIP record for this book is available from the Library of Congress
http://www.loc.gov

ISBNs: 978-1-64802-944-8 (Paperback)

978-1-64802-945-5 (Hardcover)

978-1-64802-946-2 (ebook)

CONTENTS

CONSIDERING TEACHING AND TEACHER DEVELOPMENT FROM AN EXISTENTIAL PERSPECTIVE

An Introduction

Aaron S. Zimmerman
College of Education at Texas Tech University

Contemporary paradigms of teacher education seek to delineate what beginning teachers must know and be able to do (Darling-Hammond & Bransford, 2005). This delineation establishes a shared set of standards for the teaching profession and for programs of teacher education (Grossman & McDonald, 2008). While these standards may be integral to the endeavor of preparing new professionals, it is important that teacher educators not overlook the fact that becoming a teacher is, in addition to being a function of professional training, an ontological journey.

As an introduction to the chapters included in this edited book, I will begin by highlighting three existential dimensions of being and becoming a teacher: the revelation of meaning through mood, the inescapability of wrestling with irrationality, and the responsibility of individual choice. While these three dimensions do not represent an exhaustive description of the philosophy of existentialism, these three dimensions do highlight

Problematizing the Profession of Teaching From an Existential Perspective, pp. vii–xxiii
Copyright © 2022 by Information Age Publishing
www.infoagepub.com

unique elements of teaching that may be obfuscated when teaching is conceptualized solely as work fueled by technical expertise, instrumental know-how, and rational knowledge.

ACKNOWLEDGING THE PROFESSIONAL DIMENSIONS OF TEACHER EDUCATION

I will begin, first, by acknowledging three dimensions of teacher education that can be argued to be essential to all programs of teacher preparation. Programs of teacher education are responsible for preparing practitioners who are accountable to the teaching profession; hence, upon graduation and certification, beginning teachers must be able to teach—and to think about teaching—in ways that are shared by the profession (Ball & Forzani, 2009; Darling-Hammond & Bransford, 2005; Feiman-Nemser, 2001; Lampert, 2010; Murray, 2008). With this goal in mind, programs of teacher education must provide beginning teachers with opportunities to reconsider beliefs, to acquire knowledge, and to develop practices.

Reconsidering Beliefs

Prospective teachers enter the profession with certain presumptions about the work of teaching. Prospective teachers were once themselves students in schools, and these experiences of schooling tend to shape what these individuals believe about knowledge, teaching, learning, and schooling (Britzman, 1986; Lortie, 1975; Norman & Spencer, 2005). For example, prospective teachers who relished their own experiences in classrooms may presume that all students share this enthusiasm. Additionally, prospective teachers who themselves succeeded in school by assiduously taking notes and completing homework assignments may presume that all students can learn successfully via this method (Holt-Reynolds, 1992). Relatedly, prospective teachers may have experienced, as students, exclusively teacher-centered instruction, leading these prospective teachers to believe that teaching is, in essence, a matter of *showing* and *telling* (Barlow & Reddish, 2006; Murray, 2008). For all of these reasons, prospective teachers may enter into their professional preparation with a reductive and problematic set of presumptions (e.g., all students like school; teacher-centered instruction is effective for all students). Therefore, prospective teachers should begin the endeavor of learning to teach by becoming aware of and potentially reconsidering the beliefs that they bring to the classroom (Bird et al., 1993; Deemer, 2004; Pajares, 1993; Yerrick et al., 1997).

Acquiring Knowledge

Because teaching is sometimes assumed to be second nature (Labaree, 2000; Murray, 2008), and, because many prospective teachers have spent most of their lives observing teachers in schools (albeit from the limited perspective of being a student), prospective teachers may enter into their professional preparation assuming that they already know how to teach; additionally, beginning teachers may believe that their content knowledge is sufficient to ensure their pedagogical effectiveness. Scholars have argued, however, that there is a significant amount of professional knowledge (which cannot be assumed to be self-evident) that beginning teachers must acquire before they are able to teach proficiently and ambitiously (Ball & Forzani, 2009; Darling-Hammond & Bransford, 2005; Kersting et al., 2012; Shulman, 1987).

For example, professional teachers should be able to lead an effective classroom discussion (Boerst et al., 2011). Enacting this complex classroom practice requires not only pedagogical knowledge (Chapin et al., 2009) but also knowledge about how to anticipate, interpret, and build upon what students are thinking (Ball et al., 2008; Lampert, 2001; Stein et al., 2008). A mathematics teacher must, therefore, not only know mathematics; the mathematics teacher must also know how to represent mathematical ideas in ways that make these ideas comprehensible to others (Ball et al., 2008; Shulman, 1987) and how to interpret student thinking productively (Kersting et al., 2012; Lampert et al., 2013). Beginning teachers must also be able to interpret curriculum (Remillard & Bryans, 2004), to craft informative assessments (Bell & Cowie, 2001), and to manage behavior in the classroom (Emmer & Stough, 2000). Because these practices all require sophisticated knowledge (e.g., principles of learning theory and educational psychology), all beginning teachers should be expected to acquire this requisite professional knowledge through diligent study.

Developing Practices

Given the complexity of the classroom (see, e.g., Doyle, 1977), becoming a proficient classroom teacher requires intentional, focused, and consistent practice (Bronkhorst et al., 2014; Grossman, Compton, et al., 2009). In order to develop their pedagogical expertise, beginning teachers must rehearse a number of sophisticated practices (e.g., managing a discussion; modeling a procedure; assessing student work; responding to student resistance) and must receive constructive feedback on their enactment of these practices from experts (Berliner, 2001; Grossman et al., 2007; Hiebert et al., 2007; Lampert et al., 2013). If beginning teachers are left on their own to invent or assess their own practices, beginning teachers may find themselves to be in a vulnerable (and potentially overwhelming) position (Cochran-Smith, 2012; Lortie, 1975). In order to be considered professional teachers, beginning teachers must master specific practices that are understood to be shared practices of professional teaching (Forzani, 2014; McDonald et al., 2013). For a professional teacher, "[d]ecisions about what to do are not appropriately rooted in personal preferences or experiences but are instead based on professionally justified knowledge and on the moral imperatives of the role" (Ball & Forzani, 2009, p. 500). Learning to teach, therefore, implies being apprenticed into a professional role where the work of teaching is not idiosyncratic but is, instead, governed by shared ways of thinking and acting (Ball & Forzani, 2009; Dottin, 2009; Grossman et al., 2009; Lampert, 2010).

THREE EXISTENTIAL DIMENSIONS
OF TEACHER DEVELOPMENT

Reconsidering beliefs, acquiring knowledge, and developing practices are, as I have argued, critical professional dimensions of learning to teach. If programs of teacher education fail to delineate what it means to be a professional teacher—that is, unless beginning teachers receive clear messages about what all teachers should know and be able to do—beginning teachers may have difficulty coping with their professional responsibilities (Cochran-Smith, 2012; Friedman, 2006; Grossman & McDonald, 2008; Martin, 2004).

This paradigm, however, may be incomplete. The endeavor of learning to teach is composed of both *shared, professional dimensions* as well as *subjective, personal dimensions*. As beginning teachers reconsider beliefs, acquire knowledge, and develop practices, they will, inevitably, also attempt to make sense of their own experiences in the classroom. As a result, beginning teachers will filter the profession's beliefs, knowledge, and practices through their own subjective meanings. For this reason, the philosophy of Existentialism becomes an especially appropriate and generative theoretical framework through which to explore the phenomenon of becoming a teacher.

To develop this argument, I draw on three anecdotes from three beginning teachers. As an instructor of one of the courses during these students' fifth-year teaching internship, I was able to inquire into my students' concerns. Unsurprisingly, these beginning teachers were concerned with managing their students' behavior; they worried as to whether or not they were effective teachers; they wrestled with how to stay true to their own pedagogical values while still achieving the learning objectives of their school's curriculum (Smagorinsky et al., 2004; Veenman, 1984). I also began to develop the impression, however, that many of the issues that these beginning teachers described to me involved not only professional concerns (e.g., how to manage a classroom; how to lead a productive classroom discussion) but existential concerns as well (e.g., Do I have what it takes to be a teacher? Do I still want to be a teacher?).

In an attempt to research these beginning teachers' lived experiences (van Manen, 1990), I interviewed a set of my former students who had just completed their first year of full-time teaching. I asked these beginning teachers to narrate for me, in rich detail, meaningful and memorable experiences from their first year of teaching. The anecdotes that these teachers (represented through pseudonyms) shared with me illuminated some of the existential dimensions of becoming a teacher, including the revelation of meaning through mood, the inescapability of wrestling with irrationality, and the responsibility of individual choice.

The Revelation of Meaning Through Mood

First, let us consider the anecdote narrated by Ingrid in which she describes trying to set up her classroom two days before her first year of full-time teaching:

> I remember [that] I had this panic moment when I was sitting in my class-room, and it was so hot, 95 degrees and it didn't have air conditioning, and I was sweating through my clothes and I just sat there and I thought, "Oh my god ... I don't know, I don't know, I don't know. I don't know what I'm going to say. I don't know who's going to be in here. I don't know how to set up these desks ... I could never imagine being left in this situation.... This is overwhelming.... That was just the worst, most upsetting feeling ... I remember looking in the mirror at the end of the day, and I was sweating off my face, my hair was wet, I was so hot, and I looked like I was beaten down ... I can't believe I'm screwing it up so badly ... I remember think-ing, trying to think of a logical way to pull myself out of it without making myself look like an idiot, without exposing myself as the fraud ... I thought, "And you thought you were a big shot.... Now you found out this is really hard and you're not really as good as you thought you were.... If you think you were coming in as some kind of young phenom, trust me, you're not. You're coming in as an idiot.

Ingrid, in this moment, is not only grappling with an intellectual problem (i.e., How do I prepare for my first day of class?) but is also overcome by a very distinct mood. Notably, Ingrid's mood is not only triggered by her thoughts but also by space (the empty classroom), time (feeling that time is running out), and body (feeling exhausted and "beaten down"). In this moment, Ingrid does not experience teaching as a solely cognitive endeavor (e.g., What are the beliefs, knowledge, and practices that I require in order to teach well?). Instead, she finds herself in a very powerful moment of lived experience that has existential ramifications. Specifically, within the mood in which she finds herself, Ingrid definitively concludes that she is not a "phenom" but, rather, an "idiot," and a "fraud."

Professional principles of teaching (e.g., how to organize classroom space for productive learning) emphasize what teachers should know and be able to do; yet this *cognitive* emphasis on beliefs, knowledge, and know-how deemphasizes the revelatory potential of *moods* (Garcia & Lewis, 2014). As Heidegger (1962) argues, beings-in-the-world are always concerned with the issue of meaning, and meaning is revealed through our being-in-the-world. If we accept Heidegger's fundamental ontological premise (i.e., that *to be* necessarily implies being concerned with meaning), then, we must accept the fact that meaning matters to beginning teachers and that this meaning is revealed to beginning teachers not only through what they learn in their teacher education but also through the moods in which they find themselves. Heidegger refers to mood as a state of *Befindlichkeit*—to find oneself tuned to the world in a particular way. Through these particular "tunings," meaning is revealed.

Therefore, I argue that regardless of the beliefs, knowledge, and practices with which beginning teachers are equipped, beginning teachers may live through their classroom experiences in particular ways (i.e., they may find themselves moods, such as the "overwhelming" mood of feeling "beaten down"). These moods, in turn, hold the potential to reveal unique insights to these beginning teachers (e.g., "That was just the worst, most upsetting feelings ... [I'm] coming in as an idiot"). The critical point is that *being*—that is, moments of lived experience that involve not only cognitions but also the lived realities of body, space, and time (van Manen, 1990)—may prompt beginning teachers to consider not only practical questions such as, "What is the most effective way to set up the classroom?" but also subjective questions such as, "Am I a fraud?"

The Inescapability of Wrestling with Irrationality

Next, let us consider an anecdote by Kathryn in which she describes a dilemma of classroom management:

There was one day.... It was before [a] test ... [In class, the students are] squirrely, and I understand. That's the thing: *I understand!*, I want to [say to them,] "You know what, I understand completely, but at the same time you have to work." And I *did* explain that [to them]. But [the students] just went nuts … and…. When [I] lose it, I don't know…. When [I] lose it like that, [I'm] like, "STOP!" … I don't know, I don't even know what to do anymore, because I'm just standing there screaming, and it's like, *I'm an idiot!*... [On that day,] I just was like, "AHHHHHHHH! Your test is in 2 days!... And some of you are just running around the classroom!" … I would just revert to this one phrase, which is not good at all, but they would just be jumping around and kicking stuff and I'd be like, "WHAT ARE YOU DOING?!", and after awhile it's just not effective to just say, "What are you doing?!" because they don't know what they're doing. Why am I not doing something about [this]? I'm letting them do this. But how do I make them stop? I don't know. And they don't know. And we're looking at each other: *We don't know!* And so then they just keep doing whatever they want and I don't know what I want to do so I'm just, "AHHHH! I don't know what to do!" So, then I'll just be like, "Good thing class is over! Bye!" It's like the feeling of being trapped.

The endeavor of learning to teach, when conceived in terms of the professional dimensions of beliefs, knowledge, and practices, implies that there are beliefs that must be revised; there is knowledge that must be learned; and there are practices that must be mastered. Inherent in this paradigm is the assumption that the beliefs, knowledge, and practices generated by and for the profession of teaching have rational justification (Cochran-Smith, 2005a, 2005b) and that the beliefs, knowledge, and practices cultivated in teacher education lead, causally, to more effective teaching (Marzano, 2007; Windschitl et al., 2012). Indeed, as mentioned earlier in this introduction, such rational justification is critical if teaching is to be considered a profession in which teachers' curricular and instructional decisions are rooted in shared, professional judgment rather than in idiosyncrasy or personal preference (Ball & Forzani, 2009; Dottin, 2009; Lortie, 1975).

In the above anecdote, however, Kathryn is unable to make sense of her dilemma rationally; instead, she is caught in a paradoxical knot of her own thinking and feeling (Wagner, 1987). She feels sympathy for her students, and yet she is angry with them. She yells at her students, "What are you doing?!" even as she rationalizes that this is an ineffective way to manage the classroom. In this classroom moment, Kathryn's actions and beliefs are in conflict, and, yet she feels "trapped," compelled to respond in an ineffective and emotionally exhausting manner. Kathryn admits that this is a paradox that she does not know how to resolve and that she has been confronted with a classroom dilemma that appears to be insoluble.

The philosophical framework of existentialism can help us to appreciate Kathryn's experience of wrestling with paradoxes that seem to have no rational solutions. Kierkegaard (1946a, 1946b) argued that rationality can never fully explain an individual's existence or the choices that an individual must make; rather, the meaningful choices that an individual makes are governed by both objective truth and subjective truth. In *Fear and Trembling*, Kierkegaard (1946c) uses the story of Abraham's attempted sacrifice of Isaac to illustrate how an irrational commitment to subjective truth can play a critical role in human existence. Kierkegaard underscores how Abraham's attempted murder of his son is motivated by the irrational assumption that murder might be a God-pleasing act; Abraham, in this moment, defers to the religious rather than the ethical. In other words, Abraham's actions were inspired not by the rationality of an ethical system but instead by an irrational faith. Indeed, Abraham can only resolve his paradoxical dilemma (follow the precepts of ethics or obey the perceived will of God) by making a decision that is not beholden to any given ethical system's rationality.

Furthermore, precisely because Abraham's decision was rooted in an irrational faith, Kierkegaard is careful neither to applaud nor to condemn Abraham's choice; for, as Kierkegaard argues, there is no rational way to evaluate Abraham's choice. The existential decision that Abraham faced transcended normative ethical principles (e.g., One should not murder). Kierkegaard (1946c) argues that paradoxical moments of existence (such as when our ethics are called into question) "cannot be mediated, for all mediation comes about precisely by virtue of the universal [that is, a universal ethical principle that applies to all individuals]; [the situation] is and remains ... a paradox, inaccessible to thought" (p. 130). There is, therefore, no way to *think through* what Abraham *should* have done; rather, the resolution of the paradox that Abraham faced was possible only when he allowed himself to be unfettered by normative ethics and to take a leap of faith rooted only in subjective truth.

Likewise, Kathryn could not rely on rational thinking (or a rational system of classroom management) to resolve the classroom paradox that she faced. Kathryn understood why her students were squirrely, but she needed them to work; she did not want to yell at them, but she felt obliged to yell at them; she knew that her tactics were ineffective, but, yet she still felt compelled to employ them. By doing so, she was not embodying the teacher she aspired to be, but she felt "trapped" and unable to be otherwise.

It is also critical to note that no one can think through Kathryn's dilemma for her. Although Kathryn might benefit from learning about additional classroom management strategies (cf. Marzano, 2003), Kathryn can resolve her dilemma (i.e., How do I want to treat my students? Who do I want to be as a teacher?) only by confronting and wrestling with the paradoxes (Palmer, 1998) and tensions (Elbow, 1983) that are inherent to the (more than occasionally) irrational work of classroom teaching.

The Responsibility of Individual Choice

Finally, let us consider an anecdote by Robyn in which she describes her frustration with her students' lack of effort:

> I had a lot of kids bomb almost every [reading] quiz and [the quizzes] were not that hard, I was not trying to trick them, it was just, "Who died?" ... Just these basic questions [about the story], and a bunch of [the students], I would look at their answers, and they were ludicrous answers, and I would be like, it's not just that you're just confused where you mixed up two things, you didn't even look at the book.... There was this moment where [my students] were doing quote analysis [from *The Kite Runner*]. They just had to say who said the quote. This one girl was like, "Oh, is this one the dad?" And the dad had died like 17 chapters ago. So I was like, "No. He's dead!" I was so frustrated, and the people around her laughed and I was just like, "UGHH, you don't even know that he's dead! I talked about [his death] in class.... It was like a big moment halfway through the book, and now we're at the end, and you think that he said that? He's not even in the book anymore! What have you been doing every day when we talk about it?".... In that moment I was just like, "Ugh!" ... I was like, not only to not be reading, but to be that grossly unaware of the entire plot.... So when she was like, "It's the dad," I was like ... someone random walked into my class. And I told her that. I was like, "I can't believe you just said that. Are you serious?!" And I was kind of laughing, but I was like, "I don't even have an answer for you. I'm going to leave now." ... And the people around her laughed ... and I knew that she didn't care, but at the same time [to myself] I was like, "Is this my life?"

In this moment, Robyn is not only considering the nature of teaching. She is also considering how (and if) teaching matters to her. Motivating disinterested students is a common challenge of teaching (Cohen, 2011). Robyn, however, did not interpret her lived experience in terms of this professional predicament (e.g., "Why are my students disengaged, and what are some strategies that I can use to motivate them?"). Instead, she interpreted her experience as an existential dilemma that is uniquely her own. Robyn did not ask, "What does this moment reveal to me about the nature of teaching?" Instead, pointedly, she asked, "Is this my life?" For Robyn, the most pressing question – the question that this experience imprinted upon her— was not, "How do I motivate these students?" but, rather, "Is motivating these disinterested students the life that I want to live?"

Robyn's struggle to make sense of her own life is consistent with a fundamental premise of the philosophy of Existentialism: Shared norms can never fully mediate an individual's relationship to his or her own life. Sartre (2007) insisted that individuals are responsible for what they make of their lives because an individual's *existence* precedes the individual's *essence*. In other words, individuals exist before they take on the task of defining themselves in the world (i.e., adopting a particular essence). For this reason, Existentialist philosophers have argued that human beings can never be fully defined in objective terms (e.g., "I am a teacher") because human beings can always choose (and are perpetually asked to choose) the way in which they relate to their own lives.

Said differently, all individuals are free to ask themselves, "How do I want to live my life?" Existentialists argue that each individual is responsible for formulating an answer to this question. Thus, while the project of *being a teacher* may be defined in particular ways by the profession of teaching (Ball & Forzani, 2009; Darling-Hammond & Bransford, 2005; Grossman & McDonald, 2008), beginning teachers (and all teachers, for that matter) are always free to choose whether or not they want to pursue this project (i.e., the project of being a teacher; or, the project of being a particular type of teacher). This is, indeed, the very issue with which Robyn wrestled when she asked herself, "Is this my life?"

Robyn's anecdote illustrates that even though the profession of teaching and contemporary programs of teacher education may take it upon themselves to define what it means to be a teacher; every beginning teacher possesses the prerogative to choose how he or she wants to relate to the profession of teaching. Regardless of what the professional norms of teaching are (e.g., professional teaching involves motivating disinterested students), individual teachers are responsible for choosing whether or not they want to define their existence according to these norms and to engage in this project (e.g., the project of motivating disinterested students). In this way, Robyn's anecdote represents an exercise in existential freedom: She is asking herself who she wants to become. Indeed, neither the profession of teaching nor programs of teacher education can make this decision for any teacher. That is, the fundamental question of whether to be or not to be a teacher is an existential question, not a professional question. When Robyn asks herself, "Is this my life?" she is the one who is solely responsible for answering the question.

TOWARDS AN EXISTENTIAL FRAMING OF
TEACHER DEVELOPMENT

Currently, programs of teacher education aim to delineate what all teachers should know and be able to do. These efforts are appropriate, for, indeed, ambitious teaching should not be presumed to be an act that comes naturally. Beginning teachers must reconsider their beliefs, acquire new knowledge, and develop complex practices as they are apprenticed into the profession of teaching. Furthermore, part of being a professional requires adopting the profession's shared standards for what it means to think and act as a teacher. Teaching "is not about being oneself ... [Rather, teaching involves] suspending some aspects of one's self" (Ball & Forzani, 2009, p. 499) in the service of cultivating one's professional self.

When, however, teacher education becomes about "building" better teachers (Green, 2014), teacher education becomes mechanical and technological, operating in a mode of thought that Heidegger referred to as "machination" (*Machenschaft*). Machination is consumed with calculation and occludes subjective meaning in favor of predictable results. Kierkegaard (1946a), like Heidegger, recognized society's inclination towards rational explanation and, thereby, warned his readers against humanity's "objective tendency, which proposes to make everyone an observer, and in its maximum [seeks] to transform [each individual] into so objective an observer that he [or she] becomes almost a ghost" (p. 210). Said differently, both Kierkegaard and Heidegger exhort us to take heed of our own "subjective truths," rather than allowing "objective" and normative meanings to be the only sources of meaning in our lives. If we allow ourselves to be built solely by the meanings that society offers us, we will become observers (rather than authors) of our own lives.

I, therefore, argue that it is vital for teacher educators not to lose sight of the role that each beginning teacher's subjectivity plays in his or her (professional and personal) development. Because beginning teachers are beings-in-the-world, we can expect them to experience moods that reveal meaning, to wrestle with irrationality, and to be confronted with the freedom and responsibility to choose how they want to engage in their lives. The anecdotes and arguments presented in this introduction illuminate what Orland-Barak and Maskit (2011) have refered to as a "black box" of teaching, a hidden element of teaching that contains "an existential core which transcends issues of management [or] subject matter" (p. 446).

Although I have argued that teaching should not be conceptualized, solely, as a professional endeavor, teacher educators can and should help beginning teachers appreciate what it means to be a professional teacher (Ball & Forzani, 2009). Else, beginning teachers will enter the profession unprepared and unequipped for the multiple challenges that they will inevitably face in the classroom. At the same time, teacher educators can and should recognize that a beginning teacher's existence as a being-in-the-world precedes his or her essence as a professional teacher. Becoming a teacher is, in no small part, an existential choice and an ontological (rather than an exclusively epistemological) journey.

AN INTRODUCTION TO THE CHAPTERS IN THIS BOOK

From a variety of perspectives, the chapters in this edited book explore the manner in which the projects of teaching and learning are, fundamentally, projects of being and becoming. Some of these chapters present frameworks that teachers can use to reconceptualize their curricular and pedagogical approaches so that new experiential and ontological possibilities can be unlocked within the classroom. Other chapters focus on how teacher educators and instructional coaches can reconsider the nature of their work so that the existential concerns of preservice and early-career teachers are explicitly addressed throughout their teacher development.

The first section of this edited book, "Existentialism and Curriculum and Instruction," contains chapters that aim to illuminate existential dimensions inherent in teaching and learning. In the chapter, "Possibility and Rebellion in Sartre and Camus: Existential Possibilities for Education," James Magrini and Elias Schwieler apply Sartre's philosophy and Camus's philosophy to education, specifically by considering the manner in which existential considerations of the possible can, in turn, open up new possibilities for teachers and students in the classroom.

In the chapter, "Learning Objectives Reconsidered in Light of Existential-Phenomenology and Mindfulness," Glen Sherman highlights how learning objectives are often framed with an exclusionary emphasis on cognition, eschewing phenomenological dimensions of learning. By utilizing the philosophical frameworks of Husserl, Heidegger, and Merleau-Ponty, Sherman puts forward the notion of framing learning in terms of the accomplishment of "learning subjectives."

In the chapter, "A Precious Darkness: Utilizing Existential Loneliness to Achieve Culturally Relative Self-Actualization in the Classroom," Christopher Kazanjian and Sandra Kazanjian discuss the possibility of constructing culturally-relative self-actualization experiences in the classroom that have the potential to help students to cultivate an existential awareness of their individual selfhood. In particular, the authors call attention to the existential elements of solitude and loneliness (particularly prominent experiences for contemporary youth) and discuss how the practices of cultural humility, mindful awareness, and cognitive reappraisal can assist teachers in addressing students' existential loneliness.

The second section of this edited book, "Existentialism and Assessment," explores how the assessment of student learning can either constrain or create possibilities for students' being and becoming. In the chapter, "Under Observation: Student Anxiety and the Phenomenology of Remote Testing Environments," Tyler Loveless explores the phenomenon of remote proctoring services designed to detect student cheating during online exams. In particular, this chapter analyzes the effect of these technologies in terms of students' lived experience of feeling seen and the awareness of the physical self as existing for others. In this way, the author argues, such proctoring services may, in fact, be contributing to students' feelings of existential alienation.

In the chapter, "Assessments of Ambiguity," Steven Fleet applies the philosophy of Simone de Beauvoir to describe the manner in which educational assessments can serve as opportunities for students to construct themselves (as opposed to having assessments serve as moments in which a student's essence is predetermined and assigned by the teacher and the curriculum). This chapter describes ways in which complexity, uncertainty, and ambiguity can be utilized within assessments to provide students with the freedom to articulate their own values.

The third section of this edited book, "Existentialism and Teacher Development," explores how the philosophy of Existentialism can be applied, in particular, to the project of becoming a teacher. In the chapter, "Kierkegaard and the Power of Existential Doubt in Teaching: Transformation of Self and Profession," Dan Riordan, Paul Michalec, and Kate Newburgh discuss the critical role of doubt in the experience of teacher development, particularly in the lives of early-career teachers. The authors utilize Kierkegaard's philosophy to develop a framework that instructional coaches can use to assist early-career teachers in acknowledging and exploring their doubts as means of unlocking new directions for professional growth.

In the chapter, "Rational Communication in University Education: A Jaspersian Theory," Daniel Adsett discusses the role of freedom in the pursuit of truth within the context of the university. Adsett points out that when this freedom is unguided, there is a danger that students may adopt anti-liberal or conspiratorial ways of thinking. Adsett applies Jasper's philosophy of education to present the reader with a framework through which teacher educators and university faculty can help their students to engage in collaborative inquiry in ways that are simultaneously rational and empathetic.

In the chapter, "Foundations of Education: Absurdity and Ambiguity," Stephanie Schneider discusses her experiences with teaching and planning for a foundations of education course within her teacher education program. Utilizing the concept of the absurd, Schneider highlights a number of unresolvable dilemmas in both teaching and teacher education that are critical to consider when attempting to prepare preservice teachers for the often-dilemmatic profession of teaching.

The fourth section of this edited book, "The Teaching of Existentialism," shifts to discussing how the philosophy of Existentialism itself can be taught to university students. In the chapter, "Agency Precedes Essence: Existentialism, Ecology, and the New Materialisms," Daniel O'Dea Bradley utilizes the philosophy of Bruno Latour to discuss how the teaching of the philosophy of existentialism can not only expand students' perspectives on the nature of being in the world but can also catalyze students' questioning of the anthropocentric nature of modernity. In this way, helping students (including prospective teachers) to appreciate the principles of Existentialism may have the potential to deepen students' appreciation for contemporary society's potentially ecologically catastrophic treatment of the nonhuman world.

In the chapter, "Teaching is … Other People: Existential Reflections on Coteaching Phenomenology with Undergraduate Students," Lauren Manton, Brigid Flaherty, Cecelia Little, and Peter Costello describe their experiences in coteaching a course on Phenomenology and Existentialism in the context of undergraduate education. This chapter provides insights into how students and faculty can collaborate in the teaching of undergraduate philosophy courses, and, furthermore, how the practice of Phenomenology (with its focus on lived experience) and the philosophy of Existentialism (with its focus on being and becoming) are perhaps most effectively taught within the context of collaboration.

In sum, the aim of this edited book is to encourage readers to consider the profession of teaching through the lens of the philosophy of Existentialism as a means of pushing the work of teaching and the experience of learning towards becoming more authentic and empowering for teachers and students alike. The authors of the chapters in this edited book believe that the concepts of subjectivity, possibility, freedom, absurdity, phenomenological awareness, and doubt have potential in assisting teacher educators, university faculty, experienced teachers, and early-career teachers to reframe (and to reengage with) the projects of teaching, learning, and learning to teach.

REFERENCES

Ball, D. L., & Forzani, F. M. (2009). The work of teaching and the challenge for teacher education. *Journal of Teacher Education, 60*(5), 497–511.

Ball, D. L., Thames, M. H., & Phelps, G. (2008). Content knowledge for teaching: What makes it special? *Journal of Teacher Education, 59*(5), 389–407.

Barlow, A. T., & Reddish, J. M. (2006). Mathematical myths: Teacher candidates' beliefs and the implications for teacher educators. *The Teacher Educator, 41*(3), 145–157.

Bell, B., & Cowie, B. (2001). The characteristics of formative assessment in science education. *Science Education, 85*(5), 536–553.

Berliner, D. C. (2001). Learning about and learning from expert teachers. *International Journal of Educational Research, 35*, 463–482.

Bird, T., Anderson, L. M., Sullivan, B. A., & Swidler, S. A. (1993). Pedagogical balancing acts: Attempts to influence prospective teachers' beliefs. *Teaching and Teacher Education, 9*(3), 253–267.

Boerst, T., Sleep, L., Ball, D. L., & Bass, H. (2011). Preparing teachers to lead mathematics discussions. *Teachers College Record, 113*(12), 2844–2877.

Britzman, D. (1986). Cultural myths in the making of a teacher: Biography and social structure in teacher education. *Harvard Educational Review, 56*(4), 442–472.

Bronkhorst, L. H., Meijer, P. C., Koster, B., & Vermunt, J. D. (2014). Deliberate practice in teacher education. *European Journal of Teacher Education, 37*(1), 18–34.

Chapin, S. H., O'Connor, C., & Anderson, N. C. (2009). *Classroom discussions: Using math talk to help students learn.* Math Solutions.

Cochran-Smith, M. (2005a). The new teacher education: For better or for worse? *Educational Researcher, 34*(7), 3–17.

Cochran-Smith, M. (2005b). Studying teacher education: What we know and what we need to know. *Journal of Teacher Education, 56*(4), 301–306.

Cochran-Smith, M. (2012). A tale of two teachers: Learning to teach over time. *Kappa Delta Pi Record, 48*(3), 108–122.

Cohen, D. K. (2011). *Teaching and its predicaments.* Harvard University Press.

Darling-Hammond, L., & Bransford, J. (Eds.). (2005). *Preparing teachers for a changing world: What teachers should learn and be able to do.* Jossey-Bass.

Deemer, S. (2004). Classroom goal orientation in high school classrooms: Revealing links between teacher beliefs and classroom environments. *Educational Research, 46*(1), 73–90.

Dottin, E. S. (2009). Professional judgment and dispositions in teacher education. *Teaching and Teacher Education, 25,* 83–88.

Doyle, W. (1977). Learning the classroom environment: An ecological analysis. *Journal of Teacher Education, 28*(6), 51–55.

Elbow, P. (1983). Embracing contraries in the teaching process. *College English, 45*(4), 327–339.

Emmer, E. T., & Stough, L. M. (2000). Classroom management: A critical part of educational psychology, with implications for teacher education. *Educational Psychologist, 36,* 103–112.

Feiman-Nemser, S. (2001). From preparation to practice: Designing a continuum to strengthen and sustain teaching. *Teachers College Record, 103*(6), 1013–1055.

Forzani, F. M. (2014). Understanding "core practices" and "practice-based" teacher education: Learning from the past. *Journal of Teacher Education,* 1–12. https://doi.org/10.1177/0022487114533800

Friedman, I. A. (2006). The bi-polar professional self of aspiring teachers: Mission and power. *Teaching and Teacher Education, 22,* 722–739.

Garcia, J. A., & Lewis, T. E. (2014). Getting a grip on the classroom: From psychological to phenomenological curriculum development in teacher education programs. *Curriculum Inquiry, 44*(2), 141–168.

Green, E. (2014). *Building a better teacher.* Norton.

Grossman, P., Compton, C., Igra, D., Ronfeldt, M., Shahan, E., & Williamson, P. W. (2009). Teaching practice: A cross-professional perspective. *Teachers College Record, 111*(9), 2055–2100.

Grossman, P., Compton, C., Shahan, E., Ronfeldt, M., Igra, D., & Shaing, J. (2007). Preparing practitioners to respond to resistance: A cross-professional view. *Teachers and Teaching, 13*(2), 109–123.

Grossman, P., Hammerness, K., & McDonald, M. (2009). Redefining teaching, re-imagining teacher education. *Teachers and Teaching, 15*(2), 273–289.

Grossman, P., & McDonald, M. (2008). Back to the future: Directions for research in teaching and teacher education. *American Educational Research Journal, 45*(1), 184–205.

Heidegger, M. (1962). *Being and time* (J. Macquarrie & E. Robinson, Trans.). Harper Perennial.

Hiebert, J., Morris, A. K., Berk, D., & Jansen, A. (2007). Preparing teachers to learn from teaching. *Journal of Teacher Education, 58*(1), 47–61.

Holt-Reynolds, D. (1992). Personal history-based beliefs as relevant prior knowledge in coursework: Can we practice what we teach? *American Educational Research Journal, 29*(2), 325–349.

Kersting, N. B., Givvin, K. B., Thompson, B. J., Santagata, R., & Stigler, J. W. (2012). Measuring usable knowledge: Teachers' analyses of mathematics classroom videos predict teaching quality and student learning. *American Educational Research Journal, 49*(3), 568–589.

Kierkegaard, S. (1946a). Concluding Unscientific Postscript. In R. Bretall (Ed.), *A Kierkegaard anthology* (pp. 190–269). Princeton University Press.

Kierkegaard, S. (1946b). Either/or. In R. Bretall (Ed.), *A Kierkegaard anthology* (pp. 19–107). Princeton University Press.

Kierkegaard, S. (1946c). Fear and trembling. In R. Bretall (Ed.), *A Kierkegaard anthology* (pp. 116–133). Princeton University Press.

Labaree, D. F. (2000). On the nature of teaching and teacher education: Difficult practices that look easy. *Journal of Teacher Education, 51*(3), 228–233.

Lampert, M. (2001). *Teaching problems and the problems of teaching*. Yale University Press.

Lampert, M. (2010). Learning teaching in, from, and for practice: What do we mean? *Journal of Teacher Education, 61*(1-2), 21–34.

Lampert, M., Franke, M., Kazemi, E., Ghousseini, H., Turrou, A. C., Beasley, H., Cunard, A. & Crowe, K. (2013). Keeping it complex: Using rehearsals to support novice teacher learning of ambitious teaching. *Journal of Teacher Education, 64*(3), 226–243.

Lortie, D. C. (1975). *Schoolteacher: A sociological study*. University of Chicago Press.

Martin, S. D. (2004). Finding balance: Impact of classroom management conceptions on developing teacher practice. *Teaching and Teacher Education, 20*, 405–422.

Marzano, R. J. (2003). *What works in schools: Translating research into action*. Association for Supervision and Curriculum Development.

Marzano, R. J. (2007). *The art and science of teaching: A comprehensive framework for effective instruction*. Association for Supervision and Curriculum Development.

McDonald, M., Kazemi, E., & Kavanagh, S. S. (2013). Core practices and pedagogies of teacher education: A call for a common language and collective activity. *Journal of Teacher Education, 64*(5), 378–386.

Murray, F. B. (2008). The role of teacher education courses in teaching by second nature. In M. Cochran-Smith, S. Feiman-Nemser, D. J. McIntyre, & K. E. Demers (Eds.), *Handbook of research on teacher education: Enduring questions in changing contexts* (3rd ed., pp. 1228–1246). Routledge.

Norman, K. A., & Spencer, B. H. (2005). Our lives as writers: Examining preservice teachers' experiences and beliefs about the nature of writing and writing instruction. *Teacher Education Quarterly, 32*(1), 25–40.

Orland-Barak, L., & Maskit, D. (2011). Novices "in story": What first-year teachers' narratives reveal about the shady corners of teaching. *Teachers and Teaching, 17*(4), 435–450.

Pajares, F. (1993). Preservice teachers' beliefs: A focus for teacher education. *Action in Teacher Education, 15*(2), 45–54.

Palmer, P. J. (1998). *The courage to teach: Exploring the inner landscape of a teacher's life.* Jossey-Bass.

Remillard, J. T., & Bryans, M. B. (2004). Teachers' orientations toward mathematics curriculum materials: Implications for teacher education. *Journal for Research in Mathematics Education, 35*, 352–388.

Sartre, J. P. (2007). *Existentialism is a humanism* (C. Macomber, Trans.). Yale University Press.

Shulman, L. S. (1987). Knowledge and teaching: Foundations of the new reform. *Harvard Educational Review, 57*(1), 1–22.

Smagorinsky, P., Cook, L. S., Moore, C., Jackson, A. Y., & Fry, P. G. (2004). Tensions in learning to teach: Accommodation and the development of a teaching identity. *Journal of Teacher Education, 55*(1), 8–24.

Stein, M. K., Engle, R. A., Smith, M. S., & Hughes, E. K. (2008). Orchestrating productive mathematical discussions: Five practices for helping teachers move beyond show and tell. *Mathematical Thinking and Learning, 10*, 313–340.

van Manen, M. (1990). *Researching lived experience: Human science for an action sensitive pedagogy.* SUNY Press.

Veenman, S. (1984). Perceived problems of beginning teachers. *Review of Educational Research, 54*(2), 143–178.

Wagner, A. C. (1987). "Knots" in teachers' thinking. In J. Calderhead (Ed.), *Exploring Teacher Thinking* (pp. 161–178). Cassell.

Windschitl, M., Thompson, J., Braaten, M., & Stroupe, D. (2012). Proposing a core set of instructional practices and tools for teachers of science. *Science Education, 96*(5), 878–903.

Yerrick, R., Parke, H., & Nugent, F. (1997). Struggling to promote deeply rooted change: The "filtering effect" of teacher's beliefs on understanding transformational views of teaching science. *Science Education, 81*(2), 137–160.

SECTION I

EXISTENTIALISM AND CURRICULUM AND INSTRUCTION

CHAPTER 1

POSSIBILITY AND REBELLION IN SARTRE AND CAMUS

Existential Possibilities for Education

James M. Magrini and Elias Schwieler
College of Dupage, Stockholm University

ABSTRACT

Seeking a reconceived view of contemporary education, which remains in the grip of social efficiency, this chapter focuses on Jean-Paul Sartre and Albert Camus, thinkers embracing the unique existential view of human "potential" above "actuality," which runs counter to the tradition in Western metaphysics. We show how this idea lives at both ontological and historical levels as related to education. Through Sartre, we explore the "life-projects" of students with the understanding that learning occurs in its most authentic form as a living and dynamic "process," and should not be sought in any "actualized" concrete or objectified results standing outside or beyond either the individual or the educational process itself. We relate Sartre's phenomenological ontology of conscious intentionality, nothingness, and the potential for finite transcendence to an understanding of learning and curriculum development favoring a line of *process-product* curriculum (existential) over the more traditional form of curriculum grounded in the antiquated *product-process* (technical) model for learning. In Camus, we analyze Rebellion and the aporetic-tension between freedom and justice, which must be enacted in terms of identifying, critiquing, and changing ideas and practices that heedlessly exceed the ethical limits of the human community of learning. The fragile balance between freedom and

Problematizing the Profession of Teaching From an Existential Perspective, pp. 3–24
Copyright © 2022 by Information Age Publishing
www.infoagepub.com

3

justice must be acknowledged and respected in dialogue, for each holds the potential to degenerate into and manifest as authoritarian subjugation and social injustice. Through "generosity," a mode of revelatory attunement, it is possible to gain access to a world where ongoing acts of rebellion, grounded in critical communication, instantiate original practices of education in terms of epiphanic events of learning. Remaining true to these philosophers, we offer intimations of a view to education understood as "existential" in nature, however, we refrain from establishing definitive and indelible principles for education derived from their philosophies; to do so, would betray the fundamental understanding of existentialism.

Maxine Greene, a well-known advocate of existentialism in education, stresses the issue grounding this chapter: the pursuit of a viable definition of the human being. Greene (1973) observes that many educators have erroneously "tried to *fix* human nature and then to develop a theory of education based on their notion of what the human being (so defined) ought to be" (p. 76). This view runs counter to the understanding of the human being found in existentialism, which lies beyond traditional views of *rationalism, idealism,* and *materialism*. In contemporary education, *Social Efficiency* embraces a view of the human consistent with behaviorism, overlooking the ontological aspects of being human that Sartre revealed, and the *Scholar Academic* view, grounded in the polarity between epistemological authority (educator) and subordinate (student), obscures crucial normative or ethical implications for our lives that Camus so insightfully recognized and urgently communicated. As we show, for Sartre and Camus, the definition of the human being that educators should consider is existential in nature, focused on ontology, freedom, authenticity, values, and the urgency of Being. In addition, Greene rightly considers the important "question of authority" in relation to existentialism and education, arguing for "efforts to stimulate the energy, the consciousness, the pathos involved in serious choice" (pp. 284–285), that is, the ontological and existential demand to become and create a self.

Sartre's (1995) existential epigram, "existence precedes essence" (p. 35), is familiar to most educators, but far less familiar is the ontological issue grounding this epigram highlighted and developed by Sartre in *Being and Nothingness,* namely, the technical Aristotelian metaphysical distinction between *potential* over and above *actuality.* Rather than privileging *actuality,* Sartre asserts that *possibility* is the most primordial way we are structured ontologically. In essence, we do not merely have possibilities, our Being is grounded in the "possible" for continued self-overcoming or transcendence. Sartre (1984) understands possibility or the "possible" in ontological terms, as a component of the structure of *Being-in-the-world,* stressing the unfinished, *nihilating,* and *transcendent* nature of *Being-for-itself* (p. 150). We encounter the Aristotelian metaphysical notion of *actuality* above *possibility* in current models for structuring education and curriculum, where the "work" or end-result of the process (i.e., what is learned) stands outside the process as an objectified, determinate end, which is valued as the concrete instantiation of the *actualization* of learning.

This, however, erroneously indicates that students learn only when accomplishing preestablished objectives that are determined by educational authorities. In this view, the process or *lived experience* of learning is devalued, for it is the so-called "actualized product" of education that is truly valued; the product (rather than the experience) is framed as the ultimate goal of education. Contrarily, we argue that the *lived experience* of learning should not be diminished, because the lived experience of learning fosters human *potential* in a way that embraces our *Being-in-the-world* as *Being-with-others*—that is a view embracing both ontology and the sense of normativity bound up with the values we freely choose, embrace, and "live" in the presence of others, which importantly includes the "lived" world of the curriculum. Importantly, when destructuring the traditional method of *product-above-process*, we find that what lies at the root of this problematic issue is an antiquated view of the human being upon which this method is based and created to serve. Thus, the corrective to this issue resides at a deep, primordial level, and so what is required is the radical reconceptualization of our *Being-in-the-world* as *Being-with-others*, relating to our ontological sense of "possibility," as envisioned by Sartre, and what Camus understands as "metaphysical rebellion." For, as educators, we are, along with our students, immersed in a value-laden and morally exigent world of free creation that contemporary education appears to have forgotten and so continues to obscure in both theory and practice.

To address these issues in more detail and develop our analysis of how Sartre and Camus can be seen to contribute to discussions on contemporary educational practice, we begin by describing Sartre's and Camus's philosophies from a more general position. After we have outlined what in Sartre's and Camus's thinking we want to relate to education, we devote the remainder of the essay exploring how their philosophies might provide educators with an existential foundation for their teaching practice. The essay is, in consequence, divided into four major parts: the first dealing with Sartre and the possible, the second addresses Camus's notion of rebellion, the third contributes to our understanding of Sartre, the possible, and education, and the fourth part investigates how Camus's idea of rebellion can be related to education. The essay is concluded by a summary of the major points we have touched on in the essay. Remaining true to the *non-systematic* approach of existential philosophy, our intent is to offer intimations of existentialism in education, seeking to connect with the creative imagination of readers in ways that challenge and potentially inspire the enhancement of their conception and practice of pedagogy.

SARTRE AND THE POSSIBLE

Social Efficiency and *Scholar Academic* ideology harbor a tacit Cartesian *subjectivism*, a modern view of the conscious subject. In an early essay on conscious intentionality, a corrective to Husserl's phenomenology,[1] Sartre presents a radical reconceptualization of "phenomenological conscious-ness" or *phenomenological selfhood*. Against Descartes, consciousness for Sartre (2002), "has no inside," because consciousness is always already projected out beyond itself into the world, and this "being beyond itself [*projective-transcendence*], this absolute flight, this refusal to be a substance is what makes it be a consciousness" (p. 2).[2] Consciousness does not bring the world inside of itself via ideas or perceptions; consciousness does not pas-sively receive and then process the rattle-and-hum of the external world; rather consciousness is highlighted by "movement," for it is continually stretching out, reaching out, "bursting out," beyond itself toward its proj-ects as it finds itself immersed in the world (p. 3). Consciousness exists in the mode of the *infinitival*, and against the notion of pure consciousness, all *consciousness is consciousness of something*. Consciousness (*Being-for-itself*) requires a world for its life-project, the enactment of its "possibility" in and through transcendence. However, the intimate relationship between the human and the world is highlighted by *ontological distance*, for there are aspects of consciousness that cannot be fully reconciled with the world and vice versa; there are always elements of the world, transphenomenal characteristics, which remain beyond consciousness, and this is but one instance of the emergence of the pervasive ontological presence of *nothing-ness* in Sartre's philosophy.

As stated, the "possible" is a structure of *Being-for-itself*, and consciousness and the *for-itself* exist in terms of *ontological groundlessness*—that is, human *existence* has no *essence*—and this is because of *nothingness*, the pervasive lack or privation that resides at the center of human (Being) conscious-ness. Sartre (1984) claims that the freedom revealed to us in *Anguish* (the recognition that we are condemned to freely choose a groundless project) manifests the "*nothing* which insinuates itself between motives and act," and *nothingness* shapes our motivations in action, characterizing "itself as transcendence in immanence" (p. 71, emphasis in original). *Nothingness* expresses itself through what Sartre terms "*negatites*," ways in which we experience absence, limitation, change, destruction, for example, all of the possibilities that we have neglected to choose and enact manifest *nothing-ness*. There are two main conditions of transcendent negation, two *original nihilations*: (1) consciousness is *not* its own motive, since "it is *empty* of all content" and depends for its existence on what it is *not*, and (2) conscious-ness "confronts its past and its future as facing a self which is in the mode of not-being," that is, we are no longer our past and not-yet our future, and this relates to the *nihilating structure of temporality* (p. 72). The *nothingness* of *Being-for-itself* spans the horizons of time (temporality) as a synthetic unity and involves nihilation in tripartite: In the present, we are not (no longer) our past and not yet our future, but since we are "possibility" we are also not what we are even in the present, for we are ecstatically projected, via conscious intentionality, out beyond ourselves in the moment.

Against the Aristotelian tradition in Western metaphysics, the human being can never realize or fully *actualize* its essence or life-project, because it is always on the way to discovering new aspects and unforeseen possibilities of its *Being-in-the-world*, for as Sartre (1995) articulates, "with no support and no aid," the human is "condemned every moment to reinvent itself" (p. 45). Indeed, it is *nothingness* that pushes us into the mode of questioning the world in the first instance—the exigency of learning anew—for through questioning, which presupposes an unfinished project, a lack of insight, a privation of knowledge, we seek to bridge the gap between what we are and what we are not. Catalano (1980) offers the following insightful remarks about what the process of "questioning" our existence entails in his commentary on *Being and Nothingness*:

> In questioning, the questioner wrenches from being its continuity with itself, thereby "nihilating" (*neatiser*) being in relation to other aspects of being. Furthermore, the questioner himself must be separated from any continuity with being, for only thus can he await, by his attitude of questioning, the continual possibility of the presence or nonpresence of being. (p. 66)

This notion might be said to reside at the center of a reconceived "existential" educational experience, because for Sartre, such persistent and renewed questioning driving forward our *life project* and facilitating *transcendence* keeps the *learning experience* alive and unfolding in unpredictable, but potentially rewarding, directions. For as Sartre (1984) insists, since we are separated from an essence, a reified "ego" or fully formed "I," by *nothingness*, we are driven by the "constantly renewed obligation to remake the *Self* which designates the free being" (p. 72), that is however, if our choices do not fall victim to *Bad Faith* (*mauvaise foi*) or the refusal to take our *Anguish*, our responsibility to freedom, seriously.

Because consciousness is a *negating* or *nihilating activity*, our future projects are separated from us by *nothingness*, and for this reason we reveal ourselves as the "original source" of "possibility." Just as *nothingness* comes into the world through the *for-itself*, "a being which is its own lack," so too is "possibility" inextricably linked with the *for-itself* and its distinct manner of Being, for according to Sartre (1984), possibility comes into the world only if it comes through *human reality*, that is, "a being which is for-itself in its own possibility" (p. 150). When freely enacting concrete possibilities, our life-project gathers meaning, value, and displays consistency through the choices we make, and this is because of the *ontological* structure of the *possible*, which first grants the *for-itself* "*the possibility of becoming*" and enacting its own unique and concrete "*possibilities*" (p. 80). Recalling our discussion of conscious intentionality, we are *as* possibility or "The Possible" because the *for-itself* "lacks a certain coincidence with itself" (p. 142), the possible is "*the something* which the for-itself lacks *in order to* be itself" (p. 155), in order to reveal and confront its concrete possibilities. It is *nothingness*, inherent to *existential possibility*, which engenders the pursuit of our own unique set of possibilities as they emerge and are relatable to our lives, with the potential to choose, enact, and appropriate the possibilities we deem valuable.

To be clear, we can set and achieve (actualize) goals, but this is not the same as "actualizing" our *existential possibility* in such a way that we succeed in bringing our life-project to fruition through actualization. For we cannot actualize the *existential* "possibility" that structures our way of being, for as stated, it is an *ontological* structure, providing a "schematic outline" of the *for-itself* (p. 155). Instead, we reveal it, acknowledge it, and live through it *as* possibility, which manifests in the concrete act of living beyond what we are in the moment as directed toward what we are *not*, what we might become, and this process instantiates our *finite transcendence*.

For Sartre, "transcendence" has more than a few meanings, all of which live beyond the notion of *vertical transcendence* as a form of religious salvation. Our use of transcendence is described by Barnes (as cited in Sartre, 1984): "Transcendence often refers simply to the process whereby the For-itself goes beyond the given in a further project of itself" (p. 807). Sartre (1984) emphasizes that transcendence presupposes the human's "escape-from-itself" as directed toward one or another possible future (p. 152), while simultaneously anticipating the "return toward the existing in terms of the lacked [*nothingness*]" (p. 147). The process inspiring the movement of our *Being-in-the-world* is *transcendence*, occurring through interpreting and reinterpreting our world and existence, when standing out and going beyond what we are in present moments, with the potential—as *possibility*—for continued transcendence in and through the return to ourselves, in order to once again remake our lives. When discussing transcendence, it is crucial to mention that as we choose possibilities related to our project, we engender a "double property," that is, our projects are at once bound up with "*facticity* and a *transcendence*," the "two aspects of human reality" that are related in terms of their "valid coordination" (p. 98). To speak of "coordination," presupposes an understanding of the differences separating these two modes of Being. *Facticity* refers to "factical" aspects of our existence, expressive of our connection(s) to the *in-itself,* for example, the historical epoch within which we were born, our genetic makeup and heritage; these are aspects of our *Being-in-the-world* that cannot be altered.

However, our life-projects demand that we work within the limitations set by *facticity* in order to authentically enact our possibilities in *transcendence*.

Importantly, human transcendence pushes the *for-itself* towards values and valuation, through which it assesses and interprets what has been given—manifesting through choices made via the immersion in and transmission of heritage—in light of furthering its project. It is then through reassessment and reinterpretation that the *for-itself* transcends the given and becomes *other*, affirming in the moment of choice its values, and as Sartre (1995) continually stresses, human values are inseparable from the choices made (p. 56). Consider the following: Person *x* has Eastern European and Mediterranean genetic lines, *x* cannot change this aspect of her existence, but *x* can choose the manner in which she embraces and appropriates (values) her given heritage, for example, *x* can freely choose to value *only* her Mediterranean lineage with its specific cultural traditions at the exclusion of her Eastern European lineage. But importantly, this idea also relates to education and the choices students make. Following Sartre, we understand that student *x* is free to choose and embrace specific values—despite, and even in direct opposition to, the values held and transferred by *x*'s teacher—that contribute uniquely to furthering the development of *x*'s personal "projects" that instantiate the "lived" process of *learning*.

CAMUS AND REBELLION

The text that we will focus on in our reading of Camus is his last major work, *The Rebel: An Essay on Man in Revolt* [*L'Homme Révolté*] (1951/1991). More of a historical reflection on rebellion than an existential-ontological analysis in the manner of Sartre, *The Rebel* still addresses some of the themes already broached in our reading of Sartre's work. For example, the themes of possibility and actuality are of importance to an understanding of Camus's notion of rebellion. But the two most salient concepts in Camus's essay, two concepts that have consequences for our reading of Camus's thinking in relation to education, are justice and freedom. As we will see, it is in the tension between justice and freedom that authentic rebellion develops.

Camus's essay was received with mixed reviews, and also became part of the famous hostility and polemics between Camus and Sartre, which also finally ended their friendship. Part of the polemics was about the idea of revolution and how communism in the Soviet Union was or was not part of the oppression of the Russian people. One of Camus main arguments in *The Rebel* is, precisely, the totalitarian surge of Marxism stemming from its teleological, transcendent, messianic view of history. However, to get to the critique of the teleological-transcendent character of revolt, Camus begins by revisiting his idea of the absurd, which in turn leads him to his opening and chief example of rebellion consisting of how the slave rebels against the master. The absurd, which was the central theme of his earlier work *The Myth of Sisyphus*, is in *The Rebel* juxtaposed to nihilism. These two existential stances, Camus states, are founded on a contradiction. As he writes concerning the absurd: "The absurd is, in itself, contradiction" (Camus, 1951/1991, p. 8), and he goes on to explain: "It is contradictory in its content because, in wanting to uphold life, it excludes all value judgments, when to live is, in itself, a value judgment. To breathe is to judge" (Camus, 1951/1991, p. 8). To be more precise, about the aporia at the core of absurdist and nihilist reasoning, Camus maintains that

> if we deny that there are reasons for suicide, we cannot claim that there are grounds for murder. There are no half-measures about nihilism. Absurdist reasoning cannot defend the continued existence of its spokesman and, simultaneously, accept the sacrifice of others' lives. The moment that we recognize the impossibility of absolute negation—and merely to be alive is to recognize this—the very first thing that cannot be denied is the right of others to live. Thus the same idea which allowed us to believe that murder was a matter of indifference now proceeds to deprive it of any justification; and we return to the untenable position from which we were trying to escape. In actual fact, this form of reasoning assures us at the same time that we can kill and that we cannot kill. It abandons us in this contradiction with no grounds either for preventing or for justifying murder, menacing and menaced, swept along with a whole generation intoxicated by nihilism, and yet lost in loneliness, with weapons in our hands and a lump in our throats. (Camus, 1951/1991, pp. 7–8)

Here, we find the aporia of justice and freedom expressed within the context of suicide-murder, absurdism-nihilism, which as Camus asserts leaves us incapable of neither absolute justice nor absolute freedom. "The absurd, considered as a rule of life," writes Camus, "is therefore contradictory" (Camus, 1951/1991, p. 9). This means, according to Camus (1951/1991), that rebellion takes place because of, but also despite, this impasse. However, the rebellion to which the aporia of freedom and justice gives rise has more often than not ended in repression, tyranny, totalitarianism. It is the history of these failed attempts of rebellion which makes up the majority of Camus's essay. Thus, the aim of his essay is "to face the reality of the present, which is logical crime, and to examine meticulously the arguments by which it is justified" (p. 2). Logical crime, meaning, to kill in the name of a higher purpose (e.g., the French Revolution, Marxism), or because God is proclaimed dead and there are no values—everything is allowed—which means murder cannot be considered a crime (e.g., de Sade, Nietzsche). What it boils down to in *The Rebel* is how revolt is connected to politics and violence throughout history, and how we can counter the violence and repression stemming from acts of rebellion and conceive of an authentic notion of rebellion. As John Foley (2008) agues in his study of Camus:

> Camus's investigation of the problem of political violence begins with this realization that the absurd condition is the human condition, that it describes not just the experience of the individual in whose consciousness the recognition of the absurd necessarily begins, but the character of all human experience. This recognition permits an important reorientation of the absurd premise, a reworking that permits the emergence of the ethics of revolt. (pp. 56–57)

This realization is also reflected in Camus's statement that introduces an existential-ontological dimension to revolt: "I revolt—therefore we exist" (p. 22). Now, the ethics of revolt that Foley suggests has its origin in Camus's insistence on the necessity to continuously reflect on and examine the essence and nature of the act of rebellion; this, Camus argues, is necessary in order to be able to avoid rebellion degrading into totalitarianism, violence, and murder. In other words, it is in the fact that rebellion is contradictory, founded in aporia,[3] which also makes it into a potentially ethical act.

The ethical, then, is contradiction. It is the contradiction that a slave faces when rebelling against his/her master: that is, how, as the oppressed, to avoid reverting to violence and becoming the oppressor. Again, we find here the tension of the aporia between freedom and justice. As stated, Camus exemplifies this contradictory tension by the conflict inherent in the master-slave dichotomy, a dichotomy, however, which always runs the risk of being reversed, so that the slave becomes the master, and the master becomes the slave, when there is no measure that limits neither freedom nor justice. As Camus (1951/1991) argues:

> In order to exist, man must rebel, but rebellion must respect the limit it discovers in itself – a limit where minds meet and, in meeting, begin to exist. Rebellious thought, therefore, cannot dispense with memory: it is a perpetual state of tension. (p. 22)

This statement opens up for a discussion of the potential of authentic rebellion.

We will not conduct a detailed reading of Camus's historical analysis here, but instead, after this brief introduction to what he means by rebellion, focus on how he conceives of rebellion as a positive act: that is, as an existential-ontological potential in the human being for authentic revolt. Thus, the question becomes what an authentic rebellion is and what it entails. These questions compel us to negotiate the contradictory tension between freedom and justice, to find a middle way to avoid the excesses of totalitarianism and tyranny. Consequently, Camus's guiding words are unity and moderation, which keep rebellion from falling prey to its own absolute and extreme endpoints. "Rebellion," writes Camus (1951/1991), "at the same time that it suggests a nature common to all men, brings to light the measure and the limit which are the very principle of this nature" (p. 294). Thus, justice moderates freedom, while freedom moderates justice; Camus is, in other words, arguing for a failsafe that can rescue authentic rebellion from becoming a totalitarian apparatus. As he states:

> The real madness of excess dies or creates its own moderation. It does not cause the death of others in order to create an alibi for itself. In its most extreme manifestations, it finds its limit, on which […] it sacrifices itself if necessary. (p. 301)

At the same time, moderation is inseparable from rebellion: "Moderation, born of rebellion, can only live by rebellion" (Camus, 1951/1991, p. 301). Hence, rebellion that exceeds itself and its own self-imposed limits ceases to be rebellion and becomes totalitarian with systematic violence and repression as its ultimate consequences. Authentic rebellion, on the other hand, is always a rebellion against the violence of excess, and the excess of poverty and suffering; authentic rebellion finds its ethical potential in the actuality of the present, for example, the slave recognizes a limit past which s/he will not go, where rebellion is the only answer to the demand of the master, while this limit is also the measure of rebellion, the ethical actuality of the situation that should not be transgressed. The recognition of this limit, furthermore, is what makes the slave come to an awareness of his/her own existence and suffering as well as the existence and suffering of others; in other words, the absurdity of the human condition.[4]

SARTRE, EDUCATION, AND THE POSSIBLE

Although Sartre did not write explicitly on education, we claim that it is possible to find relevant material relating to a philosophy of education in his existential philosophy that guides and inspires *praxis*. However, we note that any attempt to establish rigid principles or indelible tenets for structuring an "institutional" view of education that remains true to existential philosophy is a bastardization and betrayal of existentialism. We note that several prominent philosophers have written on Sartre and education, however, as is unique to this reading, the topic of existentialism in relation to the curriculum has yet to be explored.[5] Space does not allow for an in-depth analysis, but here, in a speculative manner, we attempt to relate Sartre's ontology of the "possible" to envisioning, planning, and enacting of the curriculum.

Although not referencing Aristotelian metaphysics, contemporary educational philosophy and curriculum theory tacitly embraces the privileging of *actuality* above *possibility,* a view that establishes the trajectory of education in advance of the *lived experience* of learning.[6] In this limited view of curriculum, learning begins at a theoretical or objective remove from the ever-evolving "lived" ontological experience of both teachers and students. The "lived" process of learning is antecedent to the formalization of schooling, and this we term the *existential* or *lived-curricula* of the human being. The *product-process* model of curriculum, grounded in the *analytic-empirical* model for research, forecloses our ontological projection toward possibilities that is necessary for existential self-transformation, that is, *transcendence* in relation to our unique and freely chosen *life-projects.* In the *product-process* model of curriculum-making, which includes conception, implementation, and assessment, two problematic issues relating to Sartre's ontology arise: (1) the conception of the human being to *be educated* emerges primarily from cognitive psychology and the educational sciences, and (2) curriculum privileging *actualization* over and above *potential/possibility* in its definition of "learning" and "education," devalues the "lived" process of learning. Based on our reading, Sartre inspires the following queries: From whence does education's *curricular vision* emerge? From what source or origin does it draw its gathering power? What is the fundamental view of the human being that education adopts?

If we remain true to Sartre's existentialism, *who* and *what* we hold the *potential* to become through learning cannot be established in advance of the unfolding of the process of education, for it is engaged action and choice that defines us and not detached theoretical reflection on our Being. First, based on Sartre's view of conscious intentionality, there is no "objective" perspective from which to know the world; we cannot adopt a "God's eye" view of the world (*sub specie aeternitatis*) and objectively and accurately capture it in knowledge. Second, there is no human nature or essence for psychology or the learning sciences to capture in knowledge, objective or otherwise, this because *Being-for-itself* lacks a hypostatic center or essence (underlying substance as *hypokeimenon*), rather it is, as Sartre emphasizes, ontological *possibility.*

To consider curriculum in terms of the *product-process* model for education retains both Aristotle's metaphysical privileging of *actuality* above *potentiality* and the epistemological model associated with Cartesian dualism, embracing the subjective-objective divide of which Sartre is highly critical. In Sartre, we encounter a human being who lives as *possibility* beyond the subject-object divide; knowledge is not situated at an objective remove from the thinking, consciously involved student; rather, knowledge is a form of understanding (*intuition*) within which the student intimately participates, as she is situated within the world of her thoughts-and-activities. The student does not bring her learning "inside," like the spider in its web, "digesting" and assimilating what has been transferred to her from an "objective" and authoritative source.

Sartre's existentialism inspires thinking on different ways to potentially approach curriculum-making. Specifically, it engenders thinking in the direction of a modified *process-product* form of curriculum-making, or better, an approach to education and curriculum attuned by way of an ontological vision of *Being-for-itself* in the world.[7] For example, in the traditional relationship between the *curriculum-as-plan* and the *curriculum-as-enacted*, as grounded in the *product-process* model for education, what it means to be educated is determined (*curriculum-as-plan*) in a manner antecedent to the implementation and enactment of the curriculum. In this model, the "process of learning" (or means to the end of the curriculum's objectives) does not consider seriously what might be called the non-systematized, ever-evolving *lived-curriculum* of the student. This, as related to Sartre, might be said to represent the *way-of-Being* or *way-of-learning* of the student as her *life-projects* unfold as *transcendence*. Based on our ontological understanding of the *for-itself*, the student *is* and *lives* the potential for opening and enacting new possibilities of its *Being-in-the-world* in various ways that cannot be accurately predicted in advance of confronting, assessing, and freely choosing the concrete possibilities emerging for appropriation.

When Sartre (1984) describes knowledge, he claims that all knowledge is *intuitive* in nature, and while more than a few of Sartre's declarations are meant to jolt us awake from our dogmatic slumbers, he is simply indicating that knowledge of ourselves and the world (despite the manner in which that knowledge obtains, be it through deduction, induction, abduction, discursive argumentation, or perceptual insight) is relative and meaningful to us in intimate ways because it contributes to furthering our *life-projects* (p. 240). It is a way of knowing and understanding that is *owned*, so to speak, for it is not given to us from an external source by way of an epistemic authority, but rather is unique to our own concerns and issues comprising our ever-changing and developing *lived-curriculum*.

Educators embracing *product-process* model for curriculum believe that learning can be controlled because the educational "environment" is structured and manipulated in such a way as to demonstrate *predictable* outcomes through the application of *learning theories* or "learning strategies" (Ornstein & Hunkins, 2004), for example, the teaching and application of *meta-cognitive theories* (Darling-Hammond & Bransford, 2007). With the primary focus on the interplay between the *curriculum-as-plan* (conceived and worked out prior to "lived world" learning situations) and the *curriculum-as-enacted* (the learning plan as put into action, or theory, as it is applied to structure and direct educational *praxis*), the process of learning is viewed, assessed, and valued in light of its "fidelity" to the original educational schema codified in the curriculum plan in terms of ends (i.e., learning objectives to be actualized). The teaching techniques employed as the curriculum is enacted are valued only in so far as they also serve the end of meeting the preestablished objectives. This, as we have stated, in terms of relating to human freedom and the necessity of free-choice in the enactment of our ever-developing *life-project*, represents a turn from or *fleeing-in-the-face* of our inherent ontological *possibility* to pursue authentically what we choose to *become*.

Sartre inspires us to reconceive the manner in which curriculum functions in terms of existentialism, and ultimately it is the *lived-curriculum*—the student's *life-project* as *projected-transcendence* into her open possibilities, and the knowledge and understanding that accrues as this project is enacted—that should be incorporated in a critical and dialectical manner within the other aspects of curriculum-making introduced above. Thus, the ontology of the human being should inform the *curriculum-as-planned* and attune in *praxis* the *curriculum-as-enacted*, as the curriculum unfolds. In essence, a *process-product* vision of curriculum would find its inspiration in "The Possible," unfolding in such a way that the student's possibilities, which the process of education reveals, are valued, and incorporated in ways that enhance the curriculum's development. In this way, the enactment of the curriculum would be consistently inspired by (and attuned and re-attuned by) the evolution of the student's *curriculum-of-life*. Such a view of curriculum, we might call it "existential" in conception and enactment, responds to and is influenced by the unique and unpredictable unfolding of the student's *life-project* which, outside of the single fatality of death, remains open to new and unforeseen possibilities that are always on the approach from out of the learner's indeterminate future.

Within the context of an existential conception and enactment of curriculum, the traditional understanding of "terminal ends" in curriculum-making are re-conceived in a *process-product* view in terms of educational objectives that are tentative, malleable, and fluid, since these educational "benchmarks" would develop and change in tandem with the ebb-and-flow of the student's development. Indeed, we might define educational goals and benchmarks as actually *dwelling-in* and *emerging-from* because educational goals, within this curricular framing, are immanent as *potential* within, the unfolding of a curriculum attuned to ontological *possibility*.

For the *lived-curricula* of students, the unique possibilities of those involved in the learning, with their ontological predisposition for *transcendence* ("learning"), becomes paramount to the task of education. Learning, and this for Sartre, as we have seen, is nothing other than the *for-itself* transcending itself as the "not-yet," always occurs through "action," that is, it never occurs at a remove from the visceral realities and contingencies of the situation of the classroom or at a remove from the lives of those actively immersed and invested in the learning.

Instead of asking the typical question common to traditional curricular theorists and specialists, such as, "Did the student actualize her potential as learner in meeting the proposed educational objective?", Sartre inspires other questions, such as (1) How might education benefit from an understanding of the human being that the tradition has overlooked? (2) How might education, when considering the notion of human *possibility*, approach students in ways that acknowledge the contributions they might make to the evolution of the learning process? (3) Why is the student's *life-project* indispensable when conceiving, enacting, and assessing an education that lives beyond dualism? Such existentially inspired questions have monumental implications for education's reassessment and re-conception of both student learning and the evaluation thereof along with raising concerns about the manner in which we approach the *institutionalized* process of teacher education.

Meditating on and offering rejoinders to such *original questions*[8] might serve to turn us from the belief that true learning comes about only when there is an obsessive focus on concrete, determinative results that are measured against definitive standards of achievement, which are expressible through calculable statistics that are employed to "accurately" gauge the achievement of learning outcomes. *Original questions* shape and guide the manner in which we confront the "existential" issues of learning that defy categorical explanations, the type of issues bound up with personal meaning and value, issues that push questioning to its limits and contribute to the provisional and fluid scaffolding of a *process-product* view-and-practice of curriculum and learning that embraces educational *possibility* above the *actualization* of learning. The attempt to formulate thoughtful and enlightened rejoinders to such questions would push us as educators toward the serious consideration of Sartre's ontological notions of *possibility, freedom,* and *nothingness.*

CAMUS, REBELLION, AND EDUCATION

We will introduce our discussion of Camus and education with a quote from Richard Shaull's (2014) "Foreword" to Paulo Freire's *Pedagogy of the Oppressed*:

> There is no such thing as a neutral educational process. Education either functions as an instrument that is used to facilitate the integration of the

younger generation into the logic of the present system and bring about conformity to it, or it becomes "the practice of freedom," the means by which men and women deal critically and creatively with reality and discover how to participate in the transformation of their world. The development of an educational methodology that facilitates this process will inevitably lead to tension and conflict within our society. But it could also contribute to the formation of a new man and mark the beginning of a new era in Western history. (p. 34)

Education has historically been a significant part of religion and the political, and so of religious and political violence; it has been used as an instrument, sometimes as a weapon, and at times as a repressive censoring process for the purpose of indoctrination; at times, however, it has been used in the name of social justice, equity, and equality. Now, we argue that it is the contradictory tension between freedom and justice in Camus's idea of rebellion, which can either provide a possibility for education as a practice of freedom, as Schaull has it, or make it degenerate into an instrument of social efficiency in which entrepreneurship and employability are the outcomes of a bureaucratic and mechanical system of education in which freedom and justice are empty words and thinking and creativity are dead concepts without real significance.

In the latter form of education, transformation and change stagnate and turn into fixed and inflexible programs for learning that are measured against rigid outcomes that stifle thinking and critique while awarding blind adherence to ready-made paths of learning. Just as for authentic rebellion, education, to be authentic, has to remember and reimagine its origin, if we, taking our cue from Camus, see education as grounded in freedom and justice. Thus, what we aim to argue for is an existential education where rebellion, in Camus's sense of the word, plays a necessary and invigorating role to keep learning alive.[9]

In this sense, education as it relates to rebellion is political[10]; but it is also ethical. Peter Roberts (2008), in his reading of Camus's short story "The Guest," states as much when he writes, "Teaching and learning are ethical activities, where judgements about what and whom to favour must be made across the educational lifespan" (p. 531). What Roberts implies here is that teaching and learning involve decisions which are inherently ethical in character and that come to govern the way we approach education —for example, as an endeavor which aims to develop new senses of self and community in a creative and critical manner; or, for that matter, education seen as an instrument to form and shape people in accordance with dominant ideologies.

An education that takes its cue from Camus's notion of the rebel and rebellion would emphasize the importance of continuously questioning the choices made in the name of education. As Aidan Hobson (2017) writes regarding the learner and rebellion in his book *Albert Camus and Education*: "It is a revolt against a perception of their world where potential had been assigned without consent" (p. 62). That is, a limit has been recognized, a limit which the learner cannot go beyond without rebelling, and so the formative potential in education is thus actualized by the "assignment without consent." Educational revolt as ethics is a continuously subversive and self-subversive movement, where its disruptions shape the formation in language of a fragile unity between ethics, education, teacher, and learner. This unity, however, is a unity founded on the contradiction and aporia of justice and freedom. Education as authentic rebellion is, in consequence, a balancing act; like walking a tightrope, education demands courage and the willingness to face the danger of falling and thereby potentially breaking the unity that the act of rebellion made possible in the first place.

The question then becomes where we can find examples that stage such rebellion and danger, examples that can serve as performative acts of transformation. We argue that such examples can be found in works of art, and that art, education, and rebellion form a tripartite potentiality, which has the possibility to navigate freedom and justice within self-formation and the formation of community, and which is necessary for existential education to take place. Certainly, Camus as well as Sartre explored the potential of art to address the existential and indeed absurd human condition in their numerous novels and plays. However, the example we would like to refer to here is Sophocles's *Antigone*, a work of art which brings together many of the themes that explain authentic rebellion (in Camus's sense of the term).

Importantly, Antigone is a rebel, she is caught between the contradiction of two rights—the right to properly bury her brother, and the rights of Creon, the ruler and king, that is, her duty to obey him. In short, Antigone is torn between the laws of the Gods and the laws of men (sic). This contradiction of two rights is the aporia, the tension between *pantaporos* and *aporos*—everywhere and nowhere—that Heidegger (1996) describes in his famous analysis of *Antigone*.[11]

When Creon denies Antigone to bury her brother, she reaches a limit that cannot be crossed, and she defies Creon's decree and buries her brother, for which she is condemned to death. Creon changes his mind, but before he can save Antigone, she has hanged herself. Her suicide causes Creon's son and wife to subsequently commit suicide, and Creon is consequently punished for his hubris, that is, for insisting on overruling divine law.

Is it enough to teach Sophocles's *Antigone*, or any other work of art, to instill authentic rebellion in our students? The answer is, of course, no; authentic rebellion is always a performative event and most often not planned. There is no curriculum of rebellion; it rather happens when we reach a limit, more precisely when we act on that which limits us, be it knowledge, understanding, censorship, repression, bondage, or slavery. There is no descriptive or prescriptive rebellion; instead, rebellion in education happens in a similar way as we experience art, namely as an epiphanic event. This is what Camus (1951/1991) speaks of as the work of beauty in *The Rebel*. "The procedure of beauty," he writes, "which is to contest reality while endowing it with unity is also the procedure of rebellion" (p. 276). Antigone thus teaches us about rebellion, about reaching the limit where rebellion can take place, but it does not teach us to rebel. For this, an active and performative reading (or procedure) of the work of art must be conducted. Art as well as education must, in consequence, be enacted and made to happen for there to be authentic rebellion.

However, the foundation of an education based on the thought of authentic rebellion is what Camus calls "generosity." Generosity is the attitude or mood (*Stimmung*, to use Heidegger's term) through which both students and teachers can prepare for an education based on authentic rebellion. Generosity here means being open to the thought of the absurd and to approach education through the "procedure of beauty," that is, by what we have elsewhere called being open and releasing ourselves to the original event of learning.[12] Speaking about the Spanish prisoners who, during the Spanish civil war, refused communion because the Catholic priests had made it obligatory, Camus (1951/1991) defines what we as teachers and students must strive for also when it comes to education:

> This insane generosity is the generosity of rebellion, which unhesitatingly gives the strength of its love and without a moment's delay refuses injustice. Its merit lies in making no calculations, distributing everything it possesses to life and to living men. It is thus that it is prodigal in its gifts to men to come. Real generosity toward the future lies in giving all to the present. (p. 304)

This, we might conclude, is the authentic potential of existential education as rebellion.

CONCLUSION

In this chapter we have attempted to present what an existential education based on the thinking of Sartre and Camus might focus on as a response to the pressure of *Social Efficiency* and *instrumentalism* present in today's education on all levels. Our response has thus taken its departure in how the *potentiality* or *possibility* of the human being as learner and its Being-in-the-world can counteract the repressive systematicity and bureaucracy of standardized outcomes-based education seen as *actuality*. And, indeed, Sartre and Camus in their respective philosophies provide a rich array of possibilities to develop an alternative existential education which builds on each learner's essential way of being, that is, Being-as-potentiality. Whether we take the perspective of Sartre's ontological existentialism or Camus's rebel, we are given new ways to approach students and learners from out of their potentiality, beyond the actuality of ready-made scripts for learning and the calculative measuring of prescribed educational outcomes. Existential education, in consequence, entails the opening up of our potentialities as learners, which is in line with what Camus calls the generosity of authentic rebellion.

To revisit Greene's (1974) statement quoted at the outset of the chapter, the foundation of education, and specifically an existential education, involves a "dominating interest in human freedom, authenticity, and the elusiveness of Being" (p. 67). These three key ideas discussed by Greene, "freedom, authenticity, and the elusiveness of Being," are embraced by Sartre and Camus in their existential philosophies, regardless of their disagreements that were most explicitly expressed in the public feud that followed the publication of Camus's *The Rebel*.

The three main existential issues mentioned by Greene are also the building blocks of the counteractive existential education that we have attempted to outline in this chapter. In the end, if we approach education with generosity and an openness toward the potential in and of each learner, conceived as an *unfinished project* that is perpetually directed out and beyond itself as *ontological possibility*, we, as teachers and colearners, can initiate the beginning of a reflection and a thinking through of an equally elusive notion as that of Being, namely, justice: an existential education, we suggest, should consider the Being of justice and the justice of Being. We view our reading of Sartre and Camus in this chapter as both an introduction and invitation to such a consideration.

REFERENCES

Arendt, H. (1961). The crisis in education. In *Between past and future: Six exercises in political thought* (pp. 173–196). Viking Press.
Barnes, H. (1971). *An existentialist ethics*. Vintage Books.
Camus, A. (1991). *The rebel: An essay on man in revolt* (H. Bower, Trans.). Vintage Books.
Catalano, J. (1980). *A commentary of Jean-Paul Sartre's being and nothingness*. University of Chicago Press. (Original work published 1951)
Darling-Hammond, L., & J. Bransford. (2007). *Preparing teachers for a changing world: What teachers should learn and be able to do*. Jossey-Bass.
Detmer, D. (2005). Sartre on freedom and education. In van der Hoven & Leak (Eds.), *Sartre today: A centenary celebration* (pp. 78–91). Berghahn Books.

Due, R. (2005). Freedom, nothingness, consciousness: Some remarks on the structure of *Being and Nothingness*. In A. van der Hoven & A. Leak (Eds.), *Sartre today: A centenary celebration* (pp. 30–42). Berghahn Books.

Foley, J. (2008). *Albert Camus: From the absurd to revolt*. Acumen.

Gelven, M. (1972). *Winter, friendship, and guilt: The sources of self-inquiry*. Harper and Row.

Gibbons, A., & Heraud, R. (2007). *Creativity, enterprise and the absurd: Education and the Myth of Sisyphos. A challenge to an educator.* https://pesa.org.au/images/papers/2007-papers/heraud2007.pdf

Greene, M. (1973). *Teacher as stranger: Educational philosophy for the modern age*. Wadsworth.

Greene, M. (1974). *Literature, existentialism, and education*. In D. Denton (Ed.), *Existentialism and phenomenology in education: Collected essays* (pp. 63–87). Teacher's College Press.

Heidegger, M. (1996). *Hölderlin's hymn "The Ister"* (W. McNeill and J. Davis, Trans.). Indiana University Press.

Hobson, A. (2017). *Albert Camus and education*. Sense.

Magrini, J. (2014). *Social efficiency and instrumentalism in education: critical essays in ontology, phenomenology and philosophical hermeneutics*. Routledge.

Magrini, J. (2015). Towards a phenomenological understanding of the ontological aspects of teaching and learning. *Linguistic and Philosophical Investigations, 31*(1), 134–147.

Ornstein, A., & Hunkins, P. (2004). *Curriculum foundations, principles, and issues*. Pearson Press.

Roberts, P. (2008). Teaching, learning and ethical dilemmas: Lessons from Albert Camus. *Cambridge Journal of Education, 38*(4), 529–542.

Sartre, J.-P. (1984). *Being and Nothingness: A phenomenological essay on ontology* (H. Barnes, Trans.) Washington Square Press.

Sartre, J.-P. (1995). The humanism of existentialism. In W. Baskin (Ed.), *Jean-Paul Sartre: Essays in existentialism* (pp. 31–62). Citadel Press.

Sartre, J.-P. (2002). Intentionality: a fundamental idea of Husserl's phenomenology. In D. Moran & T. Mooney (Eds.), *The phenomenology reader* (pp. 1–4). Routledge.

Schwieler, E., & Magrini, J. (2015). Meditative thought and *gelassenheit* in Heidegger's thought of the 'turn': Releasing ourselves to the original event of learning," *Analysis and Metaphysics, 14*(1), 7–37.

Shaull, R. (2014). Foreword. In P. Freire, *Pedagogy of the oppressed* (M. B. Ramos, Trans.). Bloomsbury.

Sprintzen, D. (1978). *The drama of thought: An inquiry into the place of philosophy in human experience*. University Press of America.

Stenhouse, L. (1986). *An introduction to curriculum research and development*. Routledge.

Tyler, R. (1949). *Basic principles of curriculum and instruction*. University of Chicago Press.

Willhoite, F. H., Jr. (1961). Albert Camus' politics of rebellion. *The Western Political Quarterly, 14*(2), 400–414.

NOTES

1. Due (2005) recognizes that Sartre is critical of the inherent "idealism" in Husserl's phenomenology, where "intentional acts of consciousness [are] directed towards a meaning-bearing or noematic object" (p. 41). Sartre instead contends that consciousness relates directly to being, and this assures that Sartre's ontological project avoids the *idealism* identified in Husserl, for Sartre, "consciousness does not have to form sense impressions, ideas or representations of some kind, nor does it relate to objects as meaning-bearing structures," for it exists "immediately and directly as a relation to being" (p. 42).

2. Sartre (2002) sets this view off from both "realism and idealism," which he wryly terms "digestive" forms of philosophy, claiming that consciousness in such views, an interior repository for ideas and perceptions, is analogous to a "spider's web," which traps things inside and covers "them with a white spit and slowly [swallows] them, reducing them to its own substance" (p. 1). In the case of realism, ideas (representations of reality) partially digest the external world, sapping it of much of its immediacy and vigor, and as related to idealism, our perceptions digest and assimilate the entirety of the external world.

3. As Annabel Hertzog (2007) argues in her essay "Justice or Freedom: Camus's Aporia": "Camus strives to reconcile politics and ethics, while at the same time believing they necessarily contradict each other. His works of fiction, as well as his essays, speeches, and interviews show that, throughout his career, his concern never diverged from his aporetic attempt to reach an 'agreement' between two concepts that he regarded as incompatible: justice and freedom" (p. 188).

4. In Fred Willhoite's (1961) words in his essay "Albert Camus Politics of Rebellion": "Camus believed that the first requirement of a society which will cease to create despair in men's hearts is to restrict justice to the modesty and earthly character which epitomizes the true rebel—the man who is fully aware of and responsive to the limitations and potentialities of the human conditions" (p. 411).

5. Detmer (2005) argues that Sartre's views on literature and authenticity in writing carry potential educational implications, because literature in Sartre's view, as an "engaged" activity, focuses on thinking, speaking, and writing as these issues are grounded in questions that are crucial for education: What is it that both teachers and students want to change about their "life-projects" by engaging in the effort to learn? Why should they be concerned with one issue as opposed to another, what import does issue x have for contributing to the free development of their unique life-projects? Barnes (1971) claims that by attending to Sartre's philosophy, teacher's might draw the inspiration required to rise to the challenge of encouraging students to actively pursue answers for themselves, which can occur only when the context of education ceases to embrace the pedagogical position that knowledge should be imparted to, or deposited in, their students (the "banking-model of education"). It is now 2021, and we continue to be critical of this outmoded

manner in which to envision education as transfer and learning in terms of the "additive" or *edifice model* of knowledge accumulation.

6. We encounter the *product-process* line of curriculum-making in the in the Tyler (1949) *rationale*. To provide a bit of history relating to Tyler's curriculum philosophy, *Social Efficiency* and *instrumentalism* in education embraces scientific techniques originally developed for industrial manufacturing. Franklin Bobbitt applied these to education, giving birth to the "technical" model that manifests in the curriculum-making of Ralph Tyler. His philosophy of education is grounded in a behavioral model, where the process of education seeks to shape, influence, and control the students' behaviors, and we must add, in a potentially determinate and predictable manner. As Tyler states, "for a given [educational] objective to be attained, a student must have experiences that give him the opportunity to produce the kind of behavior implied by the objective" (p. 65). Education in this view is the planned and controlled interaction between the "learner and the external conditions," manipulated by educators, "in the environment to which he can react" (p. 63). *Social Efficiency* might be linked with positivism and materialism, but undoubtedly, whether tacitly or explicitly, as we claim, it embraces the subject-object split, and so in radical opposition to Sartre it views consciousness as an interior realm within which we process and form representations of ideas (subjective), which have their origin in external (objective) stimuli. For an extensive analysis and critique of this phenomenon that continues to impede our educational practices from an ontological, phenomenological, and hermeneutical perspective (see Magrini, 2014, 2015).

7. Stenhouse's (1986) *humanist curriculum* challenges the dichotomy and hierarchy between actuality and potential, albeit in terms that do not reflect Greek metaphysics, or the work of phenomenology as encountered in Heidegger and Sartre or the existentialism embraced by Camus. We note for readers that Stenhouse's philosophy and practice of curriculum-making is expressed in terms of a systematic and thematic view of education grounded in definitive principles emerging from a unique view of *secular humanism*, and as we have stated, this type of so-called structured or "doctrinal" view of education and curriculum-making is antithetical to Sartre's approach to phenomenology and existentialism. For example, Sartre already, in a *non-systematic* manner—in opposition to the format of a traditional philosophical treatise—intimated the fundamental ideas that found their way into *Being and Nothingness*—consciousness, contingency, and absurdity—in his first fictionalized work of philosophical literature, the novel, Nausea (*La Nausee*, 1938).

8. In relation to the themes of this essay, we stress that "original questions" are types of questions primarily concerned with the relationship between the human and the world (ontological) and the ways in which humans attempt to navigate their way through the world with others (normative). Original questions are linked with "inquiry" as opposed to "investigation," per se, and instead of providing "solutions" to problems of a technical nature, their unique focus is on what we might call existential or "ontological mysteries" (Gelven, 1972; Sprintzen, 1978). Original questions frame and direct our

encounters with *meaningful* issues that defy categorical explanations and demand our repeated attention and inquiry, for example, issues deemed "existential" in nature, such as death, interminable suffering, and the persistent search for *human* understanding and meaning in a meaningless universe, which has been stripped of transcendent values.

9. Andrew Gibbons and Richard Hereaud (2007) touch on similar thoughts in their conference presentation on Camus and education, titled "Creativity, enterprise, and the absurd: education and the Myth of Sisyphus. A challenge to an educator," focusing on the "enterprise paradigm" in education, with its focus on life-long learning and determined and systematized learning outcomes, which kills creativity and stifles existential self-realization as the overall aim of education.

10. Worth noting is that Hannah Arendt (1961), in "The Crisis in Education," traces the political in education to the Greeks and to Rosseau: "From this source there was derived at the start an educational ideal, tinged with Rousseauism and in fact directly influenced by Rousseau, in which education became an instrument of politics, and political activity itself was conceived of as a form of education" (p. 176).

11. In a similar way that we have approached freedom and justice in Camus, Heidegger (1996) notes that in *Antigone* "everything that is essentially permeated by its counter-essence. The two main figures, Creon and Antigone, do not stand opposed to one another like darkness and light, black and white, guilty and innocent. What is essential to each is as it is from out of the unity of essence and non-essence, yet in a different way in each case" (p. 52). In Camus, in the same way, freedom finds its essence in its counter-essence, which is justice, and vice versa. This is also how for authentic rebellion the necessary unity between justice and freedom is achieved in Camus.

12. See Schwieler and Magrini (2015), "Meditative thought and Gelassenheit in Heidegger's Thought of the "'Turn': Releasing Ourselves to the Original Event of Learning," especially our analysis of Heidegger's thinking concerning *Gelassenheit* (releasement) in relation to education, which has significant similarities with Camus's notion of the generosity of rebellion.

CHAPTER 2

LEARNING OBJECTIVES RECONSIDERED IN LIGHT OF EXISTENTIAL-PHENOMENOLOGY AND MINDFULNESS

Glen L. Sherman
Saint Elizabeth University

ABSTRACT

Learning objectives in higher education typically omit consideration of authentic phenomenological mindfulness. This chapter considers how subjectivity is brought into the creation of learning goals in learning *subjectives* by first reviewing the origin and development of learning objectives, which were based on a limited, cognitive conception of knowledge and psychological science more generally, as observable and measurable. Cognitive learning objectives came with a promise that the affective domain would eventually be incorporated; this was never adequately realized due to its uniqueness as a phenomenon that exceeded the original epistemological framework. Even subsequent efforts within a broader cognitive psychology (e.g., metacognition, the self-system) and the information processing perspectives proved inadequate to expand the notion of learning objectives to fully account for subjectivity. An alternative, existential-phenomenological conception of the lifeworld, embodiment, and authentic self-realization and releasement, based upon concepts from Edmund Husserl, Maurice Merleau-Ponty, and Martin Heidegger form the basis for a more adequate educational psychology.

Problematizing the Profession of Teaching From an Existential Perspective, pp. 25–44
Copyright © 2022 by Information Age Publishing
www.infoagepub.com

Mindfulness, or mindful awareness, is a means of achieving this type of awareness of self. Cultivating mindful awareness in higher educational settings provides students with enhanced concentration, self-awareness, and understanding, cognitive attunement to themselves and their broader environments. Such insight may facilitate the integration of subjectivity into the learning process, the subject matter of learning, and vocational and career choices. As such, learning subjectives incorporate these dimensions of learning. Encouraging students' self-exploration of their relation to courses' subject matter and incorporating career counseling into curriculum provides concrete examples of how learning subjectives work in educational practice.

Student learning and knowledge in higher education are typically defined by objectively measurable goals and outcomes. In turn, these entail the development of cognitive skills and critical thinking in conjunction with a particular body of knowledge. Curriculum is object-focused, with subjectivity addressed in cognitive skill development required to know the object. This conception of learning stems from assumptions about mind and reality, the divide between subject and object, inherited from the modern Western philosophical tradition.

Having stated these assumptions, we are in a better position to consider their implications for teaching and learning. I will examine how learning objectives are typically conceived, and the kinds of educational goals to which they lead. I will consider how, if the outcome of learning focuses on predetermined learning objectives, authentic phenomenological mindfulness remains marginalized and irrelevant. Alternatively, through a review of key representatives from existential and phenomenological philosophy and psychology and the contemporary mindfulness literature, I will demonstrate how subjectivity may be brought into the creation of learning goals. There are similarities between tenets from both Maslow and Bugental, on achieving the authentic self, Husserl's philosophy of consciousness and the lifeworld, Heidegger's contemplation of being, Merleau-Ponty's phenomenology of perception, and current thinking about mindfulness, in so far as they may inform what would be different and vital about creating "learning subjectives." I will conclude with a few examples of what this looks like in actual practice.

The phenomenological perspective, the region *between* subject and object, facilitates this inquiry with an alternative conception of mind which elevates the idea of mindfulness from its frequent instrumental use in education as a stress management technique or solution for mental health problems, toward the deeper intentions of ancient mindfulness philosophy and psychology and its potential to assume a more integral place in higher education's curriculum. I then address the question: In an era when university studies are so frequently conceived as goal-directed, how might phenomenology and mindful attention *improve* learning and learning outcomes? That is to say, how might "learning subjectives" contribute in a positive way to more traditional curricular outcomes?

THE MINDSET OF LEARNING OBJECTIVES

Curriculum in higher education centers on learning objectives. Prefacing a learning endeavor with objectives is a method of specifying what students are expected to learn in a given course of study. The focus is primarily on the kinds of mental skills necessary to come to know the object of study (e.g., a scientific phenomenon or a text in the humanities). Students are encouraged to develop and use their powers of critical thinking, from the simplest to most complex, to examine, remember, conceptualize, analyze, compare, and contrast; to break things down and reconstruct them in new ways to better understand them.

If we look back to the origins of learning objectives, frequently identified with the *Taxonomy of Educational Objectives* (Bloom, 1956), there are important clues regarding how we got to this state of affairs. Bloom's (1956) taxonomy is written from the perspective of behavioral educational psychology, with the associated assumption that what is real is strictly observable. Hence, in education, behavioral outcomes are best defined as what a student can do or say (volitional behavior) that demonstrates what they have learned and what they know. The authors acknowledge that as a result, only "those educational programs which can be specified in terms of intended student behaviors can be classified" (p. 15).

Further limitations of this approach are the tripartite structuring of human being into cognitive, affective, and motoric or bodily aspects, and that Bloom's (1956) taxonomy focused solely on the cognitive, as reflected in the emphasis on the behavioral. The authors themselves described the book specifically as a "model for the analysis of educational outcomes in the cognitive area of remembering, thinking, and problem solving" (p. 2); put slightly otherwise, the focus was upon "the recall or recognition of knowledge and the development of intellectual abilities and skills" (p. 7). While the authors acknowledged broader aspects of human being and education (like student development), they settled on a limited conception of knowledge and educational objectives that were observable and measurable due to their natural scientific biases, and also because these objectives were deemed to be more manageable. Similarly, while the authors noted that the second part of the taxonomy would address the affective domain, they indefinitely deferred this endeavor because of difficulty describing its associated learning objectives and behaviors and the internal, covert nature of the feelings and emotions involved.

The very use of the term taxonomy belied the authors' bias, since the definition of taxonomy, "the study of the general principles of scientific classification ... especially plants and animals according to their presumed natural relationships" (Merriam-Webster, n.d.), emanates from the natural sciences. While this was in one way understandable, given the prevailing conception of psychological science at the time, we can now argue, from the vantage point of recognition of the *human* sciences, that observed behavior does not equal the human subject, nor the "changes produced in individuals as a result of educational experiences" or fully "the intended outcomes of the educational process" (Bloom, 1956, p. 12). As propounded by Giorgi (1970, 2009), we can assert too that the natural scientific model is not the proper one for human psychology or education.

Pring (1971) raised an important challenge and epistemological objection to separating cognition and affect. He argued that convenience, or difficulty figuring out how to conceive of them simultaneously, is an insufficient justification for separating them. He described how knowing is always infused with feeling, and, likewise, how particular feelings about something or some situation always imply judgements. As such, while separating cognition and affect may be convenient, it is not reflective of how experience occurs. "To dissect the 'cognitive' in this way is, through lack of analysis, to miss the essential unity in the development of thinking" (p. 90).

The second part of the taxonomy, *Handbook II: Affective Domain* (Krathwohl et al., 1964) was published almost 10 years later. Even then, despite efforts to broaden the scope of educational aims, the effort was impeded by the same theoretical assumptions at work in the first volume. While the authors criticized the traditional "tripartite organization" (Krathwohl et al., 1964, p. 7) of human being into cognitive, affective, and motoric aspects, and affirmed notions of the fundamental unity of the "total organism" or "whole being," they subsequently succumbed to the prevailing tradition that artificially separated these aspects with "full recognition of the arbitrariness of the *Taxonomy's* division between cognitive and affective behavior" (Krathwohl et al., 1964, p. 48). They explained that while there is a basic unity to this tri-partite structure, "to conceptualize behavior adequately" (Krathwohl et al., 1964, p. 46) one must tease them apart and consider them serially to analyze and adequately understand them. They also undid their acknowledgement of the "whole being" by speciously stating that the tripartite division of human experience is "natural" because these are categories into which teachers have historically been inclined to divide learning objectives. Of course, accepting the status quo and basing subsequent theory upon it omits adequate theoretical justification for doing so; moreover, doing so overlooks that this inclination reflects the historical Cartesian bias of mind-body duality. To state that we must not forget that one domain is always involved with the other but to fail to demonstrate *how* they are integrated is a theoretical and methodological flaw of the taxonomies. It is no wonder that the ensuing effort to define the affective realm falls short of the potential which the subjective implies.

The subjective, in *Handbook II: Affective Domain* is first equated with interests, attitudes, values, appreciation, and adjustment, or character development, based on review of affective learning objectives found in the literature up through that period of time. Their notable absence from university and college course learning objectives was attributed to faculty members' greater facility with the cognitive realm than the affective realm, hesitancy to grade students based on this affective realm of human experience (compared to a ready willingness to grade on cognitive achievement), and "deeper philosophical and cultural values" (Krathwohl et al., 1964, p. 16) which relegated the affective to personal and private matters, as opposed to the more public matter of high cognitive achievement, as reflected, for example, in public recognition of the deans' lists.

To rectify this situation, the authors wrote, "If affective objectives and goals are to be realized, they must be defined clearly; [and] learning experiences to help the student develop in the desired direction must be provided" along with "a somewhat more precise understanding of how affective behaviors develop, how and when they can be modified, and what the school can and cannot do to develop them in particular forms" (Krathwohl et al., 1964, p. 23). The authors went on to say that the descriptive list of affective characteristics from the first volume, that is, "changes in interest, attitudes and values, and the development of appreciations and adequate adjustment" (Bloom, 1956, p. 7), were too abstract, general, and imprecise to be useful if left in that vague form. So, while retaining this limited set of affective phenomena simply because they had been present in the educational literature and "seemed to indicate the behavioral components which must be provided for in the affective-domain structure" (Krathwohl et al., 1964, p. 26), they set out to organize students' levels of perception of and interaction with these phenomena. Hence, this effort was limited to the extent of students' initiative vs. passive reception of such phenomena (e.g., in music, literature), the quality of students' experienced emotion, the interrelations of values, attitudes, and philosophies of life developed, and the associated behaviors demonstrated by the student.

The authors viewed this process as a developmental progression of *internalization*, which they believed "described well the major process of the affective domain" (Krathwohl et al., 1964, p. 44). They defined internalization as incorporating something into the mind or body, adopting the ideas, values, standards, or practices of another person or society as one's own. The term internalization was chosen because "It was consistent with the behavioral point of view of education which places the focus of learning within the individual (Krathwohl et al., 1964, p. 28).

What becomes clear from this description is that behavioral psychological principles predominant at that time held sway over the definition of the affective domain. One might argue too that the bias toward the cognitive domain influenced how the affective domain was conceived and constructed. In the end, the authors acknowledged that "Much of the affective domain has been repressed, denied, and obscured" (Krathwohl et al., 1964, p. 91). Yet, using the term "internalization" limited their definition of the subjective and more complex notions of subjectivity were absent from consideration. Krathwohl (1994), one of the original authors, in a retrospective reflection many years later, acknowledged this as a problem and expressed the need for subsequent theorists to consider further integration of the domains.

More recent critiques of Bloom's taxonomy attempt to show how developments in educational psychological theory warrant revisions of the driving assumptions regarding the taxonomy and learning objectives. These critiques incorporate cognitive psychology and information processing perspectives but still ignore the problem of the unity or integration of human experience. For our purpose, the key developments are the notions of metacognition and the self-system.

Anderson and Krathwohl (2001) refined Bloom's distinctions between the six classes of learning objectives into a two-dimensional matrix. They identified four types of knowledge (factual, conceptual, procedural, and metacognitive) and juxtaposed six cognitive processes with which they may interact (e.g., remembering, understanding, applying, analyzing, evaluating, and creating). This created a dynamic analytic schema for types of learning and understanding.

Metacognitive knowledge "is knowledge about cognition in general as well as awareness of and knowledge about one's own cognition" (Anderson & Krathwohl, 2001, p. 55). As students develop greater awareness of their thinking and knowledge about cognition, they learn more effectively. This type of awareness goes by various names in different theories: "metacognitive knowledge, metacognitive awareness, self-awareness, self-reflection, and self-regulation" (p. 55). Flavell (1979), the originator of the concept, went further and included affect: "Metacognitive experiences are any conscious cognitive or affective experiences that accompany and pertain to any intellectual enterprise" (p. 906). In metacognitive thinking, one becomes aware of one's beliefs about the factors that influence the ways in which one thinks, its limitations, and the "outcome of cognitive enterprises" (p. 907). These enterprises are generally highly demanding intellectual (cognitive) activities that require strategic action. It is a kind of thinking intended to improve one's problem-solving or ability to accomplish something, by becoming aware of one's *way* of thinking about a problem, so as to modify one's strategy, if necessary. It is geared toward reflecting on and evaluating "the productivity of our own thinking" (Costa, 1984, p. 57) and taking "conscious control" (Costa, 1984, p. 60) of one's studying and learning processes. Clearly, this conception, however evolved, still represents the ongoing primacy of cognitive dimensions of human experience in relation to learning.

Marzano and Kendall (2007), in a subsequent revision, criticized Bloom's conception of knowledge as confused and overly simplistic but also built their revision on developments in cognitive theory. They distinguished further between "types of knowledge" and "the various mental operations that act on knowledge" (p. 22). They explained that developments in cognitive theory since Flavell's (1979) identification of metacognition had "established the self-system as a central aspect of human thought apart from the metacognitive system" (Marzano & Kendall, 2007, pp. 18–19). They, too, indicated that learning is dependent on levels of system processing: the self-system, the metacognitive system, and the cognitive system.

The self-system reflects a network of related beliefs and goals used to decide whether to engage in new tasks and the motivation to do so. The interaction of this arrangement of "attitudes, beliefs, and emotions … determines both motivation and attention" (Marzano & Kendall, 2007, p. 55). They wrote (similar to Flavell himself) that "the metacognitive system is in charge of conscious operations relative to knowledge that include goal setting, process monitoring, monitoring for clarity, and monitoring for accuracy" (Marzano & Kendall, 2007, p. 55). In an interesting way, they explicitly allude to Salomon and Globerson (1987), who describe metacognitive self-monitoring as being "mindful" (Marzano & Kendall, 2007, p. 55), in contrast to being automatic, in Langer's (1989) sense. This means that conscious attention is being exercised and active discriminations are being made regarding the task at hand. Ultimately, under self-system thinking (the pinnacle of these authors' knowledge schema) something akin to mindfulness emerges, although the addition of the notion of control is not exactly aligned with current, more typical notions of mindfulness:

> The key feature of this type of self-system thinking is the identification of a pattern of thinking or experiences underlying a given association along with the reasonableness of this pattern of thinking. There is no particular attempt to change these associations—only to understand them. This said, an argument can be made that awareness of one's emotional associations provides the opportunity for some control over them. (Marzano & Kendall, 2007, p. 111)

The authors tout this model as an improvement over the previous revision (Anderson & Krathwohl, 2001) and Bloom's taxonomy itself since this revised model "explicitly addresses the cognitive, affective, and psychomotor aspects of learning" (Marzano & Kendall, 2007, p. 17) and since the self-system includes the examination of emotional responses to learning situations and does not segregate or overlook aspects beyond the cognitive domain. In the end, however, this revised model does not appear to be truly integrative, since the model still prioritizes the cognitive while accounting for the other domains. Another significant problem with this way of thinking is the homunculi implied by the creation of the various systems. Describing mental systems with seemingly independent decision-makers within consciousness divides the unity of the self and creates multiple, implied selves. It also suggests that these "systems" determine what is chosen in a way that mechanizes or automatizes "choice" rather than viewing choice in terms of volition.

The issue here is finding the best way to account for the human phenomena involved in learning. In this revision, emotions are ultimately conceived as responses to the knowledge components. Once again, this places priority on the cognitive dimension of perception, thereby assuming that the rest of experience follows from that dimension. Marzano and Kendall (2007) also raised the question, reminiscent of the earlier hesitancy regarding the affective domain, about whether the metacognitive and self-system processes even lie within "the purview or responsibility of education" (p. 121) since they fall outside the domain of subject matter curriculum proper and educational goals, despite an abundance of research indicating how development of these areas of mind supports students' achievement, and that such development contributes to students' self-regulatory skills.

EXISTENTIAL-PHENOMENOLOGICAL CONSIDERATIONS

Existential-phenomenological philosophy and psychology, in contrast to behavioral and cognitive psychology, described a more holistic view of human being, providing the groundwork for a more adequate educational psychology from which to expand the current conception of learning and learning objectives. Phenomenology challenges the premise that human consciousness, thought, and reason is something separate from, and something that separates us from, an objective world. The world is not an inert or mechanical object to simply be understood by cognitive categories of understanding; rather, phenomenology describes a world brought to life in particular ways by different people or cultures, depending upon their unique engagement with, and ways of inhabiting, the world.

Edmund Husserl's phenomenology turned toward "the world as it is experienced in its felt immediacy" (Abram, 2017, p. 35) to allow its structure and meaning to be revealed and understood. This is one way of understanding the notion that consciousness is always consciousness *of* something. Yet, Husserl was not antiscience, and he believed that objectivity, understood phenomenologically, is "a striving to achieve greater consensus, greater agreement or consonance among a plurality of subjects [perspectives], rather than an attempt to avoid subjectivity altogether" (Abram, 2017, p. 38). However, that differs from a natural scientific approach to both human psychology and the world, which conceives both these phenomena as adhering to natural laws governed by reason alone.

> The "real world" in which we find ourselves, then—the very world our sciences strive to fathom—is not a sheer "object," not a fixed and finished "datum" from which all subjects and subjective qualities could be pared away, but is rather an intertwined matrix of sensations and perceptions, a collective field of experience lived through from many different angles. (Abram, 2017, p. 39)

Husserl's term for this world of experience was the *lifeworld*, "the world of our immediately lived experience *as* we live it, prior to all our thoughts" (Abram, 2017, p. 40) and preconceptualizations about the given experience. The lifeworld "is that which is present to us in our everyday tasks and enjoyments—reality as it engages us before being analyzed by our theories and our science" (p. 40).

Merleau-Ponty (1968) developed phenomenology further by recognizing the body (embodiment) or "the bodily organism" not only as the location but also the very possibility of "the experiencing self" (Abram, 2017, p. 45). In this way, embodiment suggests and includes intentionality (consciousness), as well as all other aspects of human experience coequal to thought, that is, the "poised and animate power that initiates all our projects and suffers all our passions" (Abram, 2017, p. 46). It was precisely the potential of the interaction of the embodied subject and the world, the richness and depth that might emerge from deepened awareness of any moment of perception, with both its limited perspective yet potential for expansiveness, which fascinated Merleau-Ponty. According to Abram (2017), "Perception, in Merleau-Ponty's work, is precisely this reciprocity, the ongoing interchange between my body and the entities that surround it" (p. 52) which discloses to the senses new aspects inviting further exploration.

The implication of this is that at every moment, there is an implicit preceding experience that remains (structurally, inevitably) out of awareness, that we are *subject-to*, rendering consciousness translucent. Hence, the assumption that consciousness is transparent to itself, that we are thoroughly self-aware through apperception and cognitive reason alone, is mythical. The narratives we tell about ourselves are a function of *re*-flection, forever missing the immediacy it attempts to reflect upon. This aspect of experience has remained unaccounted for in the previously cited theorizing about the meaning of learning objectives and challenges the primacy of cognition as the foundation of educational psychology.

In his later work, Merleau-Ponty (1968) went on to describe a pre-conceptual "attunement or synchronization" (p. 54), an almost mutual solicitation or "reciprocal encounter" (p. 56) between the perceiver and the perceived-world. Moss and Kean (1981) described this as "the co-constituting presence of the human body and its sensorium" (p. 111). This renders the perceived world as having "a dynamic presence that confronts us and draws us into relation" (Abram, 2017, p. 56) rather than being more akin to a passive object to be perceived by a thinking subject.

> When we no longer experience the world dualistically as a collection of separate objects perceived by the mind, but instead as a moment-by-moment manifestation of interrelated phenomena [as in the phenomenalism frequently described in Eastern and current Western conceptions of mindfulness] then we experience the whole universe as sentient, as inherently luminous. (Zimmerman, 1993, p. 253)

Such attunement suggests a radiant, lively world occurring at every moment—Husserl's lifeworld and Merleau-Ponty's flesh of the world (Merleau-Ponty, 1968). Present experience is often positioned as secondary to thought *about* the world, including the theories and stories we construct—present, remembered, or projected—yet present experience precedes "the academic distinctions among affect, conation, and cognition" (Moss & Kean, 1981, p. 112), which both behavioral and cognitive models of learning have accepted.

The existential philosophical tradition, dating back to Nietzsche and Kierkegaard, extolled the importance and virtues of the individual quest for self-realization, sometimes in a spiritual or religious context, sometimes in a godless universe. More contemporary existential psychologists, represented for example by Maslow (2014) and Bugental (1981), also described the importance of authentic self-realization, the actualization of individual human potential, in the quest for fulfillment, happiness, and well-being, as well as the overcoming of impediments to this quest. To achieve fulfillment, the individual needs to become fully aware of their true desires, talents, capabilities, and resources, and have or be willing and able to create the opportunities in their life to bring these to fruition, including the working through of whatever obstacles or impediments are encountered. The ideas of growth and development of the individual accompany such a pursuit. Certainly, Dewey (1916) was concerned that educators assist students with developing more of an appreciation for their present aims, interests, and purposes in education, rather than remaining strictly future-focused, and situating students' thinking within their broader human experience, so as to foster better engagement and growth. Yet, as Noddings (2007) suggested, precisely what Dewey meant when he said that students should experience a "personally unified curriculum" (p. 40) remained unclear.

Martin Heidegger, in his later thinking, shifted from an earlier focus on the existential aspects of human being (Dasein), to the broader matter of Being in general, how it is that Being manifests itself at all, and how it is possible that the world appears as it does. In the *Discourse on Thinking* (Heidegger, 1959/1966), Heidegger used the term "meditative thinking" to capture a kind of thinking that is "open to what is given" (p. 24), involving "an annulling of the will" (p. 25) and exceeding "the exercise of any subjective human power" (p. 25). Meditative thinking is the way Heidegger "proceeded from man to Being" (p. 37). Von Eckartsberg and Valle (1981) put it this way: "Meditative thinking is a 'thinking' that overcomes the limits of willful ego-consciousness and the separation inherent in the subject-object split" (p. 290). They also added that Heidegger's emphasis on the clearing of Being "puts him close to the illumination tradition of the East" (p. 291) and that "a personal path of thinking ... can show the way" (p. 307) to insight and understanding.

For philosophy, the "way" to accomplish this type of thinking is to walk along a path to Being, as the three interlocutors do in the dialogue, "Conversation on a Country Path about Thinking" (Heidegger, 1959/1966). As John Anderson put it in his introduction to Heidegger's Discourse on Thinking (Heidegger, 1959/1966): In meditative thinking, man opens to Being and resolves for its disclosure ... it is taking a stand which reveals Being, a kind of dwelling in being" (p. 26). Put otherwise, "meditative thinking is an opening of man to something, as is emphasized by calling such thinking releasement" (p. 28). Releasement (*Gelassenheit*) is one of the key words Heidegger used in his later philosophizing to capture this conception of approaching Being. It is significant for our purpose since it is more passive than active in its suggestion for achieving its objective.

In this conception, meditative thinking is always situated but grants us "the possibility of dwelling in the world in a totally different way" (Heidegger, 1959/1966, p. 55). "Yet releasement toward things and openness ... do not befall us accidentally. Both flourish only through persistent, courageous thinking" (Heidegger, 1959/1966, p. 56). While such meditative thinking and releasement is not strictly an act of will, it does require intentionality of practice or a particular mindset: "releasement awakens when our nature is let-in so as to have dealings with that which is not a willing" (Heidegger, 1959/1966, p. 61).

What is particularly important here is Heidegger's (1959/1966) conjunction of the idea of meditation with philosophical thinking (as opposed to calculative or representational thought—cognition, which is subsequent to it) as the way to Being, a larger vision of what *is*. Heidegger himself said:

> anyone can follow the path of meditative thinking in his own manner and within his own limits. Why? Because man is a *thinking*, that is, a *meditating*,

being. Thus meditative thinking need by no means be "high-flown." It is enough if we dwell on what lies close and meditate on what is closest … each one of us, here and now. (p. 47)

For Heidegger, this type of thinking "means being free from discursive, categorizing activity and open for Being" (Zimmerman, 1981, p. 272). In the dialogue in the *Discourse on Thinking*, the interlocutors suggest that this kind of thinking involves waiting, allowing ourselves to remain present for what is occurring in experience. This is quite consistent with the experience of reality that mindfulness practice opens up.

Many authors have noted the similarities between Heidegger's (1959/1966) work on releasement and eastern, Buddhist thought. Staumbaugh (1970) compared *Gelassenheit* with the Eastern ideas of non-attachment and nonclinging (in Buddhist psychology attachment and clinging to objects or human identities are sources of human suffering). Mehta (1970) pointed out that Heidegger's thesis of the inadequacy of objectifying thought in approaching Being is very similar to fundamental premises in the Far Eastern and Indian traditions. Stark and Washburn (1977) described how egocentricity, with its false assumptions about what is required to develop a satisfying sense of identify and self-worth (and the futility to which this leads) is also a main source of suffering. This, it has been argued, is due to the inevitable, structurally impossible lack of coincidence between consciousness and that with which it is identifying as its self-image; this suffering, it has been argued further, is also due to the intersubjective need for recognition or approval from others. What is required, therefore, "is a change in understanding, not a change in being" (Stark & Washburn, 1977, p. 280).

Zimmerman (1981) suggested something similar, when he wrote, "The suffering produced by the dualistic experience of the world cannot be alleviated by any action taken by the ego, but only by releasement from egoistical self-understanding" (p. 258). He went even further, explaining that putting oneself in a place of openness to Being (clearing a place where this may occur) does not directly come from subjectivity but is the openness in which subjectivity itself may occur. "In the eclipse of the self there occurs the dawning of Being" (p. 276). In such a place, releasement may occur, where "the ego gives way to what is more fundamental—openness" (p. 246). Zimmerman pointed out that "Presently, Being reveals itself to Western man as objectivity" (p. 252).

This exploration of key aspects of existential-phenomenology reveals the often overlooked immediacy of experience critical for a more adequate educational psychology. Our penchant for scientific thinking and explanation, presumed to be "objective" knowledge, accounts for the appeal of learning *objectives*, since they coincide with this more limited conception of the world. However, in this account, the more immediate, lived experience phenomenology describes—the *subjective*—is overlooked. How might lived experience be incorporated into educational psychology so that it too becomes a basis of educational aims (*learning subjectives*)? For this, I turn to mindfulness.

MINDFULNESS AND HIGHER EDUCATION

Mindfulness, or mindful awareness, typically (but not solely) cultivated through meditation practice, promotes concentration and awareness upon a point of focus, such as the breath, reflecting "wordless, bare attention" (Gunaratana, 2011. p. 35). As Husserlian phenomenology also affirmed, "The mind can never be focused without a mental object" (Gunaratana, 2011, p. 45). Through personal discovery, mindful "egoless" awareness (Gunaratana, 2011, p. 83) reveals the impermanence of both the self and experience. Mindfulness also attests to the process of perception described by Merleau-Ponty, that "What you are looking at responds to the process of looking" (Gunaratana, 2011, p. 33).

Mindfulness is essentially about discovering and coming to better understand the nature of one's own mind and how it interacts with the phenomenal flux of the world. It is a psychological activity, like the educative process and, thus, has great insight and benefits to offer education. Yet, unlike the explicit focus in higher education on the development of the conceptual mind, "During meditation, we are seeking to experience the mind at the preconceptual level" (Gunaratana, 2011, p. 126). Mindfulness is what happens in experience before we define it in words, phenomenology's focus.

Olendzki (2014), from a Buddhist psychological perspective, captured the conjunction of the phenomenological, intentional consciousness and mindfulness perspectives when he described how "A well-concentrated mind serves as a tool capable of zooming in below the threshold of ordinary awareness to reveal mental functioning more precisely" (p. 66). Specifically:

> every moment of consciousness emerges from the interaction of a sense organ and a sense object, and involves an act of interpretive perception, a feeling tone ... and some form of emotional and volitional response. In its simplest configuration, therefore, experience always consists of a single-pointed focus . . . along with the basic and universal mental functions of feeling, perception, intention, and attention. (p. 66)

Hence, mindful awareness precedes the conceptual thinking and activities reflected in Bloom's taxonomy and its revisions. While learning objectives are self-consciously constructed and determined to be essential for a student's learning, and while their potential for refinement of particular analytic skills in thinking are capable of producing highly evolved, refined knowledge of the object, what is overlooked and omitted from this process of defining what is to be learned, is what the student most essentially brings to the learning situation and what may either facilitate, inhibit, or otherwise inform learning. Greater mindful awareness of the mindset and accompanying emotions the student brings to their studies in the educational setting, knowledge for instance, of their desires, intentions, and perhaps inhibitions, can lend itself to greater subjective awareness on the part of the student, that can then better inform the cognitive work they set out to do upon the matter at hand. Lieberman (1985) articulated the importance in existentially informed education of the individual being awakened to, owning, and appropriating their own selfhood in the process of learning. Mindful awareness facilitates this self-ownership.

Langer's (1989, 2016) Western understanding of mindfulness noted that attention is best paid when the stimulus is varied and when individuals are encouraged to have curiosity and openness to novelty. She encouraged moving beyond the intake of bare facts taken as objectively true, and, rather, encouraged taking varied perspectives on the meaning of those facts and the creation of new categories with resultant creative, flexible thinking. Similarly, Eastern mindful awareness of sense experience and the phenomenal flux of that experience, cultivated through mindfulness practice, can contribute in a meaningful way to loosening the grip of standard, possibly outworn categories of cognitive understanding in both personal and academic problem-solving and work. Reber (2014), citing Ritchert and Perkins (2000), said that exploring the environment closely, instead of speeding through it, sensitizes us to the environment's details, resulting in openness to new information, possibilities, and perspectives. Another way of putting this is in terms of *reperceiving*, a type of metacognitive awareness, or meta-perspective "at the heart of the change and transformation affected by mindfulness practice" (Shapiro et al., 2006, p. 383). This offers a more holistic way of integrating this cognitive aspect of experience.

Reperceiving is a *"shift in perspective"* (Shapiro et al., 2006, p. 377 [emphasis original]) that allows us to witness our own experience. It is "the awareness of an observing consciousness that is both *a part of* and *apart from* the experience" (McCown, 2014, p. 1090). It is from the intention of inhabiting this mental space of meta-awareness that the attention and non-judgmental attitude of mindfulness become possible. It is similar to the *epoché* in phenomenology within Husserl's methodology, in which one may "dispassionately observe or witness the contents of one's consciousness" (Shapiro et al., 2006, p. 381) and out of which fresh descriptions of experience, as well as a loosening of standard attachments to thoughts, emotions, perspectives, and even self-narratives, become possible.

For Langer (2016) bringing mindfulness to education means encouraging active learning, research, and writing rather than the presentation of facts or drills. This is based on her conception of intelligence, which at its heart, is phenomenological and constructivist. While students may remain at an automatic level of perception, within preconceived categories of understanding (as in phenomenology's natural attitude), doing so runs the risk of "confusing the stability of our own mindset with the stability of the phenomenon itself" (p. 129). Similar to Abram's (2017) description of phenomenological experience, Langer (2016) wrote, "At every moment in a mindful state, we are learning something, we are changing in some way . . . interacting with the environment so that both we and the environment are changed" (p. 132). This promotes self-understanding and the individual's unique perspective on the world. In this sense, what emanates from the student (what comes from learning) should comprise both what resides within the student's perspective and what is being offered from the environment to either supplement, complement, or even replace what was previously known. For Langer, "the ability to explore the world and understand experience" (p. 117) reflects intelligence more adequately, and this differs from the capacity to achieve a predefined outcome which may be limited in its application to alternative settings and further may "inhibit the capacity for exploring the skills best suited to an individual's goals" (p. 118).

Saarinen and Lehti (2014) also discussed the importance of subjective intentions deriving from introspection and internal dialogue, which influence "potential outcomes" and "set a direction for action and indicate an orientation" (pp. 1122–1123) distinguished from the achievement of measurable goals. While mindfulness may not always improve educational outcomes directly, mindfulness "opens the mind for subsequent knowledge acquisition. This means that a mindfulness intervention does not necessarily replace direct instruction but, in some cases, could precede it in order to prepare the student's mind for the materials to come" (Reber, 2014, p. 1063).

Mindfulness recognizes that students do not and cannot leave their emotional baggage at the door when they enter the classroom, and that the mind is not "a neutral tool that can be used to regard inner emotional states from an objective viewpoint but is itself permeated by and molded by the very states it is trying to observe" (Olendzki, 2014, p. 63). Hence, a potential benefit of cultivating mindfulness in higher education is that it may be "extended into *behavior* through acting, speaking, or thinking with equanimity, and can strengthen and develop into a personality *trait* through systematic practice" (Olendzki, 2014, p. 67). What better form of empirical observation could there be in the classroom or laboratory than when it is also accompanied by adequate self-awareness, clarity, and emotional regulation so that so-called objective observation is freer to observe? Along this line of thinking, Weare (2014) said:

> Mainstream schools in the West have naturally been immersed in the dominant paradigm of "doing" and "thinking," and "the achieving self" as the only way to experience the world, tackle its challenges, and find satisfaction and meaning. They have simply not to date had the vital but simple tools that Eastern contemplative practice offers to help them realize their core ambitions, to help students look inwards into the organ through which all their experience is filtered, their own minds, and undertake the kind of clarifying and stilling practices that shape and cultivate these minds and help them process experience more effectively. (p. 1049)

If "[c]oncentration is a strong, energetic [single-pointed] attention to one single item" (Gunaratana, 2011, p. 70) and is "our microscope for viewing subtle internal states" (p. 64), then the concentration and mental acuity facilitated by meditation and mindfulness more generally, should become available for and contribute to the mental activity involved in academic work. This "[c]oncentration can be forced into growth" (Gunaratana, 2011, p. 110) and through it, the mind gains "power and intensity" (Gunaratana, 2011, p. 144). We frequently talk about the problem of student engagement. A solution is that the "phenomenological experience of mindfulness is the felt experience of engagement" (Langer, 2014, p. 11). In mindfulness practice, for instance, the repetitive redirecting of the wandering mind back to the object of focus (e.g., the breath) builds the power of concentration in a student. Concentration brings about greater mental clarity and awareness of thoughts and feelings as they arise. They can be let go of as distractions, or retained for later reflection, if they might offer meaningful insight. The "gentle, patient mindfulness" (p. 74) brought about through the process of meditation can enhance students' awareness of distractions from their studies, and may contribute to grit, resilience, and self-discipline, key factors in academic persistence and success.

"Insight meditation is the practice of moment-to-moment mindfulness. The meditator learns to pay bare attention to birth, growth, and decay of all the phenomena of the mind" (Gunaratana, 2011, p. 161), that is, that which is most *subjective*. Meditation demonstrates the connectedness of sensory perception, mental, affective, and bodily phenomena, as phenomenology portrays. Meditation also enhances mental flexibility, instills an inquisitive spirit, and an openness to "truth in any form, from any source, and at any time" (p. 162). These qualities and values are consistent with academic success. So, too, the ethical ethos brought about through mindful awareness (the loving friendliness and compassion which emanates from things like recognition of the universality of the breath amongst all living beings) might inform the content chosen to focus on (choice of major), the rigor with which work is attended to, the quality of work produced, and the choices made with regard to the career-related applications of knowledge—all related to *learning subjectives*.

Mindfulness practice has the potential to open students to aspects of themselves and their world that have remained unknown to them. Teaching for critical thinking alone (particularly about curricular material and applications of that material not freely chosen) produces questionable educational outcomes. Khong (2003) described how development of right mind can lead to right livelihood and vocation. This suggests that students may benefit from greater orientation to practices that lead to opening themselves up to suitable careers, rather than willful decisions based on externally based motivations and reasons. This process of self-discovery is a process of acknowledging the facticity (or thrown-ness) of student's existential realities and situations (their actualities), a realization of, or reckoning with, their current thinking and feeling about who they are and what they want to do with their vocational lives, opening themselves up to perhaps as yet undiscovered, unrecognized, or unacknowledged aspects of themselves and their experience (their potentialities), and considering a strategy for how obstacles might be overcome. Career development counselors have long known the importance of this process, but for the most part, it has remained outside of curricular concerns. *Learning subjectives* in higher education would be directly associated with this practice and may lead to more mindful outcomes contributing to the well-being of self and society. Following are two examples of how this works in practice.

While most curricula in major courses of study are progressive in nature, promoting over time deeper and more sophisticated forms of thinking by students *about* the subject matter, very little formal attention is paid to the process of discovery regarding students' individual *relation to* the subject matter, how they arrived there, what they bring to the educational situation, what the curricular material *means* to them, and what their aims and purposes are in pursuing their courses of study. Learning subjectives build these questions into the curriculum in order that students might be better grounded in their majors and courses of study *as* they take in and process the information and learn to achieve higher levels of analysis. This contributes to solidifying their purpose and objectives in understanding. Devoting a one or two credit course that each major is required to take midway through their course of study, one which explicitly invites self-assessment and self-reflection about their vocational desires as they further pursue the major, their hopes for their next educational or occupational steps beyond graduation, and assisting them with thinking through how to get there and what components to consider to enhance and enrich their upper level educational experience, is one way to accomplish this.

A typical learning subjective in a course like this is: Students will be able to articulate their reasons for studying major X, and related to this, their current goals, and aspirations for after graduation. Another example is: students will be able to articulate activities and steps they can begin taking during the final two years of their undergraduate career to better prepare for professional life after graduation (e.g., identify additional personal, service learning, campus activities, and internship experiences that will not only further students' career portfolios, but also deepen their understanding of what this course of study means to them and their personal relation to it). Another means to accomplishing this is to require students to work individually with a career counselor at the university's career services office in conjunction with the curriculum, and as a requirement for the course. The learning subjective related to this is: Students will meet with a career counselor to explore their current thoughts, feelings, and goals with regard to their major, in order that they are better able to articulate and confirm their choice of major, specify what more specifically they wish to do with it beyond graduation, and the steps they will take to achieve their career goals.

When educators refer to "subject matter," they are often referring to "object matter." What would *subject matter* be, if it were chosen as a product of mindful reflection on and awareness of what is of greatest value to a student? The conjunction of Western mindfulness, calling for a revised epistemological approach to evolving categories of understanding in tune with the ever-changing world of experience, and Eastern mindfulness, fostering right decision-making for self and others, would seem to hold great benefit for more holistic outcomes in higher education. Integrating mindful thinking may be viewed as the next evolutionary step in higher education in order to integrate the currently disparate cognitive, affective, and motoric aspects of human being into the domain of learning outcomes, so we might move from learning *objectives* to learning *subjectives*.

REFERENCES

Abram, D. (2017). *The spell of the sensuous: Perception and language in a more-than-human world*. Vintage Books.

Anderson, L. W., & Krathwohl, D.R (Eds.). (2001). *A taxonomy for learning, teaching, and assessing: A revision of Bloom's taxonomy of educational objectives* (Abridged edition). Addison Wesley Longman.

Bloom, B. S. (Ed.). (1956). *Taxonomy of educational objectives: The classification of educational goals—Handbook I: Cognitive domain*. Longman.

Bugental, J. F. T. (1981). *The search for authenticity: An existential-analytic approach to psychotherapy*. Irvington Publishers.

Costa, A. L. (1984). Mediating the metacognitive. *Educational Leadership*, *42*(3), 57–62.

Dewey, J. (1916). *Democracy and education*. Macmillan.

Flavell, J. H. (1979). Metacognition and cognitive monitoring: A new area of cognitive-developmental inquiry. *American Psychologist*, *34*(10), 906–911.

Giorgi, A. (1970). *Psychology as a human science: A phenomenologically based approach*. Harper & Row.

Giorgi, A. (2009). *The descriptive phenomenological method in psychology: A modified Husserlian approach*. Duquesne University Press.

Gunaratana, B. H. (2014). *Mindfulness in plain English*. Wisdom Publications.

Heidegger, M. (1966). *Discourse on thinking* (J. M. Anderson & E. H. Freund, Trans.). Harper & Row. (Original work published 1959)

Khong, B. S. L. (2003). Buddha, being, and the Black Forest. *The Humanistic Psychologist*, *31*(4), 37–111.

Krathwohl, D. R. (1994). Reflections on the taxonomy: Its past, present, and future. In L. W. Anderson & L. A. Sosniak (Eds.), *Bloom's taxonomy: A forty-year retrospective. Ninety-third yearbook of the national society for the study of education* (pp. 181–202). The University of Chicago Press.

Krathwohl, D. R., Bloom, B. S., & Masia, B. B. (1964). *Taxonomy of Educational Objectives: The classification of educational goals—Handbook II: Affective domain*. David McKay Company.

Langer, E. J. (1989) *Mindfulness*. Addison-Wesley.

Langer, E. J. (2016). *The power of mindful learning* (2nd ed.). Da Capo Press.

Lieberman, C. (1985). The existentialist "school" of thought: Existentialism and education. *The Clearing House*, *58*(7), 322–326. https://www.jstor.org/stable/30186413

Marzano, R. J., & Kendall, J. S. (2007). *The new taxonomy of educational objectives* (2nd ed.). Corwin Press.

Maslow, A. H. (2014). *Toward a psychology of being*. Sublime Books.

McCown, D. (2014). East meets west in the pedagogy of the mindfulness-based interventions. In A. Ie, C. T. Ngnoumen, & E. J. Langer (Eds.), *The Wiley Blackwell handbook of mindfulness* (Vol. II, pp. 1085–1104). Wiley Blackwell.

Mehta, J. L. (1970). Heidegger and the comparison of Indian and Western philosophy. *Philosophy East and West*, *20*(3), 303–317. https://www.jstor.org/stable/1398312

Merleau-Ponty, M. (1968) *The visible and the invisible: Followed by working notes* (A. Lingis, Trans., C. Lefort, Ed.). Northwestern University Press.

Merriam-Webster. (n.d.). Taxonomy. In *Meriam-Webster.com dictionary*. Retrieved December 30, 2020, from https://www.merriam-webster.com/dictionary/taxonomy

Moss, D. M., & Keen, E. (1981). The nature of consciousness: The existential-phenomenological approach. In R. S. Valle & R. von Eckartsberg (Eds.), *The metaphors of consciousness* (pp. 107–120). Plenum Press.

Noddings, N. (2007). *Philosophy of education* (2nd ed.). Westview Press.

Olendzki, A. (2014) From early Buddhist traditions to Western psychological science. In A. Ie, C.T. Ngnoumen, & E. J. Langer (Eds.), *The Wiley Blackwell handbook of mindfulness* (Vol. I, pp. 58–73). Wiley Blackwell.

Pring, R. (1971). Bloom's taxonomy: A philosophical critique (2). *Cambridge Journal of Education*, *1*(2), 83–91. https://doi.org/10.1080/0305764710010205

Reber, R. (2014). Mindfulness in education. In A. Ie, C. T. Ngnoumen, & E. J. Langer (Eds.), *The Wiley Blackwell handbook of mindfulness* (Vol. II, pp. 1054–1070). Wiley Blackwell.

Salomon, G., & Globerson, T. (1987). Skill may not be enough: The role of mindfulness in learning and transfer. International Journal of Educational Research, 11(6), 623-637.

Saarinen, E., & Lehti, T. (2014). Inducing mindfulness through life-philosophical lecturing. In A. Ie, C. T. Ngnoumen, & E. J. Langer (Eds.), *The Wiley Blackwell handbook of mindfulness* (Vol. II, pp. 1105–1131). Wiley Blackwell.

Shapiro, S. L., Carlson, L. E., Astin, J. A., & Freedman, B. (2006). Mechanisms of mindfulness. *Journal of Clinical Psychology*, *62*(3), 373–378 https://doi.org/10.1002/jclp.20237

Stark, M. J., & Washburn, M. C. (1977). Ego, egocentricity, and self-transcendence: A Western interpretation of Eastern teaching. *Philosophy East and West, 27*(3), 265–283. https://www.jstor.org/stable/1397999

Staumbaugh, J. (1970). Commentary on Takeshi Umehara's "Heidegger and Buddhism." *Philosophy East and West, 20*(3), 283–286. https://www.jstor.org/stable/1398309

von Eckartsberg, R., & Valle, R.S. (1981). Heideggerian thinking and the Eastern mind. In R. S. Valle & R. von Eckartsberg (Eds.), *The metaphors of consciousness* (pp. 287–311). Plenum Press

Weare, K. (2014). Mindfulness in schools: Where are we, and where might we go next? In A. Ie, C.T. Ngnoumen, & E. J. Langer (Eds.), *The Wiley Blackwell handbook of mindfulness* (Vol. II, pp. 1037–1053). Wiley Blackwell.

Zimmerman, M. E. (1981). *Eclipse of the self: The development of Heidegger's concept of authenticity.* Ohio University Press.

CHAPTER 3

A PRECIOUS DARKNESS

Utilizing Existential Loneliness to Achieve Culturally Relative Self-Actualization in the Classroom

Christopher Kazanjian
El Paso Community College

Sandra Kazanjian
Western Hills Elementary School

ABSTRACT

This chapter explores culturally relative self-actualization experiences in the classroom that cultivate an existential awareness of students' unique sense of selfhood. The existential given of isolation as a being entails solitude and loneliness. However, youth that experience loneliness anxieties may be fearful of existentialism altogether. Existential loneliness is an experience of sincere solitude where the person faces the realities of existence in courageous and compassionate ways. The authors discuss three approaches to helping students explore existential loneliness: cultural humility, mindful awareness practices, and cognitive reappraisal. When teachers engage existential loneliness, they develop a multicultural humanistic curriculum for children to find enlightenment and healing in the face of existential trauma.

Problematizing the Profession of Teaching From an Existential Perspective, pp. 45–69

The effects of the novel SARS-CoV-2 corona virus or COVID-19 has deeply marred the well-being of youth around the world. The effects of the super-spreading virus cause(d) isolation, restrictions for gatherings, economic hardships, and the restructuring of the psychosocial atmosphere. People across the world have seen fundamental changes to personal and professional lives, mental and physical well-being, and have been shaken with the reality of mortality.

COVID-19 caused a violence to the world that traumatized the physical and emotional well-being of youth (Houtepen et al., 2020; Purkey et al., 2020). For example, emotional and sexual abuse toward children, regardless of geographic location increased during the pandemic (Blosnich et al., 2020). Populations of refugee and internally displaced youth were at higher risks for challenges to well-being, socioeconomic hardships, and higher risks of COVID-19 exposure (Fegert et al., 2020). Initiatives such as the U.S. Federal Child Abuse Prevention and Treatment Act as well as agencies the World Health Organization designate child abuse/maltreatment as the an intentional or unintentional behavior to harm, abuse, neglect, or expose a child to abuse (emotional, physical, sexual), violence (as witness or victim), expose to risk of physical or psychological harm, or live with people that have mental disorders, substance abuse, or are incarcerated, all of which can inhibit the well-being of the child and his/her development, survival and dignity in the context of the relationship of the caretaker (Tsehay et al., 2020).

The pandemic increased the frequency of adverse childhood experiences (ACEs) which will result in lifelong effects (Atchison et al., 2020; Maunder et al., 2020; Lorenc et al., 2020). ACEs are a category of childhood adversity that include 10 subcategories of experience: abuse that is sexual, emotional, physical, or neglect for emotions or necessities, domestic violence, guardian separation, substance abuse or incarceration, and living with someone that has a mental disturbance. The consequences of trauma have been documented as lifelong physical and psychological affects that reduce the quality of life, by increasing the incidence of mental disturbance, cognitive impairment, socio-emotional problems, somatization disorders, gastrointestinal disorders, accelerated aging, and even reducing life expectancy by up to 20 years (Colich et al., 2020; Cozolino, 2014; Kalia & Knauft, 2020; Lorenc et al., 2020; Park et al., 2020; Yağci et al., 2020).

The realities of mortality and isolation were brought forth during the pandemic with terrifying intensities. The daily reports of death tolls and infection rates were alongside school closures and stricter social guidelines. The avenues of childhood that were once used for coping with life challenges became limited, as playgrounds, after-school activities, sports programs, and playgrounds were reduced to the household or online interactions (Fegert et al., 2020). The limited time and opportunities for interactive play or sociality that stimulate time-sensitive neural growth spurts and advance select abilities during developmental periods were reduced (Cozolino, 2020).

The natural unfolding developmental processes were either impeded or hastened by death anxieties and ACEs. These negative stressors can the potential to speed up biological aging, causing precocious puberty (Colich et al., 2020). In addition to accelerated aging, long-term negative stress for children alters the healthful development of the hippocampus and medial prefrontal cortex, causing functional deficits, neural malformations, and emotional regulation problems (Tsehay et al., 2020). Constant vigilance for threats to mortality alongside ACEs result in implicit and explicit memory formation that enact the parasympathetic and vagal activation to freeze the child, making youth become removed from growth-promoting explorations of existential concerns

This chapter will explore the existential foundations for developing a multicultural humanistic psychological praxis to alleviate loneliness anxieties and support a growth-promoting exploration of existential loneliness. When teachers support students in their existential loneliness, they develop a curriculum for students to find enlightenment and healing during existential trauma. Youth learn to access their solitude as a guide to creating a meaningful and fulfilling life.

NEUROBIOLOGICAL CONSEQUENCES OF EXISTENTIAL ANXIETY

Existential anxiety is present when the threat of loneliness, mortality, loss of meaning, or restriction of freedom results in a rigidity of living that interrupts the natural flow and growth of life. These anxieties are not remedied by superficial changes or modifications to one's life and go beyond the effects of acute stressors.

Stress, according to May (1977) is a psychological term that has origins in engineering and physics as a way to measure levels of what a structure or person can handle. However, stress should not be synonymous with anxiety because

> the term "stress" is still weighted heavily on what happens *to* and *on* the person. This makes sense in its original use in the areas from which it is borrowed—in engineering the concern is how much stress a heavy car makes *on* the bridge, or whether a building can withstand the stress *on* it from an earthquake. In the area of engineering, consciousness is irrelevant. (p. 111)

Stress can be helpful for growth and motivation, or it can be a source of inner turmoil. Anxiety is *"how the individual relates to stress, accepts it, interprets it. Stress is a halfway station on the way to anxiety. Anxiety is how we handle stress"* (p. 113). Anxiety is when a person interprets stress in such a way where the values s/he lives by or their corporeal being is under threat of attack or annihilation.

Although existential anxiety can fall under the category of generalized anxiety, it is primarily focused on the fear, dread, or worry about one's fundamental aspects of existence as a being (i.e., death, existing as a solitary being, meaninglessness, and responsibility of choice). Where anxiety can come from careers, relationships, and even threats from bullies, existential anxiety creates a suffering of the entire being in its ability exist. Generalized anxiety and acute stress may stem from existential concerns, but the only way to differentiate it would be to discover the meanings that informs the rigid patterns of living.

No science should be used to ascribe the value of a being or be used to validate an emotional state—the findings of research are just mere traces of an infinity of sides to a phenomenon (Sapolsky, 2017). When students experience existential anxiety, the natural neuroplasticity of the brain that enables them to learn about and facilitate new associations, knowledge, sensations, images, and behaviors in a community of people come to a halt (Cozolino, 2014). Particularly, when circumstances in the school or classroom trigger associations to previous trauma, the sympathetic nervous system (SNS) activates, and glucocorticoids are released. The body then switches to survival processes in order to endure the threat (environmental trigger) and students respond by either fight, flight, or freeze (Sapolsky, 2017). To help regulate hormones that coordinate responses to potential and imminent threats, the hypothalamic-pituitary-adrenal (HPA) axis facilitates necessary measures for short-term survival. This includes using energy stores, altering immune and endocrine system functions, and increasing focus of attention (Cozolino, 2014). When the stress system is activated for long period of time, the body begins to breakdown and can cause long-term damage. There is much more happening beneath the surface of students that act out, retreat, or remain silent—there is an existential survival schemata functioning as it has come to know best.

EMOTIONAL CONSEQUENCES OF EXISTENTIAL ANXIETIES

The increasing rates of mental disturbances for youth 5 to 14 years of age have become a major global concern (Folayan et al., 2020). The pandemic increased the prevalence and gravity of many mental disturbances, while creating new stress-related problems that youth with vulnerabilities and disadvantages now face (Çoban & Tan, 2020; Fegert et al., 2020; Park et al., 2020). Traumas experienced during the developmental years put youth at a higher risk for long-term emotional disturbance and physical ailments (Read et al., 2020; Yağci et al., 2020). Cozolino (2020) observed that adult misconceptions

> of childhood as a time of innocence and fun can lead us to underestimate the impact of negative childhood experiences. There certainly appears to be considerable evidence to support the claim reflected in our societal resistance to accepting the incidence, scope, and magnitude of early trauma. (p. 221)

For primary and secondary level students, there is no getting over loss of loved ones or the loneliness thereafter. There are ultra-fast processing systems the amygdala facilitates that never forget—it remembers as a way to compile a survival reference guide in times of fright, shame, and hurt. These are holistically generalized throughout the person to influence and sustain a survival paradigm that teachers often mistake as acting out or delinquency. However, trauma does not determine the person. There is always choice for how to live, heal, and create meaning. Existentialism empowers youth to create meanings that promote growth, enlightenment, and compassion.

Equitable educational opportunities for underserved students (vulnerable and hidden populations as well) touched by existential angst means training educators with culturally responsive pedagogies (Lorenc et al., 2020; Purkey et al., 2020). Pedagogies need to be tailored, adapted, or added to make learning accessible and relevant to culturally relative existential paradigms. Furthermore, underserved children do not have as many opportunities for lessons to explore existential concerns through their relationships with others. Their education is primarily composed of rote memorization and behavioral management (Hammond, 2015).

Growth-promoting relationships with teachers helps students interconnect brain regions that stimulate new ideas, creativities, and understandings and expression of emotions (Cozolino, 2014; Kazanjian, 2021; Presti, 2016). Growth-promoting relationships in the classroom offer security, safety, and the conditions that cultivates courage within youth to explore their mortality and loneliness. Existential loneliness is a precious darkness that holds limitless potentials and meanings. Teachers must empower students with the courage and resources to explore the flow of eternity in its purest form; the loneliness of *being*.

THE PRECIOUS DARKNESS:
STARING INTO THE ABYSS OF EXISTENTIAL ANGST

The existential reminders of mortality and loneliness were constant during the COVID-19 pandemic. Death was the subject of unremitting breaking news media displaying mortality rates. Students were reminded that their lives and the lives of loved ones were under threat, all while the previous sense of normal quickly faded. COVID-19 shook routinized lives and habitual patterns of thought and behavior as people awakened to existential realities (Bland, 2020).

The threat of COVID-19 transcended international and cultural borders to cause foundational changes to education systems worldwide (Calder et al., 2020). Schools were transformed with mandatory masks requirements, social distancing guidelines, classes were required to transform into a virtual experience, while enrollments dropped, and budgets were impacted. Pre-pandemic worries and challenges were overshadowed with the realization that life would be fundamentally different in the years to come (Bland, 2020). However, by helping students develop an existential awareness, they become empowered with the courage to face realities as they are (Kazanjian, 2021). Existentialism supports students to choose how to live and who to become.

Existential canon has its roots in Western philosophy and art, as it has been recorded and disseminated as cultural epistemological resources for engaging existential givens (Camus, 1991; Yalom 1980). The 19th and 20th century thinkers, such as Søren Kierkegaard, Fyodor Dostoevsky, Martin Heidegger, Jean-Paul Sartre, Friedrich Nietzsche developed existential philosophy as a distinct, yet interconnected field of thought, analysis, and praxis. These existentialists championed a doctrine that promoted living by subjective meanings, where there is no predetermined structure or fate to anyone's life other than how a person chooses to live (Yalom, 2009).

According to Yalom (1980), the four existential concerns that provide fundamental psychological dynamics for each person's reality are "death, freedom, isolation, and meaninglessness" (p. 10). Furthermore, Yalom's (2015) clinical research on the prevalence of existential concerns reveal narratives that "deal with anxiety about death, about the loss of loved ones and the ultimate loss of oneself, about how to live a meaningful life, about coping with aging and diminished possibilities, about choice, about fundamental isolation" (p. 211). Existential psychology has been utilized for training educators and counselors to help students shift focus from the analysis of the past to how they engage existential givens in the here-and-now (Yalom, 1980). Although the past has fundamental influences and contains important meanings, an existential praxis proffers that the tense of living always be the *present*.

Although existentialism is often misconstrued (i.e., by pop culture and even scholarly writings) as a gloomy preoccupation with death; in actuality, it is an optimistic paradigm for empowering young adults to determine the meanings in their lives. The acknowledgement of mortality is a motivational key to challenging the social norms and external cultural values—ultimately allowing a critical reasoning of prepackaged socio-cultural meanings (Kierkegaard, 1959; Sartre, 1966; Yalom, 2015). Appreciating the finite nature of existence helps students create purposes in life, that motivate them to live mindfully and sincerely. Perhaps even some may choose to live diligently as a tribute to a loved one that transitioned.

In existential educational praxis, students come to realize that they have the responsibility to determine their own lives, where the student "is nothing else but that which he makes of himself" (Sartre, 1948, p. 28). This empowerment also means acknowledging that existence precedes essence, but does not seek to explicitly change or challenge students' religious or cultural beliefs, that is for them to determine (Moustakas, 1995). Although this existential perspective can bring mystery and vitality to life, it can also be scary for youth because its inherent angst of death and in the onus of writing each meaningful page of one's life story (Kierkegaard, 1959). In existentialism, choices matter and reflect the students' responsibility to create their meanings in life (Sartre, 1966; Yalom, 1980). Existentialism reveals that the nature of the human being is entirely plastic, able to adapt and survive where it is conducive to thriving; things can be unconditioned, and the future chosen in the present (Bradford, 2020). In this paradigm, young adults accept their failures and limitations as part of the human condition. This self-acceptance combats feeling of shame or guilt from absurd socio-cultural meanings or norms (Gnaulati, 2020).

Although critical in nature, the existential canon has a Euro-American orientation and carries with it the historical summation of bias, assumption, and privilege associated with Western paradigm for understanding the self and world. To engage this, scholars and practitioners have fused existentialism and phenomenology with a humanistic psychological perspective to fashion a existential-humanistic psychology. This perspective seeks to transcend cultural contexts to understand greater barriers to human growth; to actualize human potential beyond the constraints of sociocultural contexts (Hocoy, 2019). However, existential-humanistic psychology has also been criticized for proffering middle to upper class values, where self-actualization is a process that assumes all people have the resources, time, and money to satisfy needs to climb Maslow's hierarchy (Hocoy, 2019). In actuality, underserved and marginalized groups struggle to meet the basic survival needs and do not have equitable opportunities to climb Maslow's hierarchy as privileged populations experience.

Since the Civil Rights and multicultural education movements of the mid to late 20th and 21st centuries, existentialism has widened its lenses to embrace Eastern and indigenous existential paradigms. This has served to deepen understandings, discussions, and representations of existential phenomena (Mika & Peters, 2015). Western philosophy has a history of marginalizing non-Western paradigms, in which existential educators today must still work to critically analyze and deconstruct findings through a process of positionality in order to liberate or empower other existential paradigms from colonization and subjugation (Mika, 2015; Spinelli, 2019). Colonization of existential world paradigms of indigenous people has caused cultural destruction that has taken away primary tools for exploring/creating meanings (Salzman & Halloran, 2004).

For educators engaging students that are mindful of their existential loneliness, the question becomes, "What, then, can existentialism and humanism offer to the individual caught in this trap? How can she re-discover her own humanity" (Tubbs, 2013, p. 478)? A multicultural humanistic psychological framework can help educators focus on the existential foundations for culturally relative self-actualization processes situated within a diversifying global context in order to promote students' holistic growth and well-being (Kazanjian, 2021).

In a multicultural humanistic psychological praxis, existential issues are creatively explored and expressed, where underlying existential themes emerge. Coming to terms with the complexity and mystery of existence allows students the opportunity to get in touch with an inner flow of creativity and authenticity that resonate with their cultural and environmental circumstances (Bland & DeRobertis, 2017). This existential awareness is a constant source of resilience, awe, strength, and faith. Deconstructing the comforting illusions of certainty, belief, and assumptions of cultural knowledge awakens students to the growth-promoting power of their existential solitude (Moustakas, 1956).

ALONE WITH MYSELF:
AN AGE OF EXISTENTIAL-DISTANCING

Contemporary pop cultural artistic artifacts have the ability to represent and facilitate an exploration of existential loneliness or anxieties, through meanings and imaginations. For example, the popular Netflix Original Korean drama *My Holo Love* (Hye-Young, 2020) depicted a lonely female protagonist that encounters a beta-test pair of Holo Glass—eyeglasses that reveal an attractive artificial intelligence hologram man named Holo that can not only pass the Turing test but has also developed the capacity for empathy and who eventually falls in love with the protagonist. This drama depicts the theme that humans need empathy and relationships. With modern technology, if we cannot find someone to know what it means to be us, we create them and an illusion of reality.

Young adulthood is a critical developmental phase of puberty during 10 to 19 years of age, where holistic maturations develop deeper motivations for social relationships to become more numerous, complex, and intimate (van Roekel et al., 2018). Inherent in this phase is a sense of loneliness. Loneliness is comprised of (and perhaps misperceived as) undesirable negative emotions that stem from an incongruence between the desired and actual quality or number of relationships in a social sphere (Franssen et al., 2020; Zhang et al., 2018). Loneliness is part of every life stage but can be intense during young adulthood, where sincere and authentic social support is needed but sometimes lacking due to inability, failure, immaturity to establish complex relations (Çakir & Çetinkaya, 2020).

Moustakas (1961) discovered that loneliness is an essential component of being human and carries inimitable feelings of emptiness, nothingness, and angst. Loneliness has growth-promoting effects by revealing new opportunities, values, paths that are presented anew with each day (Luiggi-Hernández & Rivera-Amador, 2020). The terror of loneliness is intense at first, but if one embraces it with compassion, s/he will surpass the pain and suffering to reach inner sources that restore vitality and purpose.

For young adults, loneliness can come with physical illness, the death of a loved one, changing schools, social rejection, ACEs, but also being creative or expressive. From the existential foundations of a multicultural humanistic psychology lens, loneliness is an incomparable organic experience of emancipation for the purpose of realizing the self. There is no exile or estrangement in loneliness, because as Moustakas (1961) described,

> Loneliness involves a unique substance of self, a dimension of human life which taps the full resources of the individual. It calls for strength, endurance, and sustenance, enabling a person to reach previously unknown depths and to realize a certain nakedness of inner life. (p. 8)

Students must learn to accepted loneliness with compassion, tolerance, and mindfulness to better express emotions, tend to relationships, and to live more diligently.

EXISTENTIAL LONELINESS: SOLITUDE AND BROKEN LIFE

There are two significant ways in which students can experience loneliness intensely: existential loneliness and loneliness anxiety. Existential loneliness is an intrinsic and organic reality of human life in which there is both pain and triumphant creation emerging out of long periods of desolation. In existential loneliness man is fully aware of himself as an isolated and solitary individual. (Moustakas, 1961, p. 24)

Within the spectrum of existential loneliness there is a *loneliness of solitude*, which designates a content state of being, where the person is alone and finds harmony with the wonders and conundrums of life, the environment, and the universe (Moustakas, 1972). Also within existential loneliness is *loneliness of a broken life*. Students experience this when life has become irreparably altered from trauma, death, crisis, physical maladies or injuries, exclusion, or pain. With loneliness of a broken life, the way students relate to, lives in, and labors in the world are fundamentally altered.

When intense life challenges are present, students may venture into their loneliness to discover inner resources and abilities in order to understand, adapt, survive, grow, and creatively express in relevant ways. Existential loneliness brings about new spheres of awareness that offers compassionate understandings of life, appreciation of the miracle of the living moment, and mindfulness of a self that experiences the world with each breath. However, when one denies the darkness of existential loneliness, the result, as Yalom (1980) described, can be isolation denial, where young adults seek escapism as a way to deny existential realities (Luiggi-Hernández & Rivera-Amador, 2020). Isolation denial typically results in living with the loss of authenticity and seeking to dissolve the self into others, material things, or cultural avenues that become abstract tools to alleviate inner angst—a loneliness anxiety ensues.

LONELINESS ANXIETY: ESCAPING THE DARKNESS

Loneliness anxiety is present when young adults are estranged from their selves as feeling and conscious beings (Moustakas, 1961). Inherent in loneliness anxiety is the vague existential angst, whose discomfort motivates one to adopt ready-made panaceas, such as gaining power, social statues, buying things, trying to conform to unattainable standards, or establishing strict rules over one's life. Loneliness anxiety encourages students to find authoritarian routine, safety, predictability, confirmation, and power over their lives and emotions; this exhausting endeavor results in more loneliness anxiety and despair at never being able attain what was initially sought (Moustakas, 1961). As Western culture fosters (with social media as its fastest vehicle) loneliness anxiety for youth, it also offers remedies for the symptomology. This false therapy inhibits authentic attunement, living, and relating to others in a fundamental way—the result is a vague and constant torment of emptiness.

The activities students take on to mitigate loneliness anxiety are more than just defense mechanisms against death anxiety (Bland & DeRobertis, 2017). The situation is much more convoluted, with a long history of social incubation. Maladaptive coping strategies for existential concerns during crises means keeping busy. Preoccupation has become a necessary strategy to ward off loneliness anxiety, whether it be through binge-watching dramas, browsing social media, online shopping, or finding the perfect place to take the next selfie. Time is the enemy that must be killed in order to avoid realities. Loneliness calls one back with feelings of emptiness, despair, or fear, which are in need of attention, compassion, and healing.

FALLING TO PIECES:
HEALTH EFFECTS OF LONELINESS ANXIETY

Loneliness has historically been a health concern for people with advanced age, but recent research has discovered that it is a major concern for children and young adults (Franssen et al., 2020). During COVID-19, the developmental phases for youth were confounded by variables such as social distancing, mortality reminders, and loss of family or loved ones, that exacerbate the pressures of adapting to adulthood and social roles. Due to the rising unemployment rates and decline of income during the pandemic, mental disturbance, domestic violence, suicide ideation, and substance abuse increased (Biondi & Poduti, 2020; Blosnich et al., 2020; Fegert et al., 2020; Luiggi-Hernández & Rivera-Amador, 2020). Çakir and Çetinkaya (2020) stated that one out of five young adults have an emotional disturbance, where 4 to 5% of the current global adolescent population suffers from depression. Depression often results in decreased quality of life and is frequently suffered with anhedonia, sleep disturbances, fatigue, diet problems, and irritability (Danneel et al., 2019).

Physically, loneliness anxiety poses serious threats and has deleterious physical effects to youth, as it has been associated with higher instances of chronic disease and pain, diminished well-being, obesity, substance abuse, cardiovascular disease, sleep disorders, and even early death (Barreto et al., 2020; Franssen et al., 2020; Reinhardt et al., 2020; Segerstrom et al., 2019). These ailments remove a young adult from age-normative goals or activities, which increase the severity and effects of state loneliness. Furthermore, loneliness often results in lower social support due to fewer positive social relationships—which can lower life satisfaction, self-esteem, and exacerbate mental disturbances (Franssen et al., 2020).

VIRTUAL WORLDS:
LONELINESS AMONG FOLLOWERS AND FRIENDS

The internet is a vital source of social interaction, education, and informational research. Of the world population, 42% or 3.196 billion people that use social media, with an average time of just over 6 hours of use (Ergun & Alkan, 2020). For university student groups on Facebook and Hungarian writing websites, 82% report Internet use every day, and 60% of teenagers reported daily usage. Both groups reported spending almost 3 hours a day on weekends for just social media (Prievara et al., 2019). Online platforms for social media and networking are two of the main uses of the Internet. These can be used for professional or personal profiles to interact with distant family, friends, professionals, or sources for group interaction in common interests. However, some social networking usage is to compensate for lack of social-emotional skills and present the danger of dependency. Prievara et al. (2019) discovered that "loneliness plays a central role in youth's problematic Internet use that may also stem from the lack of social support from peers as well as from parents" (p. 1017).

For example, internet social networking is now a litmus test for many young adults to judge whether they are socially desirable, and through this process, vulnerability can beget loneliness anxiety. The dynamics for the need to belong and to discover identity in adolescence is explored in peer groups, family, and solitude. For those that fail to appreciate the failures and struggles of this developmental period, loneliness and low self-worth can result (Çakir & Çetinkaya (2020). The greater exposure and use of social media has led to opportunities to develop new psychological phenomena, such as social media disorder (SMD) or problematic internet use (PIU) (Ergun & Alkan, 2020; Prievara et al., 2019). These maladaptive or addictive behaviors result in compulsive and extended use of the internet (via cell phone, social media) which causes loneliness anxiety, habituation and the need for more usage, withdrawal, and emotional disturbances, and deteriorating real life social relationships (Garakouei et al., 2020). Public spaces that once encouraged human interaction are now lonely places, where cell-phone usage has replaced the mindfulness of others and the environmental contexts.

CULTURAL PARADIGMS: COMFORT IN COMMUNITY?

Culture is a vital resource for students to explore existential loneliness or it can be a source of loneliness anxiety. Each student's cultural worldview and intersectional identity are largely influential for the values, meanings, and behaviors influence one's loneliness (Barreto et al., 2020; Bland, 2020;

Franssen et al., 2020). The most frequent classifications of cultures are those of collectivism and individualism, but it has been found that loneliness is ubiquitous to every paradigm.

For cultures based in collectivism, there is a high value on interdependence in close social and family networks. Group harmony, relying on each other, social acceptance, and serving the family unit/community are endemic qualities to collectivistic cultural paradigms (Sapolsky, 2017). A collectivistic cultural paradigm also promotes cultural awareness, community, genuine or authenticity, and finding the connections or spirituality to people and the world (Grier & Ajayi, 2019; Johnson & Vallejos, 2019). Whereas, the unique qualities of an individualistic culture can be seen from its members seeking personal success, improvement, and distinction, where they often talk in first-person singular, acknowledge themselves by their profession rather than relationships (such as a parent or sister), define successes at what they are personally good at intrinsically, rather than situationally, remember past events where they are the focus, rather than what relationships were formed or cultivated (Sapolsky, 2017). Often agreed is that cultures based in individualism have a great value placed on self-reliance, and on loosely formed social networks (Barreto et al., 2020).

Loneliness in both collectivistic and individualistic paradigms have wide spectrums of surface level differences. However, the existential givens of death, freedom of choice, isolation, and meaninglessness take people beneath superficial cultural differences into the existential connective tissue of the human condition. The cultural paradigm that one is familiar with is important to the initial exploration of existential loneliness, and educators must appreciate this paradigm. It is in existential loneliness that one's cultural paradigm is transcended, and solitude may enlighten one to cultural relativity.

CULTURALLY RELATIVE
SELF-ACTUALIZATION IN THE CLASSROOM

Utilizing the existential foundations of a multicultural humanistic psychological pedagogy means developing culturally relative self-actualization experiences in the classroom as a means to support diverse groups of students in exploring their existential angst through existential loneliness. COVID-19 increased the incidence rate and exacerbated mental disturbances. Students that experience loneliness anxiety due to ACEs from COVID-19 would benefit from engaging existential loneliness in the classroom through lessons that engage culturally relative self-actualization processes.

Culturally relative self-actualization is a transcendental process over personal and local needs to fulfill potentialities within form and function, as it is meaningful to one's cultural paradigm (Kazanjian, 2021). Young adults actualize potentials of the real or conception of self and/or group/community in order to find new ways of being and create meanings (Johnson & Vallejos, 2019). The cultural paradigms establish the processes for self-actualization, as these will be the guides, resources, and tools in which to recognize and challenge loneliness anxieties in order to explore existential loneliness.

For the educator, the first step is to begin developing the lifelong process of cultural humility; which is an open-mindedness, critical self-reflection, and cultivation of culturally diverse growth-promoting relationships, that help one transcend his/her cultural paradigm to form an existentially oriented positionality (Johnson & Vallejos, 2019; Rosen et al., 2017; Soheilian et al., 2014). Cultural humility opens the possibilities of other interpretations, understanding how stories that are made with a focus on how bias and privilege have influenced values and decisions, and to dispel fatalistic assumptions for the possibility of future actions/stories (Miller, 2017; Morley, 2008). With increasing cultural diversity in classrooms across the United States, educators may be unfamiliar with many existential paradigms of students. Cultural humility helps educators walk humbly amongst new worlds of meaning, while questioning and updating previously learned cultural knowledge.

Educators that develop cultural humility are most likely to inspire this open-minded disposition and cultural self-awareness to their students. Cultural humility as a process is similar to Moustakas's (1994) use of Epoché in phenomenological inquiry. The word Epoché has Greek origins to designate the abstaining from judgement or to refrain from perceiving something the way it has always been. Cultural humility may utilize Epoché as a way for understanding cultural biases, meanings, and privileges. Epoché,

> encourages an open perception is that of reflective-meditation, letting the preconceptions and prejudgments enter consciousness and leave freely, being just as receptive to them as I am to be unbiased looking and seeing. This meditative procedure is repeated until I experience an internal sense of closure. As I do, I label the prejudgments and write them out. I review the list until its hold on my consciousness is released, until I feel an internal readiness to enter freshly, encounter the situation, issue, or person directly, and receive whatever is offered and come to know it as such. (p. 89)

Cultural humility benefits from Epoché because educators can challenge previous beliefs, ideas, and acknowledge privilege. The educator is able to discover new elements of cultural bias and privilege within reflection, but most importantly, within each new encounter.

One fundamental aspect of helping students explore existential loneliness (and to deconstruct loneliness anxiety) as a means to support culturally relative self-actualization processes is by establishing a nurturing, growth-promoting relationships (Atchison et al., 2020; Mead, 2020). Growth-promoting relationships are preventative and protective to the effects of anxieties by means of supporting emotional management (Tsehay et al., 2020). Rogers (1989) outlined a growth-promoting relationship as "one in which one of the participants intends that there should come about, in one or both parties, more appreciation of, more expression of, more functional use of the latent inner resources of the individual" (p. 40). However, being kind and compassionate to students as they explore both types of loneliness also means that the educator must diligently practice his/her own existential mindfulness of loneliness and critical analysis of loneliness anxieties.

Growth promoting relationships are formed from the Rogerian conditions of empathy, congruence, and unconditional positive regard. Educators can establish these with students by opening spaces for self-exploration and expression. Trusting the students to accomplish tasks through creativity and self-discovery opens opportunities for teachers to encounter the student as a person. When students are able to express themselves, educators can empathically relate and explore the student's world of meaning.

After the educator has decided to practice cultural humility and established a growth-promoting relationship, we recommend utilizing the diligence of mindful awareness in an existential framework. Mindfulness meditations or mindful awareness practices (MAPs) have been shown to have a positive correlation to emotional well-being for young adults. Research has also shown MAPs are effective at promoting well-being at the cellular level, where telomere length and activity are found to be healthier (Presti, 2016). Public schools are effectual and convenient places (even virtually) to help youth develop their diligence of mindful awareness for engaging loneliness anxiety and existential loneliness. For example, students that are feeling angry, sad, or the desperate need to check their phone for text messages, can begin by acknowledging and learning to develop a vocabulary for the emotions that motivate behavior. An active way to introduce students to this process is by the guiding questions posited by Moustakas and Perry (1973):

> What am I feeling at this moment? What is happening within me right now? What is my mood? Do I feel tensions in my body? If I listen carefully, can I actively be in touch with the source of my discontent? What do I want? What do I prefer? How many different levels of awareness can I reach

when I am alone? Can I describe each feeling? What thoughts and feelings stand out? (p. 3)

Statements such as, "Right now, I am feeling ..." or "I am aware that ..." are helpful in this diligence. Becoming mindful of how the body experiences negative emotions develops interoceptive awareness, self-validation, and self-compassion that leads to empathy with others. Also, mindfulness develops a sense of hope, enlightenment, and optimism for growth amidst existential uncertainties and anxieties (Kazanjian, 2021). Educators must become practitioners for supporting student exploration of existential loneliness and loneliness anxieties amidst the intersectionality of cultural values, self-identity, race, world views. (Grier & Ajayi, 2019)

Mindfulness for young adults actively regulate and manage internal states that are associated with loneliness anxiety in order to grow as a person. Zhang et al. (2018) used a mindfulness-based curriculum for loneliness psychoeducation to help increase self-awareness in an 8-week study with young adult college students in China as a means to reduce feelings of loneliness. After the experimental trials, students reported a decrease in levels of state loneliness compared to control groups. As the researchers stated, "Mindfulness training enhances the capacities to disengage and de-identify with the perceived social threat, which leads to reduced loneliness" (Zhang et al., 2018, p. 376). The cognitive benefits helped young adults to develop a nonjudgmental awareness to emotions, which helped them accept unpleasant or unavoidable social experiences and thus, reduce loneliness feelings.

Mindful diligence has its foundations in Eastern (i.e., Buddhist and Taoist) religion, culture, and philosophy from 2,500 years ago and has been gaining popularity in secular Western culture, psychology, holistic medicine, and education (Harley, 2018; Harpin et al., 2016; Larrivee & Echarte, 2018; Williams et al., 2018). Mindfulness practice offers deeper levels of self-awareness in existential loneliness in the impermanence of life—where the stream of experiences flow with the passage of time (Brody et al., 2018). The culturally relative self-actualization processes are supported by mindfulness because they help students become attuned to physical and cognitive aspects of experiencing existential loneliness as they become attuned to life environments and circumstances (Meesters et al., 2018; Williams et al., 2018).

The privilege of experience in mindfulness is for the practitioner—the educator is a facilitator, and the meanings of awareness are left to the students to explore (or critically reason) through their cultural paradigm. Loneliness anxiety takes one out of alignment with the aspects of a cultural paradigm (i.e., love, belonging, relationships, self-integration to contribute to a community) that support well-being and self-actualization.

Realignment with culturally relative self-actualization processes begins by being mindful of how one experiences loneliness anxiety, the conditions in which it arises, and deconstructing negative patterns of thought and behavior. Students must learn to develop an intent to focus on existential loneliness, and to learn to create time and space for a diligence to know how it is to experience the world that touches their inner core of being, that is always flowing, growing, and eternal. In the face of mortality reminders or threats, loneliness anxiety, and isolation, students can learn to return to themselves in existential mindfulness.

The practice of an existential mindful awareness through a multicultural humanistic psychological lens, allows us to appreciate its secular Buddhist foundations. However, Western religious mindfulness practices may also have similar benefit. For example, the Christian method of askesis is a contemplative meditation that does not seek to remedy emotions, but understand them in their relationship to the contexts—self in the world (Larrivee & Echarte, 2018). Research has shown that mindfulness-based practices have helped students develop greater abilities to focus on studies by practicing focusing on the self and relationships with the world (Halland et al., 2015; Tsur et al., 2016). The result is an appreciation of the dialectical tensions that come about from isolation and our freedom to be, all while figuring out a sense of meaning. Mindfulness practices are preventative measures, especially during existential crisis for lessening the degree of loneliness anxiety, and creating positive self-evaluations and life satisfaction (Tan et al., 2016). To begin facilitating a mindfulness of existential loneliness, we recommend the following:

- Begin with a focused breathing technique, where students count breaths or pay attention to the natural breathing rhythm.
- Direct students to ground the body by focusing on sensations (i.e., grounding to the chair or floor) (see aforementioned questions by Moustakas & Perry, 1973).
- Begin to appreciate the flow of thoughts, concerns, and preoccupations as a means to help them continue to flow.
- Begin facilitating the mindful awareness of existential loneliness with the following questions: Who is it that feels lonely, anxious, or the need to reach out to others? Who am I right now, and what direction do I follow in becoming more of myself? What words do I use to describe myself that no one else recognizes? What do these thoughts and feelings that I experience right now mean to me in the universe? How does it feel to know that I have a finite time in this life? What do I want to accomplish, and what motivates me to do so? Can I find comfort in knowing that only I

can know what it is to experience the world as me? Just as it is for others? How can loneliness help me know others and my world? What meanings do I want to achieve, that will satisfy my deepest values before I leave this life?

After these questions, it is also important to help students reflect on the process of existential mindful awareness practices (i.e., personal written reflection, group discussion, Socratic method, etc.) and the content. The processes of existential mindfulness (how one explored through) are equally as important as the content derived.

The last strategy is called cognitive reappraisal, and it falls within mindful diligence as a means to help students explore existential loneliness to support their culturally relative self-actualization processes. Cognitive reappraisal is an emotional regulation strategy where students mindfully shift perspectives from an initial appraisal of a situation and the emotions elicited to a different existential perspective in order find meaning or resources to meet a goal or regulate emotions in healthful and constructive ways (Adolphs & Anderson, 2018). For example, failing at a social relationship challenge may cause guilt and shame, ultimately leading to loneliness anxiety (fear of rejection and incompleteness without others). As Kalia and Knauft (2020) declared, "When demands exceed available resources, the situation is appraised as threatening" (p. 3). However, a cognitive reappraisal can help discover vital inner resources and meanings, as one begins to appreciate the complexity of the situation and the other person. Data from this situational analysis will empower students to learn and grow in order to enhance relationships. Asking critical questions such as "What emotions and body sensations are happening in me as the event happened? How is it to experience this event as this other person? Could I have misperceived this situation? What does this incident mean in the greater stream of my existence? What do I want it to mean?" In the face of existential loneliness, students need resources as a means to find empowerment, and educators can provide these resources.

During episodes of loneliness anxiety, cognitive reappraisal is advantageous to becoming mindful of the cognitive and somatic interconnections and interdependencies in an environmental circumstance. Focusing on the internal responses to external stimuli allows students to realize how each individual has a different experience, and that there are available inner-resources to manage the challenge of existential realities. Kalia and Knauft (2020) discovered that "individual differences in the habitual use of reappraisal to regulate emotions moderates the relationship between ACEs and perceived chronic stress" (p. 12). Emotional regulation through cognitive reappraisal lessened the detrimental effects of chronic stress, while adding to the individuals' cognitive flexibility to adapt and overcome environmental challenges. Cognitive reappraisal is important to lessening the effects of ACEs throughout life, as well as immediate existential anxieties and traumas caused by the pandemic. The negative habits formed as a result of loneliness anxiety also come with distorted recursive meanings that reinforce habits. Educators empower students by teaching them to critically think about judgements, conclusions, and habits, so that meanings are reappraised in an existential lens. The goal is to deconstruct loneliness anxieties so that students can explore their deepest concerns in existential loneliness.

CONCLUSION

The COVID-19 pandemic has exacerbated the rate and severity of ACEs, mental and somatic health disturbances, and loneliness anxieties across the world. Young adults will have adverse lifelong effects from these circumstances that can result in lower quality of life satisfaction, long-term health maladies, and academic, economic, or professional challenges. Loneliness anxieties promote habitual use of technology, social media, materialism, over involvement, and over working as a means to distract one from the existential angst pervasive in the pandemic. Reminders of death were constant, where in the first two months of 2021, an average of 4,000 people died from COVID-19 every day.

Students in public schools, either online format or re-entering the restructured social environment, bring with them existential anxieties and concerns that they may not have the tools to explore or engage. The existential concerns of death, isolation, meaninglessness, and freedom may be too intimidating or scary for some. That is why educators must engage in an existential pedagogy to help them embrace the darkness as a guide to living diligently.

With the rapid forces of globalization increasing diversity and complexity of student demographics, the authors recommended to utilize a humanistic multicultural humanistic psychological pedagogy to develop cultural humility. The existential foundations of this framework allow it to adapt to the existential complexity of current circumstances, and for educators to become students to different culturally relative self-actualization processes. Discovering the existential paradigms that are embedded into cultural worldviews will help educators create strategies to help students deconstruct loneliness anxieties. By using techniques such as mindful awareness practices and cognitive reappraisal, educators support students' exploration of existential loneliness as an empowering and meaningful experience. This exploration will realign students with their cultural paradigm's self-actualization processes. Along students' paths toward existential self-realization processes, they will challenge old cultural judgements in favor of cocreating inclusive/interconnected meanings; recognize and deconstruct loneliness anxieties in order to live in the here-and-now; and they will not turn away from the existential darkness, but greet is as a precious source of wonder and strength.

REFERENCES

Adolphs, R., & Anderson, D. J. (2018). *The neuroscience of emotion: A new synthesis.* Princeton University Press.

Atchison, C. G., Butler, J., & Damiano, P. (2020). Adverse childhood experiences: A model for effective 21st-century clinical–community partnerships. *American Journal of Public Health, 110*(4), 450–451. https://doi.org/10.2105/AJPH.2019.305556

Barreto, M., Victor, C., Hammond, C., Eccles, A., Richins, M. T., & Qualter, P. (2020). Loneliness around the world: Age, gender, and cultural differences in loneliness. *Personality and Individual Differences*, 1–6. https://doi.org/10.1016/j.paid.2020.110066

Biondi, G., & Poduti, E. (2020). Self-harm behavior in preadolescence: An integrated intervention model pediatric-psychologist. *Pediatric Reports, 12*(2), 15–16.

Bland, A. M. (2020). Existential givens in the COVID-19 crisis. *Journal of Humanistic Psychology, 60*(5), 710–724. https://doi.org/10.1177/0022167820940186

Bland, A. M., & DeRobertis, E. M. (2017). Humanistic perspective. In V. Zeigler-Hill, T. K. Shackelford (Eds.), *Encyclopedia of Personality and Individual Differences* (pp. 1–19). Springer International.

Blosnich, J. R., Henderson, E. R., Coulter, R. W. S., Goldbach, J. T., & Meyer, I. H. (2020). Sexual orientation change efforts, adverse childhood experiences, and suicide ideation and attempt among sexual minority adults, United States, 2016–2018. *American Journal of Public Health, 110*(7), 1024–1030. https://doi.org/10.2105/AJPH.2020.305637

Bradford, K. (2020). The subject matter of psychology: Psyche, Dasein, non-self. *Existential Analysis: Journal of the Society for Existential Analysis, 31*(2), 336–350.

Brody, J. L., Scherer, D. G., Turner, C. W., Annett, R. D., & Dalen, J. (2018). A conceptual model and clinical framework for integrating mindfulness into family therapy with adolescents. *Family Process, 57*(2), 510–524. https://doi.org/10.1111/famp.12298

Çakır, O., & Çetinkaya, A. (2020). Time spent on the internet, blood pressure, and loneliness in adolescents: A cross-sectional study. *Erciyes Medical Journal / Erciyes Tıp Dergisi, 42*(1), 30–36. https://doi.org/10.14744/etd.2019.68815

Calder, A. J., Novak, L. F., & Lane, A. (2020). We're all going crazy now: how the COVID-19 pandemic can promote more compassionate clinical perspectives. *Journal of Humanistic Psychology, 60*(5), 639–646. https://doi.org/10.1177/0022167820938615

Camus, A. (1991). *The myth of Sisyphus and other essays*. (J. O'Brien, Trans.). Vintage International.

Çoban, A., & Tan, O. (2020). Attention deficit hyperactivity disorder, impulsivity, anxiety, and depression symptoms mediating the relationship between childhood trauma and symptoms severity of obsessive-compulsive disorder. *Archives of Neuropsychiatry / Noropsikiatri Arsivi*, *57*(1), 37–43. https://doi.org/10.29399/npa.23654

Colich, L. N., Rosen, M. L, Williams, E., & McLaughlin, K. A. (2020). Biological aging in childhood and adolescence following experiences of threat and deprivation: A systematic review and meta-analysis. *Psychological Bulletin*, 1–44. http://dx.doi.org/10.1037/bul0000270

Cozolino, L. (2020). *The pocket guide to neuroscience for clinicians*. W. W. Norton & Company.

Danneel, S., Bijttebier, P., Bastin, M., Colpin, H., Van den Noortgate, W., Van Leeuwen, K., Verschueren, K., & Goossens, L. (2019). Loneliness, social anxiety, and depressive symptoms in adolescence: examining their distinctiveness through factor analysis. *Journal of Child & Family Studies*, *28*(5), 1326–1336. https://doi.org/10.1007/s10826-019-01354-3

Ergun, G., & Alkan, A. (2020). The social media disorder and ostracism in adolescents: (OSTRACA- SM Study). *Eurasian Journal of Medicine*, *52*(2), 139–144. https://doi.org/10.5152/eurasianjmed.2020.19076

Fegert, J. M., Vitiello, B., Plener, P. L., & Clemens, V. (2020). Challenges and burden of the coronavirus 2019 (COVID-19) pandemic for child and adolescent mental health: a narrative review to highlight clinical and research needs in the acute phase and the long return to normality. *Child & Adolescent Psychiatry & Mental Health*, *14*(1), 1–11. https://doi.org/10.1186/s13034-020-00329-3

Folayan, M. O., Oginni, O., Arowolo, O., & El Tantawi, M. (2020). Internal consistency and correlation of the adverse childhood experiences, bully victimization, self-esteem, resilience, and social support scales in Nigerian children. *BMC Research Notes*, *13*(1), 1–6. https://doi.org/10.1186/s13104-020-05174-3

Franssen, T., Stijen, M., Hamers, F., & Schneider, F. (2020). Age differences in demographic, social and health-related factors associated with loneliness across the adult life span (19–65 years): A cross-sectional study in the Netherlands. *BMC Public Health*, *20*(1118), 1–12. https://doi.org/10.1186/s12889-020-09208-0

Garakouei, S. A., Mousavi, S. V., Rezaei, S., & Lafmejani, A. Q. (2020). The examination of mediating effects for self-control and time management in relationship among problematic cellphone use with loneliness and educational performance of high school students. *Journal of Educational Sciences & Psychology*, *10*(1), 127–140.

Gnaulati, E. (2020). Fostering mirthful acceptance in couples therapy: An existential viewpoint. *Existential Analysis: Journal of the Society for Existential Analysis*, *31*(2), 368–379.

Grier, R. T., & Ajayi, A. A. (2019). Incorporating humanistic values and techniques in a culturally responsive therapeutic intervention for African American college students. *Journal of Humanistic Counseling*, *58*(1), 17–33. https://doi.org/10.1002/johc.12087

Halland, E., Vibe, M. D., Solhaug, I., Friborg, O., Rosenvinge, J. H., Tyssen, R., Sørlie, T., & Bjørndal, A. (2015). Mindfulness training improves problem-focused coping in psychology and medical students: Results from a randomized controlled trial. *College Student Journal, 49*(3), 387–398.

Hammond, Z. (2015). *Culturally responsive teaching & the brain: Promoting authentic engagement and rigor among culturally and linguistically diverse students*. Corwin.

Harley, J. (2018). The role of attention in therapy for children and adolescents who stutter: Cognitive behavioral therapy and mindfulness-based interventions. *American Journal of Speech-Language Pathology, 27*(4), 1139–1151. https://doi.org/10.1044/2018_AJSLP-ODC11-17-0196

Harpin, S., Rossi, A., Kim, A. K., & Swanson, L. M. (2016). Behavioral impacts of a mindfulness pilot intervention for elementary school students. *Education, 137*(2), 149–156.

Hocoy, D. (2019). The challenge of multiculturalism to humanistic psychology. In L. Hoffman, H. Cleare-Hoffman, N. Granger Jr., & D. St. John (Eds.), *Humanistic approaches to multiculturalism and diversity: Perspectives on existence and difference* (pp. 18–28). Routledge.

Houtepen, L. C., Heron, J., Suderman, M. J., Fraser, A., Chittleborough, C. R., & Howe, L. D. (2020). Associations of adverse childhood experiences with educational attainment and adolescent health and the role of family and socioeconomic factors: A prospective cohort study in the UK. *PLoS Medicine, 17*(3), 1–21. https://doi.org/10.1371/journal.pmed.1003031

Hye-Young, L. (Executive Producer). (2020, February 7,). *My Holo love* [TV series]. Netflix.

Johnson, Z., & Vallejos, L. (2019). Multicultural competencies in humanistic psychology. In L. Hoffman, H. Cleare-Hoffman, N. Granger Jr., & D. St. John (Eds.), *Humanistic approaches to multiculturalism and diversity: Perspectives on existence and difference* (pp. 63–75). Routledge.

Kalia, V., & Knauft, K. (2020). Emotion regulation strategies modulate the effect of adverse childhood experiences on perceived chronic stress with implications for cognitive flexibility. *PLoS ONE, 15*(6), 1–18. https://doi.org/10.1371/journal.pone.0235412

Kazanjian, C. J. (2021). *Empowering children: A multicultural humanistic approach*. Routledge.

Kierkegaard, S. (1959). *The journals of Kierkegaard* (A. Dru, Trans.). Harper & Row.

Larrivee, D., & Echarte, L. (2018). Contemplative meditation and neuroscience: Prospects for mental health. *Journal of Religion & Health, 57*(3), 960–978. https://doi.org/10.1007/s10943-017-0475-0

Lorenc, T., Lester, S., Sutcliffe, K., Stansfield, C., & Thomas, J. (2020). Interventions to support people exposed to adverse childhood experiences: systematic review of systematic reviews. *BMC Public Health, 20*(1), 1–10. https://doi.org/10.1186/s12889-020-08789-0

Luiggi-Hernández, J. G, & Rivera-Amador, A. I. (2020). Reconceptualizing social distancing: Teletherapy and social inequity during the COVID-19 and loneliness pandemics. *Journal of Humanistic Psychology, 60*(5), 626–638. https://doi.org/10.1177/0022167820937503

Maunder, R. G., Hunter, J. J., Tannenbaum, D. W., Le, T. L., & Lay, C. (2020). Physicians' knowledge and practices regarding screening adult patients for adverse childhood experiences: A survey. *BMC Health Services Research*, *20*(1), 1–5. https://doi.org/10.1186/s12913-020-05124-6

May, R. (1977). *The meaning of anxiety*. W.W. Norton & Company.

Mead, V. P. (2020). Adverse babyhood experiences (ABEs) increase risk for infant and maternal morbidity and mortality, and chronic illness. *Journal of Prenatal & Perinatal Psychology & Health*, *34*(4), 285–317.

Meesters, A., den Bosch-Meevissen, Y. M. C. I., Weijzen, C. A. H., Buurman, W. A., Losen, M., Schepers, J., Thissen, M. R. T. M., Alberts, H. J. E. M., Schalkwijk, C. G., & Peters, M. L. (2018). The effect of mindfulness-based stress reduction on wound healing: a preliminary study. *Journal of Behavioral Medicine*, *41*(3), 385–397. https://doi.org/10.1007/s10865-017-9901-8

Mika, C. (2015). Counter-colonial and philosophical claims: An indigenous observation of Western philosophy. *Educational Philosophy & Theory*, *47*(11), 1136–1142. https://doi.org/10.1080/00131857.2014.991498

Mika, C., & Peters, M. (2015). Blind, or keenly self-regarding? The dilemma of Western philosophy. *Educational Philosophy & Theory*, *47*(11), 1125--1127. https://doi.org/10.1080/00131857.2014.991496

Miller, C. (2017). Teachers, leaders, and social justice: A critical reflection on a complicated exchange. *Multicultural Perspectives*, *19*(2), 109–113. https://doi.org/10.1080/15210960.2017.1301100

Morley, C. (2008). Teaching critical practice: Resisting structural domination through critical reflection. *Social Work Education*, *27*(4), 407–421. https://doi.org/10.1080/02615470701379925

Moustakas, C. E. (1972). *Loneliness and love*. Prentice Hall Press.

Moustakas, C. E. (1995). *Being-in, Being-for, Being-with*. Jason Aronson.

Moustakas, C. E. (1994). *Phenomenological research methods*. SAGE.

Moustakas, C. E. (1956). *The self: Explorations in personal growth*. Harper & Brothers.

Moustakas, C. E. & Perry, C. (1973). *Learning to be free*. Prentice-Hall.

Moustakas, C. E. (1961). *Loneliness*. Prentice-Hall.

Park, Y.-M., Shekhtman, T., & Kelsoe, J. R. (2020). Effect of the type and number of adverse childhood experiences and the timing of adverse experiences on clinical outcomes in individuals with bipolar disorder. *Brain Sciences (2076–3425)*, *10*(5), 254. https://doi.org/10.3390/brainsci10050254

Presti, D. E. (2016). *Foundational concepts in neuroscience: A brain-min odyssey*. W.W. Norton & Company.

Prievara, D. K., Piko, B. F., & Luszczynska, A. (2019). Problematic Internet Use, Social Needs, and Social Support Among Youth. *International Journal of Mental Health & Addiction*, *17*(4), 1008–1019. https://doi.org/10.1007/s11469-018-9973-x

Purkey, E., Davison, C., MacKenzie, M., Beckett, T., Korpal, D., Soucie, K., & Bartels, S. (2020). Experience of emergency department use among persons with a history of adverse childhood experiences. *BMC Health Services Research*, *20*(1), 1–10. https://doi.org/10.1186/s12913-020-05291-6

Read, J., Morrison, T., & Waddingham, R. (2020). Traumas, adversities, and psychosis: Investigating practical implications. *Psychiatric Times*, *37*(7), 48–51.

Reinhardt, M., Horváth, Z., Morgan, A., & Kökönyei, G. (2020). Well-being profiles in adolescence: psychometric properties and latent profile analysis of the mental health continuum model - a methodological study. *Health & Quality of Life Outcomes*, *18*(1), 1–10. https://doi.org/10.1186/s12955-020-01332-0

Rogers, C. (1989). *On becoming a person: A therapist's view of psychotherapy*. Houghton Mifflin.

Rosen, D., McCall, J., & Goodkind, S. (2017). Teaching critical self-reflection through the lens of cultural humility: An assignment in a social work diversity course. *Social Work Education*, *36*(3), 289–298. https://doi.org/10.1080/02615 479.2017.1287260

Salzman, M. B., & Halloran, M. J. (2004). Cultural trauma and recovery: Cultural meaning, self-esteem, and the reconstruction of the cultural anxiety buffer. In J. Greenberg, S. L. Koole, & T. Pyszczynski (Eds.), *Handbook of experimental existential psychology* (pp. 231–246). Guilford Press.

Sapolsky, R. (2017). *Behave: The biology of humans at our best and worst*. Penguin Press.

Sartre, J. P. (1948). *Existentialism and humanism*. (P. Mairet, Trans.). Haskell House.

Sartre, J. P. (1966). *Being and nothingness: An essay on phenomenological ontology*. Washington Square Press.

Segerstrom, S. C., Boggero, I. A., King, C. D., Sturgeon, J. A., Arewasikporn, A., & Castro, S. A. (2019). Associations of pain intensity and frequency with loneliness, hostility, and social functioning: Cross-sectional, longitudinal, and within-person relationships. *International Journal of Behavioral Medicine*, *26*(2), 217–229. https://doi.org/10.1007/s12529-019-09776-5

Soheilian, S. S., Inman, A. G., Klinger, R. S., Isenberg, D. S., & Kulp, L. E. (2014). Multicultural supervision: supervisees' reflections on culturally competent supervision. *Counselling Psychology Quarterly*, *27*(4), 379–392. https://doi.org/ 10.1080/09515070.2014.961408

Spinelli, E. (2019). What's so existential about existential therapy? *Existential Analysis: Journal of the Society for Existential Analysis*, *30*(1), 59–79.

Tan, J., Yang, W., Ma, H., & Yu, Y. (2016). Adolescents' core self-evaluations as mediators of the effect of mindfulness on life satisfaction. *Social Behavior & Personality: An International Journal*, *44*(7), 1115–1122. https://doi.org/10.2224/ sbp.2016.44.7.1115

Tsehay, M., Necho, M., & Mekonnen, W. (2020). The role of adverse childhood experience on depression symptom, prevalence, and severity among school going adolescents. *Depression Research & Treatment*, 1–9. https://doi. org/10.1155/2020/5951792

Tsur, N., Berkovitz, N., & Ginzburg, K. (2016). Body awareness, emotional clarity, and authentic behavior: The moderating role of mindfulness. *Journal of Happiness Studies*, *17*(4), 1451–1472. https://doi.org/10.1007/s10902-015-9652-6

Tubbs, N. (2013). Existentialism and humanism: Humanity-know thyself! *Studies in Philosophy & Education*, *32*(5), 477–490. https://doi.org/10.1007/s11217-012-9354-z

van Roekel, E., Verhagen, M., Engels, R. C. M. E., Scholte, R. H. J., Cacioppo, S., & Cacioppo, J. T. (2018). Trait and state levels of loneliness in early and late adolescents: examining the differential reactivity hypothesis. *Journal of

Clinical Child & Adolescent Psychology, 47(6), 888–899. https://doi.org/10.1080/15374416.2016.1146993

Williams, C., Meeten, F., & Whiting, S. (2018). 'I had a sort of epiphany!' An exploratory study of group mindfulness-based cognitive therapy for older people with depression. *Aging & Mental Health, 22*(2), 208–217. https://doi.org/10.1080/13607863.2016.1247415

Yağci, I., Taşdelen, Y., & Kivrak, Y. (2020). Childhood trauma, quality of life, sleep quality, anxiety and depression levels in people with Bruxism. *Archives of Neuropsychiatry / Noropsikiatri Arsivi, 57*(2), 131–135. https://doi.org/10.29399/npa.23617

Yalom, I. (2009). *Staring at the Sun.* Jossey-Bass.

Yalom, I. D. (1980). *Existential psychotherapy.* Basic Books.

Yalom, I.D. (2015). *Creatures of a day and other tales of psychotherapy.* Basic Books.

Zhang, N., Fan, F., Huang, S., & Rodriguez, M. A. (2018). Mindfulness training for loneliness among Chinese college students: A pilot randomized controlled trial. *International Journal of Psychology, 53*(5), 373–378. https://doi.org/10.1002/ijop.12394

SECTION II

EXISTENTIALISM AND ASSESSMENT

CHAPTER 4

UNDER OBSERVATION

Student Anxiety and the Phenomenology of Remote Testing Environments

Tyler Loveless
George Washington University

ABSTRACT

As online learning becomes more prevalent, colleges and universities have increasingly turned to remote proctoring services that claim to detect and deter student cheating during exams. However, many students have begun to voice concerns about the discomfort and anxiety these services can cause. This chapter aims to illuminate the existential and phenomenological nuances present in student testimony by reevaluating the proctor's gaze as an objectifying and alienating force. Specifically, I argue that the anxiety students describe is a response to *feeling seen*.[1] In most cases, remote proctoring involves the surveillance of student behavior by a stranger or artificial intelligence, and the empirical literature suggests that students are often falsely penalized for innocuous or unintentional "disruptions" during their exams. Thus, rather than be "caught up" in the exam process (and invisible to oneself), students are forced to attend to their bodily comportment and engage in a self-reflective awareness of their behavior as a body *for-others*. In the most extreme cases, the proctor's gaze is not only a distraction for students; it is also alienating such that students no longer feel free to appraise the character of their own actions but must instead see themselves through the eyes of the proctor.

Problematizing the Profession of Teaching From an Existential Perspective, pp. 73–90
Copyright © 2022 by Information Age Publishing
www.infoagepub.com
All rights of reproduction in any form reserved.

What I apprehend immediately when I hear the branches crackling behind me is not that *there is someone there*; it is that I am vulnerable, that I have a body which can be hurt, that I occupy a place and that I can not in any case escape ... in short, that I *am seen*.

—Jean-Paul Sartre, *Being and Nothingness*

As online learning becomes more prevalent, colleges and universities in the United States have increasingly turned to remote proctoring services (e.g., ProctorU, ProctorTrack, Honorlock, Respondus, Proctorio) that claim to detect and deter student cheating during online exams. In response, a number of editorials and news articles have emerged detailing the discomfort and anxiety remote proctors often cause students; however, the existing empirical and philosophical literature has yet to offer a substantive analysis of these negative psychological and physiological effects. This chapter aims to illuminate the existential and phenomenological nuances present in student testimony regarding remote proctoring. Specifically, I argue that the anxiety students describe is a response to *feeling seen*. In most cases, remote proctoring involves the surveillance of student behavior by either a stranger or artificial intelligence, and the empirical literature suggests that students are often falsely penalized for innocuous or unintentional "disruptions" during their exams (Sietses, 2016, p. 15). Thus, rather than be "caught up" in the exam process (and invisible to oneself), students are forced to attend to their bodily comportment and engage in a self-reflective awareness of their behavior as a body *for-others*. Moreover, student testimony suggests that in the most extreme case, remote proctoring is more than a distraction for students; it can also be alienating such that students no longer feel free to appraise the character of their own actions but must instead see themselves through the eyes of the proctor.

THE RISE OF REMOTE PROCTORING

In April 2021, Ohio State University student Claire Krafka (2021) published a report in *The Lantern*—the school's independent student newspaper— about the university's newfound reliance on remote proctoring services. Krafka wrote, "Despite its intended goal of keeping students honest while outside of physical classrooms, online test proctoring programs, such as Proctorio, have given some Ohio State students test anxiety" (para. 1). Proctorio, founded in 2013, is one of several remote proctoring services created over the last decade in response to the growing demands of online academic programs. As the low cost and flexibility of distance learning at for-profit schools proved to be an attractive option for nontraditional students, leading research institutions in the United States began leveraging their prestige by offering online alternatives of their own (Casey, 2008), often marketed as "identical" to in-person courses (Johnson, 2017, para. 16). But with reputations on the line, research universities quickly shifted their focus to concerns about cheating as a possible foil to this new online model, and remote proctoring services were a natural response (Barnes, 2010; Hollister & Berenson, 2009; Nash, 2015).

By 2020, Proctorio reported that it had administered more than 20 million exams across 1,200 institutions (Olsen, 2021)—a statistic now reflective of the industry-at-large (Kimmons & Veletsianos, 2021)—and students began voicing their concerns. In the year that followed, student newspapers at Brandeis, Cornell, DePaul, Duke, Emory, Ole Miss, Penn State, Purdue, Syracuse, William and Mary, and many more covered student dissatisfaction with the services. Multiple petitions were launched by student groups in protest of remote proctoring, and several universities agreed to stop using the software altogether (Kelley, 2020a). Students have cited a number of concerns, including privacy violations and discriminatory practices, while also pointing out that the long-term effectiveness of proctoring services remains ambiguous as students begin to test and share techniques for circumventing remote surveillance mechanisms (Geiger, 2021; Heilweil, 2020). Moreover, empirical literature examining the severity of academic dishonesty taking place during online verus in-person exams has produced inconsistent results (Peterson, 2019; Woldeab et al., 2017).

THE "INVISIBLE" BODY

Though many of these issues have been treated at length elsewhere, student reports of increased anxiety while under the watchful gaze of remote proctors have yet to be thoroughly explored. In this chapter, I attempt to move beyond an empirical analysis and address the *lived experience* of testing under the supervision of remote proctors. By taking embodied experience as the point of departure for this investigation, I aim to uncover the existential implications of newly implemented proctoring technologies. For this reason, I employ phenomenological perspectives throughout this inquiry—regularly turning to and interpreting student testimony found in the editorials and news articles mentioned above. As a theoretical framework, phenomenology is concerned with revealing the tacit structures and conditions that shape a person's conscious experience as a being-in-the-world (i.e., a body inextricably linked to—and in constant dialogue with—the world as such). From this theoretical perspective, an individual is not considered a disembodied and unaffected "ego" of the Cartesian—now posthumanist (Vaccari, 2012)—tradition; rather, the experiences that an individual has are directly shaped by the *facticity* of their being: the specific particularities of their body (e.g., age, race, height, disposition), as well as the many cultural norms and ideological influences embedded within it. For example, when I miss a step while walking down the stairs, the flutter in my stomach reminds me that I am not merely a free-floating mind but a corporeal, perspectival being, limited by the particular physical benefits and constraints that my body affords me.

Influenced by the work of Martin Heidegger and Edmund Husserl, French phenomenologist Maurice Merleau-Ponty (1945/2012) wrote that the body is our "point of view upon the world" (p. 73). Indeed, the body is our "general means of having a world" at all (p. 147). It is through my hand that I engage with the pen on my desk, through my eyes that I admire the bird outside my window, and through my nose that I become distracted by the smell of freshly baked bread wafting through my office. Moreover, as Drew Leder (1990) has noted, "My expressive face can form a medium of communication only because it is available to the Other's gaze" (p. 11). Simultaneously seeing and seen, touching and touched, the body is not a refuge or "envelope" (Merleau-Ponty, 1964, p. 172) that protects me from an outside world but the means by which "I am immersed in it" (p. 178). "Visible and mobile, my body is a thing among things; it is … caught in the fabric of the world" (p. 163). And yet, often, it seems that I am unaware of my bodily comportment. The body's tendency to recede into the background of one's attentional field is a point that has been repeatedly discussed in phenomenological literature. For example, in *The Absent Body*, Leder noted that "While in one sense the body is the most abiding and inescapable presence in our lives, it is also essentially characterized by absence" (p. 1). He continues:

> That is, one's own body is rarely the thematic object of experience. When reading a book or lost in thought, my own bodily state may be the farthest thing from my awareness. I experientially dwell in a world of ideas, paying little heed to my physical sensations or posture. (p. 1)

Merleau-Ponty suggested in *Phenomenology of Perception* (1945/2012) that this bodily absence may be explained by the simple idea that we do not *have* so much as *inhabit* our bodies. Indeed, I do not often perceive my arm as an external object or tool; instead, as I start to pick up the mug on my desk, my movement is informed by a wealth of "preconscious knowledge" that has already determined the range of possibilities available to me without the need for "a clear and articulated perception of [my] body" (p. 83). Nor is there a need to consciously calculate the mug's distance, shape, or weight—I am already aware of such things. Though the items in my periphery are distinct physical objects in their own right, my orientation toward them is almost always as an object available *for me* such that, as Luna Dolezal (2015) has noted, "I situate my lived-body in space around them and in relation to them" (p. 22). She continues:

> I cannot see a glass bottle, for example, and observe, in an abstracted way, its material and form without immediately and pre-reflectively associating it with my body's history of experiencing such an object and hence project-ing a possible future that includes the human act or acts which it can serve. (p. 22)

As a result, my body is "already mobilized by the perception" of the objects around me (Merleau-Ponty, 1945/2012, p. 108). Moreover, my intent to reach for an object on my desk may only become clear to me once the object is already within my grasp. The prevalence of habitual motor processes in everyday activities (e.g., eating, walking, driving, speaking) highlights how rarely we consciously attend to and exercise conscious control over our bodies. The ability to move in and respond to one's surroundings with ease and confidence is possible, in some sense, only because of the prevalence of this pre-reflective, habitual knowledge. As Dolezal (2015) has noted, "We do not and (many argue) cannot move and act successfully if we thematically regard the body as an object, supposedly using rational and quantifiable judgments to control and manipulate it" (p. 22).

Thus, phenomenologists have often described the "normal" body as experientially *absent* or *invisible* insofar as we are rarely explicitly aware of our bodily comportment during everyday life. Experiences of bodily absence, termed "flow" by Mihaly Csikszentmihalyi (1975, p. 86) and Hubert Dreyfus (1999, p. 105), are perhaps most noticeable during moments of high-level cognition: Athletes, musicians, and public speakers report being "in the zone" during their most impressive performances, and almost everyone has undoubtedly experienced the realization, after driving home from work, that they have no memory of monitoring and adjusting the speed of their vehicle, signaling lane changes, or maneuvering through traffic. In *Being and Nothingness* (1943/1992), Jean-Paul Sartre analyzed the familiar example of writing. When putting pen to paper, he argued, "my hand has vanished" (p. 426):

> I do not apprehend *my* hand in the act of writing but only the pen … I use my pen in order to form letters but not *my hand* in order to hold the pen. I am not in relation to my hand in the same utilizing attitude as I am in rela-tion to the pen; I *am* my hand. (p. 426)

Moments of flow like the one Sartre describes are dependent upon the body's ability to move through and act upon its surroundings without "getting in the way" (Dolezal, 2015, p. 27). When I walk through a crowd, my body constantly shifts and maneuvers around obstacles to avoid drawing itself into my attentional field. Thus, my own physical structure is "*passed by in silence*"—a latent presence in the background of my everyday life (Sartre, 1943/1992, p. 434).

THE "VISIBLE" BODY

There are, however, many situations that can disrupt this flow. For example, if I suffer a muscular strain in my arm while exercising, my attention is immediately directed toward the point of injury. In the days that follow, even the simplest tasks in my routine—putting away dishes, walking the dog, or reaching for the mug on my desk—are plagued by a newfound awareness of muscles I didn't even know I had. Similarly, Luís Madeira and colleagues (2019) have described the experience of falling ill, when the "pre-reflexive, intimate, and familiar" features of the body become "other" and the "painful, heavy, nauseated, feverish body, now alien and out of control, is no longer *home*" (p. 278). Leder (2016) wrote that when we are ill, we are brought to a "heightened awareness of the body," now perceived as an "external threat" that encumbers our once free-flowing movement and thought (p. 16). Having entered the attentional field, the ill or injured body is regarded as an obstacle, an *object* of sorts. Indeed, the disruption of bodily invisibility often occurs during everyday performative failures, much like the way a familiar keyboard—taken for granted in everyday use—comes sharply into focus when a broken key fails to produce the intended letter.

THE BODY *FOR-ITSELF*

Though I have focused on localized and individual disputations of bodily invisibility up to this point (e.g., illness, injury, disability, pregnancy), such examples fail to get at the inherently social and discursive dynamics at play between students and their proctors. In order to evaluate the critical intersubjective dimensions of bodily self-consciousness at work during student-proctor encounters, I turn now to Sartre's account of *the gaze*—or "the look"—in *Being and Nothingness* (1943/1992) and its existential significance as an objectifying and alienating force.[2] Though at times his ontology is too heavily tied to Cartesian subject-object dichotomies, it remains particularly useful for analyzing the technologically mediated forms of communication under investigation here, in which limitations to the conveyance of gesture, tone, and eye contact only further emphasize the superficiality these forms of communication often promote.[3]

The "invisible" body already discussed above reflects the first of three ontological dimensions of embodiment introduced by Sartre: the body *for-itself*, the body *for-others*, and the body *for-itself-for-others*—the last of these three dimensions having been re-termed the "seen body" by later scholars (Dolezal, 2012; Sheets-Johnstone, 1994). The first of these, the body *for-itself*, is experientially characterized by its inconspicuous absence and familiarity. "*Lived* and not *known*" (Sartre, 1943/1992, p. 324), the body for-itself is "surpassed" as it remains in the background of my attentional field (p. 236). But, of course, my body is *not* invisible to others.

THE BODY *FOR-OTHERS*

Diverging from his description of the invisible body, Sartre (1943/1992) recalls his experience volunteering to participate in various psychology and physiology experiments. Sitting in a laboratory, and "in the Other's presence," an experimenter asked that he assess whether the light on a screen in front of him was more or less illuminated, whether the pressure exerted on his hand was more or less intense, and so on (p. 311). He wrote that, though he apprehended the objects presented to him as a self-reflective subject, he was apprehended by the experimenter as a mere object among other objects: "The illumination of the screen belonged to *my* world; my eyes as objective organs belonged to the world of the experimenter" (p. 311). Here, thematized by the experimenter's gaze, his body-as-object was "utilized and known by the Other," and he was faced with the ontic features of his physical form (p. 351). This illustration typifies the second of Sartre's ontological terms: the body *for-others*. Under the (omnipresent but often ontically absent) gaze of the Other, I acquire a conceptual self-awareness of my bodily features and instrumentality as a mediating "tool-among-tool" (p. 352). Jacob Saliba has further illuminated Sartre's familiar scene in an examination room, writing, "The doctor presses the stethoscope against my chest listening intently to my breathing patterns and objectifying me in my anatomical form; I, in turn, sit there patiently as the ground for the doctor's actions" (Saliba, 2021, para. 16). As the doctor asks me to breathe in and out, my breathing becomes stilted, and I find myself keenly aware of every movement required to accomplish this task—a task which, just before the doctor turned his gaze upon it, I completed without forethought and without effort. "There is no doubt"—as Sartre (1943/1992) surmised—my experience is one of objectification, of bodily visibility (p. 252). I *am seen* by the Other, and now *I see myself* as well.

In the next section, I connect the disruptive force of *the gaze* as outlined above to the particular functions and methods employed by proctoring services. I then turn to the last of Sartre's three ontological dimensions (i.e., the "seen body") and its often-alienating role in the constitution of reflective self-consciousness.

THE PROCTOR'S GAZE

The proctor's gaze clearly presents issues for students, many of whom report, in quite plain terms, "It feels like someone is staring at me as I take my exam" (Krafka, 2021, para. 6). In an interview about his petition to stop the use of remote proctors at Brooklyn College, a sophomore named Aharon asked that readers imagine what it would feel like if they knew a proctor was watching their every movement: "You [would] think about it the whole entire time," he said. "You can't not think about it" (Young, 2020, para. 11). Further elucidating this experience, Takashi, a student at St. Charles Community College, explicitly compared remote proctoring to common in-person test-taking: Noting the "intrusive" nature of remote proctoring, he reported that the online experience feels "like having someone standing over your shoulder" (Chin, 2020a, para. 25). Similarly, another student asked, "You know how in high school, when you'd be doing a test and a teacher would walk around and peer over your shoulder? That anxiety you feel for those 10 seconds? That's how basically all of us feel" (Harwell, 2020a, para. 18). The experience described here is undoubtedly familiar to many readers. Looking back at my time as an undergraduate, I clearly recall the uneasy feeling that eclipsed any attempt to concentrate on the exam in front of me as an instructor or proctor, tasked with monitoring the room, passed by my desk. When the heat of their gaze grazed my back, hands, desk, paper, and backpack, I too became aware of the presence of these objects. Like a spotlight surveilling the room, the proctor's gaze drifted onto my desk and, lingering for a moment, illuminated its contents. As the teacher stood behind me, tension grew in my chest, my posture tightened inward, and I became increasingly aware of my bodily comportment: I was paralyzed in this state of being-for-others, unable to move freely or direct my attention back toward the task at hand.

However, unlike the momentary disruptions that occur during in-person testing, students have pointed out that remote proctoring ensures they each remain under direct surveillance "the whole time" (Chin, 2020a, para. 25). Indeed, many services include features that explicitly remind students that they were under observation, repeatedly drawing students' attention back to their bodily comportment. Drew Harwell (2020a) of *The Washington Post* found that when students using ProctorU were "flagged" for suspicious behavior, their proctors alerted a "more aggressive specialist," known as an "interventionist," who could interrupt the exam to "demand that the student aim his or her webcam at a suspicious area or face academic penalty" (para. 24). Meanwhile, Betsy—a Rutgers University student navigating ProctorTrack—found that once her exam began, "a red warning band appeared on the computer screen indicating that [the proctor] was monitoring her computer and recording video of her" (Singer, 2015, para. 3). Moreover, "To constantly remind her that she was being watched, the program also showed a live image of her in miniature on her screen" (Singer, 2015, para. 3). As a result, students have reported being unable to give their "undivided attention . . . to the content of the test" (Krafka, 2021, para. 8). One student noted that they found the services "distracting" (Zhang, 2020), while another said that she "wasn't as focused" (Scavo, 2020). Tracy, a recent graduate, reported that she often felt as though she could only use "half of [her] brain ... to actually work on the exam" because the other half was "so concentrated on not messing up or doing anything wrong or making the wrong move" (Harwell, 2020b, para. 59). Similarly, University of Minnesota student Katrina said, "My experience with Proctorio has been nerve-wracking, to say the least. Every time I take a test I worry about accidentally acting suspicious while the camera's watching" (Chin, 2020b, para. 14). And for good reason: In an oft-cited example, more than one-third of the nearly 9,000 participants who sat for the State Bar of California's remote exam in October had their test flagged by ExamSoft for review (Kelley 2020b).

Indeed, numerous reports have emerged that proctors incorrectly flag unintentional and innocuous behaviors as cheating (Hubler, 2020). Like its competitors, Proctorio is a remote service meant to replicate the security of an in-person exam. Once the test begins, the service employs several surveillance techniques to guard against cheating: Student behavior is monitored and recorded via the computer's webcam and microphone; artificial intelligence software tracks physical movements, facial expressions, background noise, and screen activity; and several computer features (e.g., printing, web browsing, copy-pasting, etc.) are made inaccessible. However, while the methods and functionality of these services are not monolithic, the many forms of observation they introduce extend far beyond what is found in most classrooms. Live proctors at Examity (who each monitor one student at a time) say they are instructed to continuously scan their student's surroundings and "closely watch the face of the student ... [for] suspicious eye movements" (Chin, 2020a, para. 26). Meanwhile, Harwell (2020b) found that services reliant on automated software use gaze-detection and computer-monitoring to "flag students for 'abnormal' head movement, mouse movement, eye wandering, computer window resizing, tab opening, scrolling, clicking, typing, and copies and pastes" (para. 7). He continues:

> A student can be flagged for finishing the test too quickly, or too slowly, clicking too much, or not enough. If the camera sees someone else in the background, a student can be flagged for having "multiple faces detected." If someone else takes the test on the same network—say, in a dorm building—it's potential "exam collusion." Room too noisy, Internet too spotty, camera on the fritz? Flag, flag, flag. (para. 7)

As one student put it, "Stuff that people wouldn't think twice about in a real classroom was being used against us" (Harwell, 2020b, para. 3). Indeed, Thera, a student at the University of California, Los Angeles who suffers from allergies, reported that she was "intimidated" by the testing software after it repeatedly flagged her exam each time she sneezed into a tissue on the grounds that she was "looking away from the screen to view a piece of paper (Hubler, 2020, para. 22). Similarly, test-taker Cole reported that interruptions from the proctor disrupted his "train of thought" (Guthrie, 2020, para. 7). Cole noted, "When you are taking the exam at the testing center where it is normally held, nobody pops up out of nowhere, barking at you not to touch your face" (Guthrie, 2020, para. 7). As a result, students report heavily self-monitoring their own behavior—a task encouraged by the inclusion of features (e.g., self-facing cameras, red banners, proctor interruptions) that intentionally draw the student's bodily comportment back into their attentional field. It is here, however—when students begin to report (not only "distraction" but) "anxiety" about the way their proctors see them—that Sartre's third ontological dimension of embodiment becomes most relevant.

THE "SEEN BODY"

As we have seen, the gaze of others has the ability to alert the individual to (i.e., make visible) their body as an object (utilized by themselves and others) much in the same way an injury might bring one's arm into focus. Sartre (1943/1992) argued, however, that the gaze also reflects the value-laden judgments of the gazer. Thus, the *seen body* is characterized by the intersubjective, socialized manner in which "I exist for myself as a body known by the Other" (p. 351). That is to say, the third ontological dimension is distinct from the conspicuous body *for-others*, in which my superficial features, movement, and comportment are apprehended as the object of my attentional field; rather the *seen body* is characterized by first-person experiences of *shame, embarrassment,* or *alienation* as I develop a self-conscious awareness of *how I appear to the Other* (p. 358).[4] Sartre wrote, for example:

I have just made an awkward or vulgar gesture. This gesture clings to me;
I neither judge it nor blame it. I simply live it. I realize it in the mode of
for-itself. But now suddenly I raise my head. Somebody was there and has
seen me. Suddenly I realize the vulgarity of my gesture, and I am ashamed.
(p. 221)

Finding myself within the Other's attentional field, I am thrown into a
position of self-appraisal: I am suddenly faced with concern about my
outwardly appearance. Sartre further illustrated this point in an oft-cited
vignette of a voyeur jealously peeking through a keyhole to spy on his lover.
"Let us imagine that moved by jealousy, curiosity, or vice I have just glued
my ear to the door and looked through a keyhole," he writes (p. 259). At
first, he is pre-reflectively engaged in this act of voyeurism: "there is no
self to inhabit my consciousness, nothing therefore to which I can refer
my acts in order to qualify them. They are in no way *known*; I *am my* acts"
(p. 259). Immersed in this act of spying, his body recedes from his awareness.
But then, hearing someone approach, his bodily invisibility is disrupted:

All of a sudden I hear footsteps in the hall. Someone is looking at me!
What does this mean? It means that I am suddenly affected in my being
and that essential modifications appear in my structure.... First of all, I
now exist as myself for my unreflective consciousness ... I see *myself* because
somebody sees me. (p. 260)

Sartre reports that, with the appearance of the Other, his face turns red,
an "immediate shudder" runs down his back, and his *seen body* enters his
attentional field. He writes, "I am ashamed of myself as I *appear* to the
Other" (p. 222). Hence, Dolezal (2012) has noted that our self-knowledge
is largely *dependent* on the objectifying responses of other people; In the
third ontological dimension of embodiment, "I experience and am aware
of how (I think) the other sees me" (p. 13).

And yet, I am never truly aware of how I appear to others. Sartre
(1943/1992) wrote that to apprehend the Other's gaze is not to apprehend
it as-object in the world; rather, "it is to be conscious of *being looked at*"
(p. 258). Nevertheless, I have no direct access to the contents of this look.
As such, Helen Ngo (2017) has noted that the "unknowable" nature of
the Other's objectifying gaze necessarily involves an asymmetrical power
relation such that "there is a distinct sense in which the gaze leaves the
Other-as-object both revealed and exposed" (p. 140). She continues,
"to find oneself suddenly looked-at ... is to find oneself naked" and in a
"moment of vulnerability" experienced as "disempowerment" (p. 142).
Disempowerment is particularly apparent for proctored students who, to
paraphrase Saliba (2021, para. 16), must sit there patiently as the ground
for the proctor's actions. Thus, this loss of control is a constitutive element

of what Sartre (1943/1992) termed "alienation," an objectified state in which the *seen body* comes to the fore of my attentional field (p. 263).

THE ALIENATED STUDENT

Though alienation is not a necessary consequence of objectification, Sartre (1943/1992) has argued that it often arises when the subject is "vividly and constantly conscious of his body not as it is for him but as it is *for the Other*" (p. 353). An experience of alienation occurs when the *seen body*—that is, the body as it has been characterized by the Other (e.g., as shameful, vulgar, lazy, deceitful)—comes to the forefront of my attentional field but does not reflect my true intentions or desires. In a state of alienation, I feel *estranged* from myself—"in the shock which seizes me when I apprehend the Other's look . . . suddenly I experience a subtle alienation of all my possibilities" (pp. 264–265). In other words, a state of alienation is one in which I no longer feel free to appraise the character of my own actions but must instead see myself through the eyes of the Other. In Sartre's words, "my freedom escapes me in order to become a *given* object" (p. 261).

As we have already seen, students take great care to note how little control they have over their proctor's perception of them. In a remote testing environment, unconscious gestures and even events fully out of students' control may lead to disqualification: Guidelines before the exam inform students that "Changes in lighting can flag your test for a violation," and "Even stretching, looking away, or leaning down to pick up your pencil could flag your test" (Singer, 2015, para. 17). As a result, students consistently report experiencing anxiety about how their actions will be interpreted: Rachel, a sophomore using Honorlock for one of her courses, told her school paper that the experience was "so stressful … knowing that I might be accused of cheating" because "I never know if what I'm doing is going to trigger a flag" (Hill, 2020, para. 6). Similarly, Cole wrote that after a proctor interrupted his exam with the injunction "don't touch your face," he worried what other behaviors might trigger a disqualification: "I was terrified. If I got an itch on my nose, was he going to fail me? What if I moved around too much in my chair? What if I looked at the ceiling?" (Guthrie, 2020, para. 9).

As Jane C. Hu (2020) has noted, "The mere threat of being flagged can be anxiety-provoking for students" (para. 7). And yet, it is students' physiological symptoms of anxiety (e.g., fidgeting, face-touching, pencil tapping) that are most often flagged as disqualifying behaviors. Femi, a junior at the University of Texas at Austin, reported, "I feel like I can't take a test in my natural state anymore, because they're watching for all these movements, and what I think is natural they're going to flag" (Caplan-

Bricker, 2021, para. 4). His dread of the software increased further after his roommate dropped a pot in the kitchen, making a loud clang that the automated proctoring software he was using deemed suspicious. "I had to try to calm down," he said, adding that he worried if he showed any physical signs of anxiety, Proctorio would "say that suspicious activity is going on" (Caplan-Bricker, 2021, para. 4). Inaara, a second-year criminology student, summarized the situation quite succinctly: "Online proctoring really just feels like you're trying to avoid getting caught for something that you didn't even do" (Jeffrey, 2021, para. 14).

Hence, we find in student testimony a range of experiences. It must be acknowledged that for many students, the geographical flexibility of remote proctoring offers more benefits than drawbacks: For some, a moment of bodily visibility at the start of the exam may be quickly overcome as they resume their work and the proctor's presence is forgotten. For others, though, this visibility may create difficult testing conditions as frequent reminders of the proctor's presence extend over the course of the exam, disrupting their flow. And as we have seen, in the most extreme circumstances, students may even find the proctor's objectifying gaze harmful; Sartre has suggested that "By the mere appearance of the Other, I am put in the position of passing judgment on myself as on an object, for it is as an object that I appear to the Other" (p. 222). And so, we see that the proctor's gaze has the potential to awaken a self-reflective anxiety that goes far beyond mere distraction, instead creating in students an ongoing *self-conscious* awareness of how they are being perceived, their apparent lack of control over that perception, and the feelings of alienation that soon follow.

CONCLUSION

The aim of this chapter has been to begin the process of elucidating some of the under-theorized phenomenological and existential nuances present in student testimony about remote proctoring. In reconsidering the effects of the proctor's gaze as an objectifying and alienating force, it is possible to reevaluate several other lines of inquiry already emerging from the tacit *technological solutionism* that grounds the remote proctoring project-at-large (Swauger, 2020).

Perhaps the line of inquiry most immediately available involves the application of Michel Foucault's (1975/2012) incisive work on *panopticism*, in which a unidirectional system of surveillance leads prison inmates to self-enforce predetermined norms of behavior. Students take care to note their lack of recourse when sitting in a remote testing environment. As one student noted, "They can see you, but you can't see them" (Hu, 2020, para. 1); another wrote, "It's kind of like a one-sided FaceTime" (Toth,

2020, para. 3). While a proctor can clearly see the student throughout the exam, "the student cannot see the proctor's face" (Harwell, 2020a, para. 24), and as a result, has "no idea if or when" a proctor is watching (Ryan, 2020, para. 14). Thus, we find the Foucauldian "eye that must see without being seen" already present in the mechanics of remote proctoring services (p. 171).

A number of additional topics emerge from a Foucauldian analysis of the gaze as a method of norm creation. For example, the series of injunctions students face as they start a remotely proctored exam—"Don't make any sudden movements." "Look directly ahead." "Don't speak" (Cahn & Deng, 2020, para. 1)—have already proven themselves uniquely burdensome for students with disabilities (Brown, 2021; Patil & Bromwich, 2020). And numerous reports have emerged that the facial recognition and detection features built into some proctoring services are not adequately constructed to "see" students of color (Clark, 2021; Feathers, 2021). Thus, there is also a need for further exploration of the unique ontological significance these experiences of alienation pose for racialized bodies, as well as a critical engagement with the clear sense in which the proctor's gaze takes shape as yet another form of the "white gaze."[5]

In this chapter, I hope to have provided a philosophical foundation on which these many new lines of inquiry can grow. As we have seen, the more extreme forms of alienation many students experience reflect a lack of control over how their in-test actions will be interpreted by universities that—through the very adoption of remote proctoring services—have demonstrated an implicit assumption that these students are *already* suspicious, *already* guilty. Indeed, the proctoring services currently in use, with features (e.g., self-facing cameras, red banners, real-time interruptions) designed to remind students of their surveilled state and encourage self-policing, only emphasize the student's inability to avoid the shameful implications of each accusatory signal. It is clear, however, that even face-to-face, in-person proctoring has the potential to throw students into a state of being-*for-others*, distracted by a wandering gaze when concentration is needed most. Thus, as teachers and administrators consider how best to maintain academic integrity inside and outside of their classrooms, one need also consider how such measurers affect the student experience, what those measures signal to the student, and whether more forgiving, less intrusive options are available.

REFERENCES

Barnes, C. (2010). Academic dishonesty in online classes: How do we maintain the integrity of online courses? In *ICERI2010 Proceedings* (pp. 3274–3281). Madrid, Spain.

Brown, L. X. Z. (2021, June 23). How automated test proctoring software discriminates against disabled students. *Center for Democracy and Technology*. https://cdt.org/insights/how-automated-test-proctoring-software-discriminates-against-disabled-students/

Cahn, A. F., & Deng, G. (2020, December 23). Remote test-taking software is an inaccurate, privacy-invading mess. *Fast Company*. https://www.fastcompany.com/90586386/remote-test-taking-software-is-an-inaccurate-privacy-invading-mess

Caplan-Bricker, N. (2021). Is online test-monitoring here to stay? *The New Yorker*. https://www.newyorker.com/tech/annals-of-technology/is-online-test-monitoring-here-to-stay

Casey, D. M. (2008). A journey to legitimacy: The historical development of distance education through technology. *TechTrends*, *52*(2), 45–51. https://doi.org/10.1007/s11528-008-0135-z

Chin, M. (2020a, April 29). Exam anxiety: How remote test-proctoring is creeping students out. *The Verge*. https://www.theverge.com/2020/4/29/21232777/examity-remote-test-proctoring-online-class-education

Chin, M. (2020b, October 22). An ed-tech specialist spoke out about remote testing software—and now he's being sued. *The Verge*. https://www.theverge.com/2020/10/22/21526792/proctorio-online-test-proctoring-lawsuit-universities-students-coronavirus

Clark, M. (2021, April 9). Students of color are getting flagged to their teachers because testing software can't see them. *The Verge*. https://www.theverge.com/2021/4/8/22374386/proctorio-racial-bias-issues-opencv-facial-detection-schools-tests-remote-learning

Cloutier, C. (2018). Love as seeing in truth: Sartre and Stein on self-constitution. *Lumen Et Vita*, *8*(2). https://doi.org/10.6017/lv.v8i2.10505

Csikszentmihalyi, M. (1975). *Beyond boredom and anxiety: The experience of play in work and games*. Jossey-Bass.

Daly, A., Cummins, F., Jardine, J., & Moran, D. (Eds.). (2020). *Perception and the inhuman gaze: Perspectives from philosophy, phenomenology, and the sciences*. Routledge.

Dolezal, L. (2012). Reconsidering the Look in Sartre's *Being and Nothingness*. *Sartre Studies International*, *18*(1), 9–28. https://doi.org/10.3167/ssi.2012.180102

Dolezal, L. (2015). *The body and shame: Phenomenology, feminism, and the socially shaped body*. Lexington Books.

Dreyfus, H. L. (1999). The challenge of Merleau-Ponty's phenomenology of embodiment for cognitive science. In H. F. Haber & G. Weiss (Eds.), *Perspectives on embodiment: The intersections of nature and culture* (pp. 103–120). Routledge.

Feathers, T. (2021, April 8). Proctorio is using racist algorithms to detect faces. *VICE*. https://www.vice.com/en/article/g5gxg3/proctorio-is-using-racist-algorithms-to-detect-faces

Foucault, M. (2012). *Discipline and punish: The birth of the prison* (A. Sheridan, Trans.). Knopf. (Original work published in 1975)

Geiger, G. (2021, March 5). Students are easily cheating 'state-of-the-art' test proctoring tech. *VICE*. https://www.vice.com/en/article/3an98j/students-are-easily-cheating-state-of-the-art-test-proctoring-tech

Guthrie, C. (2020, August 24). I failed my PMP exam and it's COVID-19's fault. *Solarity*. https://solarity.com/i-failed-my-pmp-exam-and-its-covid-19s-fault/

Harwell, D. (2020a, April 3). Mass school closures in the wake of the coronavirus are driving a new wave of student surveillance. *The Washington Post*. https://www.washingtonpost.com/technology/2020/04/01/online-proctoring-college-exams-coronavirus/

Harwell, D. (2020b, November 13). Cheating-detection companies made millions during the pandemic. Now students are fighting back. *The Washington Post*. https://www.washingtonpost.com/technology/2020/11/12/test-monitoring-student-revolt/

Heilweil, R. (2020, May 4). Paranoia about cheating is making online education terrible for everyone. *Vox*. https://www.vox.com/recode/2020/5/4/21241062/schools-cheating-proctorio-artificial-intelligence

Hill, Z. (2020, November 5). Honorlock: How it works and who's in charge. *The Point*. https://lomabeat.com/honorlock-how-it-works-and-whos-in-charge/

Hollister, K. K., & Berenson, M. L. (2009). Proctored versus unproctored online exams: Studying the impact of exam environment on student performance. *Decision Sciences Journal of Innovative Education*, 7(1), 271–294. https://doi.org/10.1111/j.1540-4609.2008.00220.x

Hu, J. C. (2020, October 26). Online test proctoring claims to prevent cheating. But at what cost? *Slate Magazine*. https://slate.com/technology/2020/10/online-proctoring-proctoru-proctorio-cheating-research.html

Hubler, S. (2020, May 10). Keeping online testing honest? Or an Orwellian overreach? *The New York Times*. https://www.nytimes.com/2020/05/10/us/online-testing-cheating-universities-coronavirus.html

Jeffrey, A. (2021, March 3). University of Alberta students call for end to online exam monitoring. *CBC News*. https://www.cbc.ca/news/canada/edmonton/university-of-alberta-students-call-for-end-to-online-exam-monitoring-1.5933094

Johnson, S. (2017, December 27). Faculty say online programs 'cannibalize' on-campus courses at George Washington University. *EdSurge*. https://www.edsurge.com/news/2017-10-17-faculty-say-online-programs-cannibalize-on-campus-courses-at-george-washington-university

Kelley, J. (2020a, September 25). Students are pushing back against proctoring surveillance apps. *Electronic Frontier Foundation*. https://www.eff.org/deeplinks/2020/09/students-are-pushing-back-against-proctoring-surveillance-apps

Kelley, J. (2020b, December 23). ExamSoft flags one-third of California bar exam test takers for cheating. *Electronic Frontier Foundation*. https://www.eff.org/deeplinks/2020/12/examsoft-flags-one-third-california-bar-exam-test-takers-cheating

Kimmons, R., & Veletsianos, G. (2021, February 23). Proctoring software in higher ed: Prevalence and patterns. *EDUCAUSE Review*. https://er.educause.edu/articles/2021/2/proctoring-software-in-higher-ed-prevalence-and-patterns.

Krafka, C. (2021, April 22). Students raise red flags over online test proctoring. *The Lantern*. https://www.thelantern.com/2021/04/students-raise-red-flags-over-online-test-proctoring/

Leder, D. (1990). *The absent body*. University of Chicago Press.

Leder, D. (2016). *The distressed body: Rethinking illness, imprisonment, and healing.* University of Chicago Press.

Madeira, L., Leal, B., Filipe, T., Rodrigues, M. F., & Figueira, M. L. (2019). The uncanny of the illness experience: Can phenomenology help? *Psychopathology, 52*(5), 275–282. https://doi.org/10.1159/000504141

Merleau-Ponty, M. (2012) *Phenomenology of perception* (D. A. Landes, Trans.). Routledge. (Original work published in 1945)

Merleau-Ponty, M. (1964). Eye and mind (C. Dallery, Trans.). In J. M. Edie (Ed.), *The primacy of perception: And other essays on phenomenological psychology, the philosophy of art, history, and politics* (pp. 159–190). Northwestern University Press.

Nash, J. A. (2015). Future of online education in crisis: A call to action. *Turkish Online Journal of Educational Technology, 14*(2), 80–88.

Ngo, H. (2017). *The habits of racism: A phenomenology of racism and racialized embodiment.* Lexington Books.

Olsen, M. (2021, March 10). 2020 Year in review: Growth in a difficult time. *Proctorio Blog.* https://blog.proctorio.com/2020-year-in-review-growth-in-a-difficult-time/.

Patil, A., & Bromwich, J. E. (2020, September 29). How it feels when software watches you take tests. *The New York Times.* https://www.nytimes.com/2020/09/29/style/testing-schools-proctorio.html

Peterson, J. (2019). An analysis of academic dishonesty in online classes. *Mid-Western Educational Researcher, 31*(1), 24–36.

Ryan, S. (2020, December 16). Why proctoring online exams is becoming mainstream. *TestReach Blog.* https://www.testreach.com/blog-post/proctoring-online-exams.html

Saliba, J. (2021, June 24). Sartre on the body in "Being and Nothingness." *Epoché Magazine, 41.* https://epochemagazine.org/41/sartre-on-the-body-in-being-and-nothingness/

Sartre, J. (1992). *Being and nothingness: An essay on phenomenological ontology* (H. E. Barnes, Trans.). Washington Square Press. (Original work published in 1943)

Scavo, B. (2020, May 21). I don't think students should be monitored while taking online tests. [Comment on "Should students be monitored when taking online tests?"]. *The New York Times.* https://www.nytimes.com/2020/05/12/learning/should-students-be-monitored-when-taking-online-tests.html#commentsContainer

Sietses, L. (2016). White paper online proctoring: Questions and answers about remote proctoring. *SURFnet.* https://www.surf.nl/files/2019-04/whitepaper-online-proctoring_en.pdf

Sheets-Johnstone, M. (1994). The body as cultural object/The body as pan-cultural universal. In M. Daniel & L. E. Embree (Eds.), *Phenomenology of the cultural disciplines* (pp. 85–114). Kluwer Academic.

Singer, N. (2015, April 6). Online test-takers feel anti-cheating software's uneasy glare. *The New York Times.* https://www.nytimes.com/2015/04/06/technology/online-test-takers-feel-anti-cheating-softwares-uneasy-glare.html

Swauger, S. (2020, June 23). Our bodies encoded: Algorithmic test proctoring in higher education. *Hybrid Pedagogy.* https://hybridpedagogy.org/our-bodies-encoded-algorithmic-test-proctoring-in-higher-education/

Toth, L. R. (2020, April 17). Students raise concerns over virtual proctoring. *The Daily Illini*. https://dailyillini.com/news/2020/04/17/proctorio-concerns/

Vaccari, A. (2012). Dissolving nature: How Descartes made us posthuman. *Techne: Research in Philosophy and Technology, 16*(2), 138-186. https://doi.org/10.5840/techne201216213

Woldeab, D., Lindsay, T., & Brothen, T. (2017). Under the watchful eye of online proctoring. In I. D. Alexander & R. K. Poch (Eds.), *Innovative learning and teaching: Experiments across the disciplines*. University of Minnesota Libraries Publishing.

Yancy, G. (2017). *Black bodies, White gazes: The continuing significance of race*. Rowman & Littlefield.

Young, J. R. (2020, November 13). Pushback is growing against automated proctoring services. But so is their use. *EdSurge*. https://www.edsurge.com/news/2020-11-13-pushback-is-growing-against-automated-proctoring-services-but-so-is-their-use

Zhang, J. (2020, May 13). I don't think students should be monitored while taking tests. [Comment on "Should students be monitored when taking online tests?"]. *The New York Times*. https://www.nytimes.com/2020/05/12/learning/should-students-be-monitored-when-taking-online-tests.html#commentsContainer

ACKNOWLEDGMENTS

I would like to express my profound gratitude to Anna Skillings and Christopher Venner for their encouragement, counsel, and many insightful comments, without which this chapter would not be complete. I would also like to acknowledge this volume's editor and peer reviewers for their helpful notes on an earlier draft.

NOTES

1. Throughout the chapter, I use italic type to denote technical concepts and distinguish them from colloquial, nontechnical usage. Italic type is also sparingly used for emphasis throughout the chapter.
2. Sartre has often been criticized for his almost exclusively negative portrayal of the gaze as a medium for antagonism (Cloutier, 2018; Daly et al., 2020; Dolezal, 2015). However, insofar as the student-proctor relationship is one of generally opposed interests, Sartre's analysis proves useful for my purposes here.
3. See Ngo (2017) chapter four, part two for an insightful analysis of the limitations present in Sartre's ontology due to its grounding in Cartesian dualism.
4. See Dolezal (2015), especially chapters two, for a comprehensive review and application of Sartre's work on bodily shame.
5. See Yancy (2017) for a thorough account of the hegemonic status of the "white gaze" and its effects.

CHAPTER 5

ASSESSMENTS OF AMBIGUITY

Steven J. Fleet
University of Denver

ABSTRACT

This chapter applies ideas from Simone de Beauvoir's (2002) defense of existential ethics in *Ethics of Ambiguity* to considerations of assessments. Beauvoir's examination of the freedom that results from an awareness of one's subjectivity raises questions concerning the nature of authentic assessments designed to guide learning rather than emerging from the experience of learning. Since meaning and essence must be constructed by the individual, an existential view of assessment requires educators to consider how assessments can assist students as they engage in the essential construction of themselves as the narrators of their lives. Beginning with ideas concerning subjectivity, this chapter considers the importance of using complexity, uncertainty, and ambiguity to realize the freedom necessary to authentically move toward goals. Ultimately, the chapter focuses on how students who freely move toward a goal of their choosing put themselves in a position to authentically value and promote the freedom of others.

Like many of my colleagues, my most meaningful activities and assessments rise out of a moment of uncertainty, if not desperation. As a teacher in the humanities dedicated to artistic principles and the promotion of authentic experience, I find comfort in spontaneity and an energy when "creative freedom develops happily without ever congealing into an unjustified facticity" (De Beauvoir, 2002, p. 27). When I first added Camus's *The Plague*

Problematizing the Profession of Teaching From an Existential Perspective, pp. 91–109
Copyright © 2022 by Information Age Publishing
www.infoagepub.com

to my philosophy curriculum, I wanted the students to do something with the images, so I brought them back to watercolors, a medium with a hardened palette released by water that most of my students abandoned in elementary school. They produced an array of images from churches and trains to garbage heaps and lots of rats. They extracted something from the text that struck them and represented it so that the entire class could see. We saw the repetition of images, but the renderings varied. They read a common text, but everything from their comfort with the medium to how students visualize the transition from text to image brought about a diversity of expression. But I wanted more, so I asked them to return to their watercolors and paint "the idea that exists beyond the image." Silence. Then muffled conversations, a question or two, then back to work. This time, when we put the pictures up in the class there was no repetition of images. We saw renderings of emotions. We saw color used to clarify and to obscure. We saw the abstract, and we saw symbols. No painting resembled another, and we talked about how disturbing it would be if they were all alike. When we displayed the third and final image, "depict how your mind moved from the image to the idea" it created a tapestry of variety and color, a representation that the diversity of thought and perspective and expression will always be as much a catalyst to free thought as an indication of its existence. Then they eagerly spoke and wrote about the process of their experience and their expression, about their connections with the text and about how individuals construct meaning.

The means by which students interacted with text and the assessment became one in the same. Despite the values that arise from current trends in which knowledge of the assessment drives instruction, there may be benefits to not knowing our ultimate destination. Maintaining a sense of mystery and ambiguity should not be confused with abandoning a thoughtful and engaging curriculum. It instead considers that an authentic development of the mind commits to the emergence of the unexpected and the assemblage of understanding that arises in any given moment. Elliot Eisner offers the following in the conclusion of *The Educational Imagination* (2002):

> The formalized rites of passage provided by tests are likely to constrain any effort to put into practice a really broad view of human development, despite our aspirations to the contrary. Operationalism and measurement have focused so heavily on behavior that the quality of the student's experience has been generally ignored or seriously neglected. (p. 366)

While Eisner primarily references standardized tests, the idea applies to any assessment that operates as a terminal activity. The implication becomes that, regardless of what the student experiences, the parameters by which that experience can be expressed have been predetermined. Such predetermination eclipses the authentic and obscures the aims of an education that extend beyond measurement. Eisner writes, "Knowing, like teaching, requires the organism to be active and to construct meaningful patterns out of experience. At base, such patterns are artistic constructions, a means through which the human creates a conception of reality" (p. 369). As educators encourage students to build their understanding and, in the process, undertake the perpetual construction of self, it becomes incumbent to reflect on the patterns of learning that develop in schools. If we perpetuate the belief that the function of learning is to pass a test, then we do our students a disservice, the same disservice we do to them if we teach them that being ethical is a way to stay out of trouble. We teach them to act a certain way in order to achieve a certain outcome. We teach them obedience at the expense of freedom.

The *Ethics of Ambiguity* (1948/2002) by Simone de Beauvoir removes existentialism from the absurd and nourishes it with the ambiguous. She offers an optimistic and pragmatic interpretation of existential thought by arguing that free actions directed toward "constructive activities of man take on a valid meaning only when they are assumed as a movement toward freedom; and reciprocally ... open concrete possibilities to men" (De Beauvoir, 2002, p. 80). We must embrace our freedom so that we can give our lives direction. We do not "save up existence" so that we carry it to a predetermined goal, we exist so that we can act, and, in our actions, we create our relationship with the world and with others.

The pattern of authentic education, essential for the promotion of the critical thinking that makes democratic education possible should play out on every level, energized by the very fuel that it produces: freedom. The exploration of "Assessments of Ambiguity" relies on the paradigmatic substitution of "assessments" for "ethics" and considers the role that judgements play in the subjective mind. In a phenomenological sense, both assessments and ethics depend upon experience to answer questions that assist in guiding action. Assessments encourage judgements on actions and understanding so that we might better comprehend the world, just as ethics rely on our experience so that we may act in a manner that corresponds with who we want to be. An authentic combination of experience and judgement encourages a contemplation of the world that overcomes the irony of existential ethics and allows for free responsibility.

From the engaging and articulate expressions of Michael Bonnett (2009) who concludes his essay on "Education and Selfhood" urging educators to take "proper account" of the "phenomenological self, with its own felt intentionality and intelligence that is both always potentially transformatively engaged and subtly existentially enduring," to the clichés of graduation speeches "be yourself, change the world," one repeatedly encounters the ambiguous and yet fundamental goals of any ethical education (p. 369).

While the need to simultaneously encourage students to freely develop their authentic selves as well as act on their sense of responsibility informs the best intentions of educators, it tends to operate more as a hope than as a practice. The present conditions of the world, both ideologically and physically make it incumbent upon us, Bonnett (2018) urges,

> to develop arguments that intimate what would be desirable features of developing human sensibility given the oncoming circumstances in which globally we find ourselves—circumstances that possess a reality that proceeds regardless of whether we attend to it or how we chose to describe it. (p. 1308)

The exigencies of current conditions, from the erosion of democratic values to the impacts of climate change, require minds that simultaneously understand and imagine. They demand the realities of the present conditions to be freely addressed and the ambiguities to energize, in the words of De Beauvoir (2002), an "ethics experienced in the truth of life" where,

> Regardless of the staggering dimensions of the world about us, the density of our ignorance, the risks of catastrophes to come, and our individual weakness within the immense collectivity … if each man did what he must, existence would be saved in each one without there being any need of dreaming of a paradise where all would be reconciled in death. (p. 159)

Interpreting a world full of contradictions and then freely acting replaces the absurdity of existentialism with a pragmatism rooted in the ambiguity of the human condition.

Ambiguity nourishes freedom and provides a basis for the most authentic efforts of philosophy and for education. The history of Western philosophy did not expand when it merely recited Plato, it emerged when it explored the contradictions, uncertainties, and ambiguities of his dialogues. This chapter uses the existential perspective of Simone de Beauvoir to consider how assessments might help students to recognize the power that they possess to free themselves, define their relation to the world, and to authentically exit Plato's metaphorical cave. The first section, *The Liberation*, considers how the promotion of subjectivity in assessments enables student to break the chains that devalue spontaneity, creativity, and perception. The second section, *The Journey*, examines the thinking of International Baccalaureate teachers dedicated to assessments that promote authentic paths out of the cave. The final section, *The Ethical Turn*, considers how ambiguity enables one to freely act in the interest of others.

THE LIBERATION: AWARENESS AND ACTION

Existentialism, as presented by Simone de Beauvoir (2002), provides considerations for promoting authentic education by first encouraging students to see the external and artificial forces that seemingly define their existence and consequently obscure their authenticity. The remarkably artificial environment of schools provides one of the greatest obstacles to the promotion of personal, relevant, and free thinking. Within the entrenched structures and organization of educational systems, emerging from what we hope to be a well-intentioned and thoughtful curriculum, exists the experiences of students. In an environment ideally dedicated to critical thinking, creativity, and free thought, students continue to encounter bureaucratic and social realities that belie the best of educational objectives. Students must navigate between the need to think for themselves and to think mathematically at a prescribed time each day; they must simultaneously be creative and measure their success with rubrics; they take intellectual risks and then submit their learning to external "objective" measurement.

Meanwhile the school environment intensifies similar contradictions in their social interactions where students construct their identities while immersed in the complex and necessary dependence on friends and family. They learn to play roles, and they want to be themselves. When students need to practice thinking independently, their lives become complicated by a world of social media where the real and unreal, the true and false, the trivial and the sublime all perpetually present themselves in sound and color and image and text. As students reflect on their ever-expanding past, they make decisions about their futures. They find themselves participants in a world that they did not create, and in that moment, education must enable them to see themselves as creators within the world where they participate. Teachers must then value the tensions generated by the ambiguities of experience as a means of education and use assessments as tools of liberation. If students are invited to be active participants in their assessments, they are more likely to recognize the personal connections that they can make to what they learn. In turn, they become responsible for facilitating personal awareness of material outside of the self, activating the power they possess to take control of their own learning.

Existentialism did not emerge as an effort to change the world, but rather to encourage individuals to comprehend the world as it is and to use that clear-eyed capacity to rekindle their awareness of freedom, to unshackle themselves from the manipulation of prefabricated essence and to value their subjectivity. The existentialism of Simone de Beauvoir takes the ambiguities of contradictions as a means of generating and valuing personal perspectives to promote the freedom that accompanies the authentic. When applied to assessments, the judgements within education,

De Beauvoir's ontological emphasis brings forward questions of subject and object, being and becoming.

These questions encourage educators to nurture the nature of student understanding of self so that they value the reality of becoming over the illusory permanence of being. Philosophical tradition tends to cast *being* as an absolute and true state, free from the ravages of change, void of ambiguity. Being possesses permanence and in permanence there is no freedom. Consequently, structures that perpetuate the illusion of being, as a state that not only describes the facts of a given moment, but also describes conditions as they have always, and will continue to exist function as instruments of control. Traditional educational models rooted in "being" determine what should be known, and assessments measure how much is known.

Alternatively, assessments seeking to facilitate actions that promote the essential vitality of student as subject as opposed to the convenient ossification of student as object empower the self. Patrick Slattery and Marla Morris write in their article, "Simone de Beauvoir's Ethics and Postmodern Ambiguity: The Assertion of Freedom in the Face of the Absurd" (1999), "When one misrecognizes another person as being an object rather than a subject—as often happens to students in authoritarian classrooms and teachers in bureaucratic school structures—one may cause real harm to that person" (p. 27). I am not certain that the classroom must be authoritarian for this to occur, but, undoubtedly, if the external structure defines the student as "object" and students begin to accept that designation, the system has made them complicit in their own subjugation. If, however, students become contributors to their environment and genuinely establish goals that both they and the school community respect and pursue then students recognize their subjectivity and the power they possess to become the authors of their narratives.

Abstractly, educators want to promote "becoming" to create life-long learners, perpetual students who continue to question their surroundings and create new interpretations. However, the idea of the "perpetual student" does not have the same allure for young people who for most of their lives have always been students, have been given assignments, have been handed schedules, have been assigned seats, have been presented with rules, rewards, rubrics, and trained to face the judgements not only of assessments but the judgements of how others must see them based upon a number, or a letter that has consequently been prescribed to them. The frequently used retort, "That's not the grade you were given, that is the grade you earned," has never been a satisfactory consolation. In contrast, assessments that value the ambiguity of becoming lead students away from the confinements of descriptive and determinative external pressures by validating their creative impulses, by encouraging them to see the transformative power that they possess.

The shift for assessments requires that the measurable "being" not serve as a point of termination, but rather as a point of departure. De Beauvoir argues that it is essential for there to "*be* being" for freedom and choice to exist. Being is the ephemeral present (what I am) that provides the platform from which one becomes aware of possible actions (what I may be) and unleashes the pure manifestation of freedom which both enables one to act and is realized in the process of action. Free action converts object to subject (De Beauvoir, 2002). Informed by the past, action projects itself into the future providing the subject with the capacity to bring about change in the external world as well as within the self. The power of this transformative process entails genuine choice as described by De Beauvoir (2002),

> It is only when the moments of his life begin to be organized into behaviour that (the child) can decide and choose. The value of the chosen end is confirmed and, reciprocally, the genuineness of the choice is manifested concretely through patience, courage, and fidelity.... The goal toward which I surpass myself must appear to me as a point of departure toward a new act of surpassing. Thus, a creative freedom develops happily without ever congealing into unjustified facticity. The creator leans upon anterior creations in order to create the possibility of new creations.... At each moment freedom is confirmed through all creations. (p. 27)

Assessments of ambiguity promote experience, and meaningful assessments do not function as ends in themselves. They insist that the student choose the end and encourage "patience, courage, and fidelity." Ambiguity comes from student interactions, a process that many traditional assessments do not attempt to incorporate. Assessments that merely look at a final product (being) establish a standard that fails to utilize the dynamic aspects (becoming) of learning.

The process of "becoming" as liberation is the transition from moving students to assessments that measure the imposed objectivity of being (that which is predetermined and can be defined) to assessments that promote the subjectivity of becoming (that which is free and ambiguous). This process facilitates an essential movement to the authentic where one escapes from the prison of facticity by projecting one's awareness into the indeterminate future. In the moment of such a projection one acts freely and consequently takes steps to create both the possible self and to construct the world that one imagines.

The fact that ambiguity, as used by Simone de Beauvoir, has no satisfactory synonym and evades simple definition seems remarkably appropriate. If definitions begin to gravitate toward the frustrations of uncertainty, they must also incorporate the positive aspects of possibility. Ambiguity gains energy through tension, most immediately the tension between the world as it is, the facticity of existence in which we see ourselves as objects, and the transcendent subjectivity that becomes immediately apparent when we realize that we are the one's viewing ourselves as objects. If we see ourselves objectively, we know that such a vantage point can only come from ourselves as subjects. And so, we simultaneously exist as object and as subject. We are creatures acted upon and humans who can freely act; and in our actions we can alter the nature of who we are, we can reconfigure the objects that we were and in so doing perpetuate the paradox of our existence. Add to the objective world the power of institutions, the exegesis of history, the desires of others and every other force that offers clarity or control by presenting interpretations that can serve to terrify as easily as they can present the false comfort of illusory certainty and the ambiguity of our condition spirals beyond the capacity of any definition.

The complexities of prefabricated expectations surround us and so we must do more than struggle to keep them from confining us, we must find in them our capacity to act; we must find our freedom. Simone de Beauvoir (2002) writes,

> Since we do not succeed in fleeing it, let us therefore try to look the truth in the face. Let us try to assume our fundamental ambiguity. It is in the knowledge of the genuine conditions of our life that we must draw our strength to live and our reason for acting" (p. 9).

When students assume their ambiguity, they recognize their power as subjects as opposed to their dependence as objects. Education shifts from something done to them, to something that students do. Education becomes a journey toward a future yet to be made, an essential perspective because if young minds fail to believe in their power to reshape the world from what it is into what it might be; if students fail to realize that every discipline that they presently study requires the animating power of *their* perspectives and the re-articulation of *their* voices, then the present loses all significance as it will appear as nothing more than a ready-made step toward a fixed future.

THE JOURNEY: FREEDOM AND PLAY

Modern education has no shortage of assessments that seek to measure against a preexisting standard. The path to educational success is marked by a series of tests, some teacher generated, some standardized. These tests produce scores, any one of which might expand or limit opportunities. Even as colleges and universities increasingly consider "test optional" admissions, the practice of traditional assessments remains practically inextricable from traditional education. As I write this, I have a set of traditional tests that I would like to have graded by Monday. No argument, however well-reasoned, will eliminate such practices, and students without the skill to take tests would be left at a decided disadvantage as they learn how to navigate the educational system. However, in over 30 years as an educator I have never had a student return to tell me how much a traditional test motivated them, provided them with confidence or had any kind of profound impact. Instead, they talk about moments that they did not even know were assessments. And yet clearly these activities provided them with a means by which they could come to recognize their capacity to think, to interact, to create, and to learn.

Assessments that ignore the process of becoming threaten to imprison students within the objectivity of measurement, reducing student capacity to imagine undertaking the journey from one state of being to another, from what they are and what they may become. Beauvoir (2002) writes "To exist is to *make oneself* a lack of being; it is to *cast* oneself in the world. Those who occupy themselves in restraining this original movement can be considered as sub-men" (p. 42). The exodus from the cave, the recognition that one lives in a state of becoming is painful but is free. This is the existential sense of responsibility and the embracing of the authentic. Slattery and Morris (1999) bring this idea back to the classroom,

> It is always a struggle to become free because we tend to want to fly away from it in anxiety; We tend to avoid wanting to make free choices since they may entail complexity and uncertainty. This is exemplified in the contradiction of students who desire freedom of expression in classroom assignments while insisting that teachers provide detailed and unambiguous criteria for assessment. It is clear that the flight toward freedom is always in tension with the flight away from freedom. (p. 27)

Existentialism becomes pragmatic in education when it vitalizes freedom and promotes authenticity. Any educational system dedicated to the advancement of democratic principles, principles in which the expressed interest of individuals emanates from their recognition that they "freely establish the value of the end that they set up" (De Beauvoir, 2002, p. 48), must actively encourage students to utilize the power they possess to shape *their* relation to the world. This comes with unpredictability and uncertainty what those who seek predefined ends and control might call "risk," but these characteristics represent an authentic interplay between consciousness and the world, between knowledge and understanding. Assessments that promote subjective expression and operate as a means of discovery fuel creativity, authenticity, and the capacity for freedom.

Encouraging students to undertake an authentic educational journey requires us to enable them to act freely in their interpretations, creations, and aspirations and provide an experience traditionally designed as an "end" and have them use it as a means. When students apply their understanding to themselves—they take the pre-existing, interpret it, and then create a personal understanding of it. Chris, an International Baccalaureate teacher, trainer, and examiner with over 20 years of experience, requests that his students explore how they see in different genres by encouraging them to consider a personal experience and then to recreate that experience:

> Because it's about you, please write in the first person. And make sure it's something you wouldn't mind sharing. So, I say, "you're going to write those 500 words." And they do that, and they come back in. And then I tell them, "The next assignment is now turn that into a scene in a play, and you can't change any of the detail in terms of plot. You've got to have the same people in it. You've got to have the same setting, but now you must write it as though you're going to see it." (Fleet, 2007)

His final request in this instruction requires students to see themselves as both object and subject. He not only asks them to recreate an experience but to reexperience their creation. Not only do they write their experience, but he asks them to cast themselves as observers of what it is they create. The dual role of creator and critic enables the student to actively foster an understanding of process as well as product, a creative combination that values the ambiguity of personal perspective. Assessments that enable students to write in the first person, for example, offer a genuine invitation to explore and use the assessment itself as a means of generating thinking, not merely demonstrating knowledge. The activation of "I" enables students to turn an exploration of a topic into an experience, turning their thinking into active interpretations.

If our awareness of our assessments drives our instruction, then we must be certain that the momentum towards comprehension and truth that students gain from our curriculum increases because of our assessments. Assessments must enable students to value their voice; assessments must empower. De Beauvoir writes in the opening chapter of *Ethics of Ambiguity* that, "To attain his truth, man must not attempt to dispel the ambiguity of his being but, on the contrary, accept the task of realizing it" (De Beauvoir, 2002, p. 13). If an assessment serves to help students realize the ambiguity of their being, it must maximize their awareness of their subjective encounters with the multiple. Awareness of possibility discovers and uncovers new meanings and possibilities. If, on the other hand, an assessment simply functions to provide a measurement or clearly compares students to a standard, it objectifies otherwise inquiring minds and helps transition them into what Simone de Beauvoir refers to as the mindset of the "serious man" where one "loses himself in the object in order to annihilate his subjectivity" (p. 45). The serious man "knows that nothing can happen through him; everything is already given" (De Beauvoir, 2002 p. 37). In this scenario, a final assessment not only functions as the terminal event of the course but contributes to the termination of the student's subjectivity and diminishes their movement toward authenticity. On the other hand, steps as easy as writing in the first person and creating an original experience produce an assessment that invites authentic reflection on the part of the student.

If an assessment funnels the experiences of students toward predetermined expectations or toward a final grade the multiple encounters that characterized the course become meaningful, not for the momentum they contributed to a student's construction of self, but for how they allow students to be measured in the end. In most cases this is then translated to a grade. The student becomes a "C student in mathematics" or an "A student in science" objectified as much by the positive as by the negative. To be "serious" is to accept one's condition as a game which measures; and this acceptance, Beauvoir 2002 writes, "bars the horizon and bolts the sky" (p. 51). Assessments of ambiguity provide opportunities for students to embrace difference and to create from ambiguity. The culminating activities that teachers set up for students must encourage them to recognize the power they possess to authentically assemble their moral selves. Authentic assessments in this model move beyond functioning as a means to measure and instead serve as a continuation of learning, expanding the dialogue between the self and the world. Ambiguous assessments do not assess students for the purpose of measurement. They remain authentic due to their effort to validate and encourage thinking. The measurable is merely an artifact, a convenient remnant left by the loftier objective of enabling students to become the assessor; enabling them to be able to see the world as simultaneously real and open to change, as an existing palette with which they can express the essence of their choosing.

Many of the best examples of this process exist in arts education. Tim, an International Baccalaureate visual arts instructor and examiner, actively invites students to reflect on their creative selves. He encourages students to emphasize the personal:

> A student in talking about his artwork is going to say, "This idea began like this and changed into this and this. I was working on this project. This happened or this happened. Or, I did this research or I stumbled upon this artist. Or, I realized I wanted to say this in my message, in my piece of artwork I wanted to have this kind of a message." It comes out in that manner through the discussion. (Fleet, 2007)

The connection between process and product that promote significant conversations between teacher and student do not need to remain in the realm of the arts. Tim asks students to explore their processes as significant endeavors of their own, not merely to produce a work of art. The emphasis is consequently placed on the experience of creating more than on the manifestation of a "final" creation. Tim repeatedly refers to art as a representation of an ongoing self-portrait, and his approach to teaching the arts encourages students to be aware that they are perpetually creating art as well as themselves. The "key questions" become statements of action, presented with active verbs: I'm creating, I'm considering, I'm proposing, I'm investigating. These statements project into the future, ripe with possibility but not burdened with expectation. All disciplines provide countless models for the promotion of freedom and the value of existentialist perspectives on the idea of assessments even in subjects students are taught to see as "serious."

Simone de Beauvoir presents the child's perspective as something that needs to be cultivated and maintained in order to prevent the stifling limitations of "the serious." Like the romantics who created sophisticated works of interpretation and lived experience while maintaining the wide-eyed wonder of childhood, Simone de Beauvoir seeks to maintain the ambiguity of adolescence, not in the pejorative but in the genuine and undervalued juggling of perspectives that characterize our early years—an antidote for the serious and a pragmatic exercise in the ethical. The formation of judgements that arise from ambiguity do not categorize or serve to limit; they connect the mind to the possibilities made manifest by free thought. Tim further explores the line between what we want students to know and what we encourage them to do.

> That is exactly what we wish our students to do.... We wish them to inform their own art with an understanding of culture and meanings, and technique and effects and media that have been utilized successfully by somebody else and to use that as the shoulders to stand on. All I want to know is, "Is it true? That's where I think some *methods* fall down, because the teacher has the goal. The teacher already knows where (he/she) wants you to go, and I hate to be manipulated. I feel when somebody knows where they're going, I feel like I'm being kneaded and played and maybe I have an issue in my own life, with having forces outside of myself and my locus of control. But, nevertheless, if there's a right answer, at least allude to me that at some point you're going to let me know what that answer is, and then I'll play your game. Alright, then I'll go ahead, and I'll let you lead me around and I'll do some thoughtful thinking about this and speculating, but I want to know at what point does the speculation cease and the answer emerge. And if there is no answer, that's fine. I'd like to know that at the beginning." (Fleet, 2007)

The challenge for educators becomes one of maintaining and cultivating a childlike and genuine enthusiasm not only in their students but in themselves. This is the model of great educators, where the assessment and the learning become inseparable and yet undeniable. Tim is right that methods lose their vitality if they seek a predetermined end. Socrates tests his interlocutors but does not judge them, he leads them by engaging them, questioning them, and enabling them to freely exercise their ability to ask essential questions. His talent for encouraging others to see beyond the distortions of puppet masters heightens the irony that Socrates was ultimately condemned by the serious for "corrupting the youth." This early model of education acknowledges the difficulties of the task. It would be far easier for the philosopher not to free the prisoners; it would be far easier for the prisoners to refuse their freedom. But ultimately, they must choose, and, in that moment, they must acknowledge the presence of their subjectivity and the existence of freedom. The choice becomes whether to embrace the uncertain or to retire to the illusions of certainty. There is not a moment when those who scored 75% or higher are free; there is simply the choice: return to the audience of the puppet masters or undergo what is described as a difficult and painful liberation. It is always easier to remain serious. Simone de Beauvoir (2002) offers a description reminiscent of Plato's cave:

> The child's situation is characterized by his finding himself cast into a universe which he has not helped to establish, which has been fashioned without him, and which appears to him as an absolute to which he can only submit. In his eyes, human inventions, words, customs, and values are given facts, as inevitable as the sky and the trees. This means that the world in which he lives is a serious world, since the characteristic of the spirit of seriousness is to consider values as ready-made things. (p. 35)

Among the most powerful tools educators possess to combat such seriousness is the contrast between the serious world and the child's perspective. Although children *find themselves cast into a (serious) universe* they seek to delay their acceptance of that reality. They utilize the tools at their disposal to suspend what they might believe to be inevitable. They imagine and they play. They enjoy their subjectivity. De Beauvoir (2002) writes,

> (The child) feels himself happily irresponsible. The real world is that of adults where he is allowed only to respect and obey. The naive victim of the mirage of the for-others, he believes in the *being* of his parents and teachers. He takes them for the divinities which they vainly try to be and whose appearance they like to borrow before his ingenuous eyes. Rewards, punishments, prizes, words of praise or blame instill in him the conviction that there exist a good and an evil which like a sun and a moon exist as ends in themselves ... he thinks that he too has *being* in a definite and substantial

> way. He is a good little boy or a scamp; he enjoys being it. If something
> deep inside him belies his conviction, he conceals this imperfection. (p. 36)

Valuing ambiguity celebrates and encourages such "imperfection." Imperfection presents challenges for assessments. Students live in a world where language and policy perpetuate the division described by De Beauvoir. They repeatedly hear their experience in school compared with the "real world" implying that the practices of education constitute something "false" and indeed measurements of success remain remarkably artificial; add to this the ironic twist that their performance on these artificial measures can have significant impact on their life after school, in the "real" world. If education seeks to liberate, it must consider how assessments might be structured so that they expand thought and encourage students to see their encounters with the world as essential, interactive, and fun.

Students adjust to living in these two worlds, and they develop practical skills when they learn to navigate a variety of environments. The problem develops when they become convinced that their "becoming," that their personal points of view, from their uncertainties to their hopes, is a temporary frivolity to be discarded in the "real" and serious world. Assessments reinforce this perspective when the measures of student success depend upon, "rewards, punishments, prizes, words of praise or blame." Within such a system, a student's desire to be right and their fear of being wrong leads them to question the validity of their subjective freedom and increases the allure of the comfortable confinements of the serious. The serious student learns to present ideas in a manner that will receive the highest grade and to solve problems in a manner that guarantees the correct solution. Students who struggle in their presentations and make errors on their way toward solutions quickly learn to categorize themselves as unworthy of the prizes and the recipients of an external as well as a self-imposed blame. Both success and failure discourage the risk-taking inherent in the exercise of freedom and as a result become different routes to the same trap.

Leslie, a history and theory of knowledge teacher laments students who just "go through the motions" likening it "to someone who goes to church … does it mean anything to them versus someone in church where it really means something? You can tell that they're really getting something spiritual from it and the other is just kind of there." She continues,

> Well, it's the same thing over and over and over again. They don't internalize it They don't get it. I think part of it is maturity and age. I had one student years ago. It was a wonderful paper. She did a dialogue between Brittany Spears and Thomas Hobbes in a bar. And it worked. It was absolutely hysterical. It was so good. She went beyond something. She took this and did this wonderful analysis based on philosophy and the idea of Freud. It was so good. And then her other dialogue was between ketchup and roast

beef on animal rights. This is the knack that I find difficult to try to teach the kids. They need to go beyond what I'm saying and take it to that next level. I'm constantly trying to find different ways to help them improve their writing and get their voice. They sometimes can't internalize it and make it their own and not just repeat back to me what I've said or what somebody else said. I find that an extreme challenge. How do you get the kids to do that? How to take your knowledge and go beyond just regurgitating it? It seems difficult. That voice thing. (Fleet, 2007)

When students authentically assemble, reconfigure and present what they learn, it emerges in a manner that is consistent with who they are. Very likely it is "maturity and age," but perhaps "internalizing thought" becomes more difficult as students move through the system and learn to play a game that traditionally encourages them not to think freely but to echo the voices of the past.

Valuing ambiguity as a means to construct the authentic self offers perspectives by which assessment can be better understood and created. In an educational era largely committed to "backward by design" it becomes that much more essential that our assessments provide students with the confidence and the power to ultimately raise the essential questions that *they* will continue to explore. In *Understanding by Design*, Grant Wiggins and Jay McTighe (2005) offer "the key questions of effective *learning*: What is important here? What is the point? How will this experience enable me as a learner to meet my obligations?" (p. 3). Significantly, these are presented as questions that students must ask themselves. However, as these questions influence how teachers create assessments, they raise several issues. What constitutes "importance" and who decides? Does the "point" indicate meaning or value? And maybe most significantly, how can "obligations" be seen as anything but an invitation to the serious? Undoubtedly, *Understanding by Design* is dedicated to promoting critical thinking, and purposeful learning, and as De Beauvoir (2002) puts it, "there is no more obnoxious way to punish a man than to force him to perform acts which make no sense to him" (p. 30). The existential perspective on these questions insists that any "obligations" be freely chosen. Assessments must then be designed to validate that choice and to provide an opportunity for students to apply their learning to the fulfillment of that choice.

THE ETHICAL TURN: RISK AND RESPONSIBILITY

Ambiguity encourages learners to direct their learning toward an end that has yet to be, and may never be, determined. Metaphors of an active mind, from palette to laboratory, create anticipation with the beauty of ambiguous possibility. How will the colors be combined? What ideas might emerge? What will be invented? What mystery will be better understood? De Beauvoir writes (2002),

> Just as the physicist finds it profitable to reflect on the conditions of scientific invention and the artist on those of artistic creation without expecting any ready-made solutions to come from these reflections, it is useful for the man of action to find out under what conditions his undertakings are valid. (p. 135)

Authentic education must build ambiguity into assessments encouraging students to take what they know and to freely apply it toward further understanding and creation with all the risks and benefits that may follow. Students must value their capacity to determine the validity of their undertakings. Good pedagogy encourages creativity and critical thinking. Effective assessments must do the same. Assessments that value process do not content themselves with measuring how much of "the big idea" (Wiggins 4) a student has mastered, they encourage students to see themselves as contributors to the construction of big ideas. Knowledge does not function as an objective, but as a tool. If, however, assessments represent a predetermined end, then teachers cast themselves as critics; the instructor or the test or the rubric will pronounce a final judgement and the processes of free thought that the student undertook to produce a final product become subordinated to measures of success, if not lost altogether.

Students must value and utilize their freedom. Existential freedom, as described by De Beauvoir (2002), provides the energy with which one may move toward an objective. Such "freedom is not to be engulfed in any goal; neither is it to dissipate itself vainly without aiming at a goal" (p. 70). The ambiguity generated by this perspective addresses the paradox of adolescence, the critical moment when young minds might transition to the serious, engulfed by inauthentic goals, or abandon all effort to pursue meaning and so to confuse freedom with selfishness and the right to do nothing. In the first case, freedom becomes reduced to obligation and obedience. In the second case, freedom exercised without direction, without authentic purpose, atomizes into a self-imposed nihilism.

If students spend the formative years of their lives experiencing a system that trains them to hit clear targets so that they can be assessed by others, they train to become functional citizens at the expense of becoming free citizens. If, however, educators perpetually encourage students to create authentic goals and to use their understanding to pursue those goals, then students use the ideas, the information, and the perspectives that they possess to construct understanding and to produce new possibilities in order to perpetuate the process. Students do not become entrapped by the facticity of being when they engage in what De Beauvoir (2002) calls "indefinite conquest":

Science, technics, art, and philosophy are indefinite conquests of existence over being; it is by assuming themselves as such that they take on their genuine aspect; it is in the light of this assumption that the word progress finds its veridical meaning. It is not a matter of approaching a fixed limit: absolute Knowledge or the happiness of man or the perfection of beauty; all human effort would then be doomed to failure, for with each step forward the horizon recedes a step; for man it is a matter of pursuing the expansion of his existence and of retrieving this very effort as an absolute. (p. 79)

It is quite possible that assessments of ambiguity are not tests at all, they are moments when students connect knowledge with possibility; when they convert not knowing where they are going into freely choosing where they want to go.

Teaching students to value their freedom and to direct their freedom toward an end of their choosing not only makes them aware of their subjectivity, but also the subjectivity of others and reduces the tyranny of objectification. Education that does not recognize the necessity of promoting freedom fails to give students the most essential tool that they need not only to develop their authentic selves, but to act in the world. Any force, from fascism and racism to climate change and the dehumanizing impacts of technology, that threatens to objectify reduces freedom and promotes tyranny. Minds capable of seeing beyond the facticity of present conditions possess the capability of finding solutions to existential threats. When education commits to the promotion of freedom the models of performance that students engage with need to make them aware of the power that they possess to bring change to the world.

An existential education does not liberate the prisoners in "the cave" with the hope that they might find their way to the forms; if the most famous educational allegory were an existential tale, to exit the cave would be to discover the formless, the ambiguous illuminated by freedom. Crossing the threshold from the darkness of the cave to the enlightenment of authenticity occurs when learners become active creators in and contributors to the world. Assessments must offer the students an authentic place from which to view their world. This vantage point allows students to see others as also necessarily free and presents young minds with an awareness that they exist "only by transcending *themselves*, and *their* freedom can be achieved only through the freedom of others. *They* justify their existence by a movement which, like freedom, springs from *their* heart but leads outside of *themselves*" (De Beauvoir, 2002, p. 156). This is the optimism that characterizes *Ethics of Ambiguity* and the hope that exists in assessments of ambiguity.

Simone de Beauvoir charts her philosophical course directly into the uncertainties of the democratic regime, elevating the perspectives of the youth, finding possibility in the formless, proudly donning the "multi-colored cloak" and valuing freedom as an antidote to tyranny (Bloom & Kirsch, 2016, 557c). Optimism and hope never come with guarantees. They come, instead, with all the risk upon which our future depends.

> If ... a child's face is so moving, it is not that the child is more moving or that he has more of a right to happiness than the others: it is that he is living affirmation of human transcendence: he is on the watch, he is an eager hand held out to the world, he is a hope, a project. The trick of the tyrants is to enclose a man in the immanence of his facticity and to try to forget that man is always...a being of the distances, a movement toward the future, a project. (De Beauvoir, 2002, p. 102)

When the active minds of such "eager *hands*" become less concerned with what they can grasp and more enthralled with what they can create, the tyranny of facticity fades away. If we take their hand, we encourage dependence; if we ignore it, we encourage selfishness. But, as educators we can provide them with the confidence to keep their hands open so that they may freely discover their power to interpret, to express and to interact, so that our students may become aware that "the trick of tyrants" can only be overcome by embracing the freedom of others, so that they may move in the direction of liberation and in that movement seek the liberation of others, so that they may become empowered by the nature of their ambiguity.

REFERENCES

Bloom, A. D., & Kirsch, A. (2016). *The Republic of Plato*. New York Basic Books.

Bonnett, M. (2009). Education and selfhood: A phenomenological investigation. *Journal of Philosophy of Education, 43*(3), 357–370.

Bonnett, M. (2018). After postmodernism: Retuning to the real. *Educational Philosophy and Theory, 50*(14), 1308–1309.

de Beauvoir, S. (2002). *The ethics of ambiguity*. Kensington. (Original work published 1948)

Eisner, E. W. (2002). *The educational imagination: On the design and evaluation of school programs*. Prentice Hall.

Fleet, S. (2007). *Aesthetic lessons in the international baccalaureate: An examination of teacher creativity in the promotion of aesthetic experience* [PhD dissertation? University of Denver]. Proquest Dissertation Publishing?

Slattery, P., & Morris, M. (1999). Simone De Beauvoir's ethics and postmodern ambiguity: The assertion of freedom in the face of the absurd. *Educational Theory, 49*(1), 21–36.

Wiggins, G. P., & McTighe, J. (2005). *Understanding by design* (2nd ed.). Association For Supervision and Curriculum Development.

SECTION III

EXISTENTIALISM AND TEACHER DEVELOPMENT

CHAPTER 6

KIERKEGAARD AND THE POWER OF EXISTENTIAL DOUBT IN TEACHING

Transformation of Self and Profession

Dan Riordan
Pacific University

Paul Michalec
University of Denver

Kate Newburgh
Books of Eden Publishing

ABSTRACT

Doubt is a common, even inevitable element of teaching. The systems in place for teacher development, however, do not have a generative or productive method for addressing doubt, instead regarding it pathologically as a sign of "weakness" or "incompetence." Using Søren Kierkegaard's framework for distinguishing between spirit and the institution of the church and drawing from our own experience as educators and coaches, we seek in this chapter to reframe doubt as a normal, healthy, and necessary aspect of teaching. To that end, we offer a practical framework for understanding doubt, not as a

Problematizing the Profession of Teaching From an Existential Perspective, pp. 113–130
Copyright © 2022 by Information Age Publishing
www.infoagepub.com

deficit, but as an instructional tool for reflection and evolving self-awareness. We see this framework as beneficial to all teachers, but particularly to novice teachers (as well as their mentors and coaches) where this reframing of doubt is an invitation for teachers to reflect and ultimately grow in their practice.

We start, first, with the premise that doubt is omnipresent in teaching. We broadly define doubt as when a teacher experiences feelings of uncertainty or a lack of confidence, which leads them to reevaluate their actions and choices. While we believe teachers of every experience level encounter doubt, we are most concerned with novice teachers as doubt left unaddressed can drain a teacher's joy and passion for teaching. Parker Palmer (2007) captures the essence of instructional doubt when he writes about his own sense of instructional inadequacy: "But at other moments, the classroom is so lifeless or painful or confused—and I am so powerless to do anything about it—that my claim to be a teacher seems a transparent sham" (p. 1). He penned these words, not as a novice fresh from his own apprenticeship, but as a veteran teacher with over twenty years of classroom experience.

Despite its recurrence as a theme in the profession, literature reviews turn up very little information on how doubt affects the teacher and thus, the classroom environment (Zimmerman, 2019). Likewise, we know of not a single standard in teacher-evaluation protocols that rewards a teacher for earnestly and honestly wrestling with doubt. It is important to pay attention to observation frameworks because they encode norms and ontological messages of what effective teaching looks like (Holloway, 2019). Thus, we can learn much from doubt's lack of presence in evaluations and research literature. In our experience coaching novice educators, doubt is often viewed as a pejorative or even shameful quality for a teacher to display. Teachers who exhibit doubt are often questioned as to their competence and even dedication. As such, it has not been investigated so much as swept under the rug to be hidden as something unworthy of a teacher. There is, then, a distinct conflict between the educational system's approach to doubt, and the personal, human needs of teachers to have tools to work with this recurring aspect of their profession.

What is needed is a new framework for understanding doubt as a precious instructional tool for reflection and evolving self-awareness. To create this framework, we draw on the work of Søren Kierkegaard. His rich descriptions, drawn from his personal experience of pain and loss (Moore, 2002), offer clear language on ways to embrace doubt and harness its energy toward teacher empowerment and agency. Kierkegaard offers these descriptions as jewels that exist in contrast to the overarching institution of the church, which, like the institution of education, offered very little room for the vulnerable human experience.

We write this chapter for instructional coaches, particularly those who work with early-career teachers. We want to reinforce that the approach of denying doubt is particularly damaging to early-career teachers. When we socialize a teacher in the early years to deny, cover up, or become shameful of their doubt, we cut off a generative route to reflection and growth. Therefore, mentors and instructional coaches who know how to use doubt as a mechanism for growth are invaluable for coaching teachers to engage with their doubt as a powerful force for their own development.

In this chapter, we will use doubt as an umbrella term for its various forms: uncertainty, questioning, trepidation, imposter syndrome, and constant reflection to name a few. As mentioned, there are two ways it can be handled. Either it can be denied and hidden, which results in a shutting down of a vital aspect of the teacher's being, or it can be used to sharpen instructional focus, mitigate hubris that can skew a teacher's perception toward unrealistic and harmful perfection, and harnessed for the purpose of deepening self-awareness. What is missing, as stated earlier, is a framework that accepts doubt in a way that invites teachers to work constructively with it as an ally. Furthermore, we believe instructional coaches play a pivotal role in helping novice teachers view doubt as a vehicle for growth and transformation and can help guide novice teachers as they navigate the challenging initial years in the profession.

We begin this chapter with a vignette, which highlights the destructive nature of doubt, especially for a novice teacher, when doubt is avoided and dismissed. After the vignette, we describe an approach, guided by Soren Kierkegaard, that through existentialism reconceptualizes doubt, or what he called "despair" as a mechanism for a teacher's growth and agency. Our data for this chapter is qualitative. We draw from teacher stories, the wisdom tradition of teaching (Hansen, 2020), and our collective experience as teacher educators coaching novice teachers toward wholeness and integration of role and calling.

VIGNETTE: ANCHORING DOUBT

In October of my first year of teaching I had set up a meeting with the principal of my school. As a new teacher, I was very motivated to do my best for my students, colleagues, and administration. I was extremely discouraged by my progress, however. I was having difficulty maintaining a positive, safe learning environment for my students. At the time, the district I was teaching in ranked among the poorest in the country. Our classrooms were overfull to the point where I actually needed students to be absent to have enough seats. I was being trained to deliver a battery of tests and was asked to find one-on-one time with each of my students to test their reading and writing skills. I did not have the classroom management skills at that point to maintain order during independent work time so that I could have meaningful assessments and conversations with each student. Worry and frustration about meeting these requirements was keeping me up at night. I was drowning, exhausted, and worn down.

Finally, I turned to my administration for help. I made an appointment with my principal to see if she had any advice for me. Sitting across from her, I communicated that I needed support with classroom management so that I could safely assess all of my students individually. I will never forget her response. She reached up and slowly pulled the glasses down her nose, regarding me over the tops of them. I remember this clearly because somewhere amidst my inner turmoil and fear was a part of me lucid enough to appreciate the absurdity of the moment. This gesture was something I'd only ever read about in books! Over the rims of her glasses, her eyes skewered me for an eternity of about ten seconds. I squirmed in shame and regretted ever setting up the meeting. A thousand sleepless nights would be preferable to this scrutiny. Finally, in a clipped voice she said, "Let me get this straight. You are telling me you can't manage your own classroom, Professor Newburgh?" (We had another absurd tradition at this school of referring to teachers as "professors.")

Laced into her words was an implicit threat that was *not* lost on me. I was teaching in New York City at the height of the recession, and many, many teachers were out of work. Any job was coveted. My application for this position had been one of literally hundreds. As a new teacher on a provisional license, I could be dismissed at will for no reason whatsoever. I was not protected by the union, nor tenure, nor any type of job security. My livelihood was fragile at best, which the principal was very quick to communicate to everyone on staff. I took a deep breath, rescinded my statement, and left quietly, figuring I would just have to get it done one way or another. I never came to her again with anything other than results, which, I am sure, was her intention for the conversation.

The toll it took on me, however, was significant. From that moment forward, my teaching days were numbered. I made it three additional years before I left the profession, contributing in a very personal way to the astronomical statistics around early-career teacher exodus. I wonder, sometimes, if in that meeting my questions and struggles had been met with curiosity, compassion, collaboration, and care, how I would have developed as a teacher. Looking back, I recognize how my principal missed an opportunity to help me embrace and lean into doubt and uncertainty. In doing so, I may have missed a pivotal point for not only remaining in the profession, but for also moving closer towards reaching my full potential as a teacher.

As demonstrated by this vignette, we believe doubt needs to be addressed, not dismissed, by instructional coaches and mentors who work with novice teachers. While we believe the content in this chapter applies to both preservice and in-service teachers, our work with early novice teachers has confirmed for us how doubt is often amplified at the start of teachers' careers when the stakes are often high, immediately present, and consequential. We also believe that by providing a conceptual framework for mentors and novice teachers to harness and utilize doubt as a catalyst for growth, we will help prevent the phenomenon of veteran teachers looking bleakly at "giving up" or chronic cynicism as their only option.

Early in a teacher's career, there may be a tendency to dismiss doubt or view it as an indictment of one's ineffectiveness. This is dangerous, as Hargreaves (2005) posits that beginning teachers can take considerable time to "establish their basic confidence and competence as professionals" (p. 970). New teachers often feel compelled to address the external imperatives of testing, covering the curriculum, managing classrooms, and meeting performance indicators, often to the detriment of their wholeness and sense of being (Holloway, 2019). Although perhaps buried and dormant, the seeds of doubt are still present and ready to burst forth, fully flowering into crippling anxiety and deep questions of how to teach with integrity when the world of the classroom no longer makes sense (Michalec, 2002). It is perhaps this unexamined deeply rooted and embedded sense of doubt that leads to instructional dissatisfaction and often high rates of teacher departure from the profession (Ingersoll & Merrill, 2013). Instructional coaches and mentors can help reframe doubt and coach novice teachers to use the presence of doubt as a catalyst for growth.

In this chapter, we argue, based on our personal experience coaching young teachers, that this sense of existential doubt about the way forward is common amongst teachers, from early career to 30-year veterans. What is uncommon, and we turn to Soren Kierkegaard for guidance here, is framing doubt as a normal, healthy, and necessary aspect of effective teaching. Pema Chödrön (2012), the American Buddhist nun, encourages us to lean into doubt and uncertainty as a way "to claim your courage, your kindness, your strength" (p. 39). Doubt should be embraced and seen just as essential to the nature of teaching as best practices (Lemov, 2010). Instead of believing that the existential crisis is fictitious, seeing it as weakness or shying away from addressing it because we don't know how, we take heart and encouragement in the struggle, suffering and pain as a gateway to more holistic and effective teaching. We agree with Annie Dillard (2013),

> In the deeps are the violence and terror of which psychology has warned us. But if you ride these monsters deeper down, if you drop with them farther over the world's rim, you find what our sciences cannot locate or name, the substrate, the ocean or matrix or ether which buoys the rest, which gives goodness its power for good, and evil its power for evil, the

unified field: our complex and inexplicable caring for each other, and for our life together here. This is given. It is not learned. (p. 94)

It is the deeps that we want to explore in this chapter, but we need a trustworthy guide, someone who has dropped over the edge, pushed against formalized structures, and knows the way back to the lived world of practice. Our navigator of choice is Soren Kierkegaard. As Kierkegaard (1941) would argue, all we have to do is choose, to make the leap past "despair" into the unknown, to follow the monsters of our doubts over the rim and into a place of sense making that is rich with ambiguity and unexpected forms of wholeness.

There is little need for external forms of technique and practice on this journey. Instead, a new skill set of faith and surrender are required. These are skills of the heart. They do not need to be learned, only practiced. A trusted mentor and guide can be helpful with this task. Palmer (2007) notes that "technique is what teachers use until the real teacher arrives" (p. 6). Palmer is not so much dismissing the importance of genuinely applied technique to address the existential conundrums of teaching, rather he is arguing that there is more to teaching than technique. To sit in existential doubt/despair is to affirm this point. The challenge is not technical but social, emotional, and spiritual.

The basic claim of existentialism that is most pertinent to our work is "the fact is that, at the deepest level, we are ultimately alone. We are basically isolated individuals who have to make sense of the world and find meaning for our lives on our own" (Guignon & Pereboom, 1995, p. xvii). This is the challenge faced by the teacher in our opening vignette, the realization of doubt, we argue, is common to all good teachers. It is normal, and, more than that, it is essential to the full formation of self. What is not normal, and what we hope to challenge in this chapter, is the way that the educational system leaves the teacher-self inhibited by standards, accountability, and performance indicators that govern the behavior and learning outcomes of teachers and students alike. Jessica Holloway (2019) argues that teachers in the United States are subject to a System of Education where "measurement, evaluation, and comparison are the necessary mechanisms for designating the quality of schools and school actors" (p. 174). And Holloway, much like Kierkegaard, argues that conformity can lead to a herd-mentality that dims the life force of both teachers and Christians. We intend to follow the lead of Kierkegaard, to elevate personal choice and agency over the self-denying herd mentality of a system that promotes normalizing behaviors of compliance and homogenization.

To be clear, we are offering a friendly critique of current models of teacher mentoring and coaching that elevate the technical over internal forms of understanding. We are arguing not for the dismissal of the technical, which can address skill-based doubt, but rather for fuller inclusion of all the ways that early career teachers experience and make sense of doubt/despair in learning to teach. We are pro-teacher preparation, from the technical to the spiritual and emotional. We seek to broaden the lens to include pain, suffering, and loss as necessary elements of good teaching. This chapter is not an either/or argument pitting the external and internal dimensions of teaching against each other. Rather, we operate within a both/and frame that places the hand and heart in conversation with each other. We agree with Palmer (2007) that, "People who start movements do so not because they hate an institution but because they love it too much to let it descend to its lowest form" (p. 170).

We will start our exploration of doubt, what Kierkegaard calls "despair," by first establishing the reliability of Kierkegaard as a guide, by showing that his critique of the Danish Church has parallels to our critique of teaching "best practices" (Lemov, 2010) and the System of Education. We, like Kierkegaard, claim that teachers, as human beings, embody both a temporal and eternal nature (Moore, 2002), and that the historic commitment and allegiance of teacher professional development to the temporal is inadequate to the task of settling—not solving—existential doubt in ways that are life-giving. In support of this move toward teacher-wholeness (integration of the objective and subjective self), informed by doubt, we will follow Kierkegaard's developmental markers of the "aesthetic," the "ethical" and the "religious." We will deepen our exploration by narrowing in on the religious dimension through the analytic categories of "resignation," "suffering," and "guilt" as defined by Kierkegaard (Guignon & Pereboom, 1995).

In the concluding sections of this chapter, we will return to the lived world of teaching, with our renewed understanding of the critical dimensions of doubt in teaching and apply that wisdom to the process of coaching and mentoring. The move toward action and the choice to embrace the ambiguity of doubt is a personal decision for each teacher, but we will show how the thoughtful presence of a coach can help ease and direct the self toward wholeness and a constructive relationship with the calling to teach.

As Aaron Zimmerman (2019) notes in his phenomenological study of two early career teachers experiencing deep levels of doubt and self-hate, if "teacher educators seek to support early-career teachers as they learn to teach, teacher educators must be willing to wrestle with threatening existential questions alongside early-career teachers" (p. 16). The heart of teacher existential doubt is the conflict between calling "as something that [gives] meaning to [a teacher's] life" (Cranton, 2016, p. 88) and institutional imperatives which leave little room for inner justifications for teaching and teaching well. Another way to express this sentiment is the difference between inner knowing and outer illusion.

PARALLELISM BETWEEN CHURCH/CHRISTIANITY AND THE SYSTEM OF EDUCATION

A core tenant and energizing impulse for Kierkegaard and other religious existentialist (e.g., Martin Buber and Paul Tillich) is the virulent critique and disdainful of the tendency of religion to promulgate rituals, practices, and dogma devoid of deep meaning (Guignon & Pereboom, 1995; Moore, 2002; Noddings, 2012). Kierkegaard (1941) refers to this mass hypnosis at the hands of the Danish Church as the "herd" that mindlessly follows without reflection, questioning, or conscious choice. We, like religious existentialists, raise skepticism about the value of systems and educational structures that are designed to guide individual teacher action toward narrow forms of meaning and purpose, action nearly devoid of choice (Holloway, 2019). In our experience, more times than not, our System of Education devalues individual choice and agency in favor of efficiency, standardization, and accountability to external authorities. In such a system, performative techniques have been accepted, valued, and normalized (Holloway, 2019). Patricia Cranton (2016), when describing barriers to adult learning, draws on Foucault's notion of "disciplinary power" which is a form of self-silencing "exercised on people themselves and others.... A normalizing gaze keeps people in line, behaving as they are supposed to behave according to the social norms of the community" (p. 96).

In order to draw from the wisdom of existentialism to inform teaching practice, we need to first draw parallels between Kierkegaard's (1941) critique of the Danish Church and our critique of the System of Education. Beyond the structural parallels, we also need to show that, at the level of institutional implementation, the mechanisms of mass inoculation, Cranton's (2016) "normalizing gaze," toward compliance and spiritual deformation are similar in both contexts. Before we move to this level of description, however, we should define the salient terms in the conversation.

By church, Kierkegaard (1941) means the Lutheran Church of Denmark, the state religion, with all of its formalities and ecclesiological structures. By Christianity, Kierkegaard meant the shriveled form of Christian practice that is curtailed and circumscribed by the theological and intellectual elite of the Church. To be a full member of the Church meant behaving in ritually prescribed fashion before one could belong; belief and personal choice, according to Kierkegaard, was a distant requirement. Individual meaning-making and choice in the face of the lived challenges of day-to-day life, had little place in this structure of power and privilege (Guignon & Pereboom, 1995; Moore, 2002).

In place of Kierkegaard's Church, we insert the System of Education that drives the practice of teaching toward unreflective consistency and compliance to structural norms. A structure or system that infringes on the sovereignty of any human being can drain one's passion and, specifically in the case of teachers, attack their professional character (Giroux, 2013; Holloway, 2019). The high priests/priestesses of the religion of education are the test makers, accrediting bodies, policy wonks, and state legislators who, like Kierkegaard's ecclesiological councils, value objectivity and formalized practice. We will note and assert, that like the Lutheran Church of Denmark, not all leaders within the System of Education adhere to these dehumanizing and self-denying beliefs. There are many educational heretics who push against or actively resist pedagogical and intellectual orthodoxy. They choose to act in the shared tradition of Kierkegaardian resistance to the numbing nature of the status quo. However, these brave souls represent a minority voice. Instead, what often dominates conversations and professional development in education are the best practices, the foot soldiers of the System of Education, associated with effective pedagogy, not fidelity to the ambiguity of craft knowledge that is responsive to self in place.

Best practices of teaching, similar to Kierkegaard's critique of mainstream Christianity, represent an incomplete representation of a fully developed sense of what pedagogy, as an individual practice, could and should look like. As teacher educators, we value and actively coach teachers along the dimensions of best practices. We also see flourishing and agency that occurs when teachers break free of the dominant ideology of structure that makes deforming claims over their individual agency and choice to act. Structure must come before freedom when considering the process of human development and thriving (Rohr, 2011). The two are bound together in mutual relationship; structure's gift is the creation of a robust container within which true freedom can emerge in the midst of the crucible of life choices. Structure is a means to human flourishing, not an ending point.

We argue that within the belief and practice paradigm of the System of Education of best practices, there is little room for doubt and uncertainty in instructional choices. As Patricia Cranton (2016) notes; "technique should not drive an educator's perspective of practice; rather, a perspective of practice should determine what technical knowledge is required" (p. 139). By perspective, Cranton means, "sociolinguistic, psychological, moral, aesthetic, and philosophical" (p. 139). Further, if a teacher is employing, with fidelity, the elements of best practices, but is still experiencing doubt, it is often seen as the fault of the teacher, not a critical questioning of the adherence to best practices over and above other considerations (Newburgh, 2019). To remedy the situation, more professional development, observation, and coaching around best practices will often follow. The existential feelings of doubt when practice falters, like Kierkegaard's questioning of the religious nobility, becomes an unwelcome distraction.

At best, doubt is acknowledged when the emotions of fear and anxiety surface, but mostly it is sidelined in the conversation or passed off to the realm of counseling and mental health. It is also seen as a "personal problem," and not the mechanistic result of the larger systems that form the teacher's context and environment (Newburgh, 2019). The potential power of existential doubt to transform the educator is mostly lost and, in its place, creeps in cynicism, fear, and an ever-growing sense of the imposter syndrome (Gallagher, 2019). The recent move toward mindfulness (Elreda et al., 2019), radical self-care (Michaeli, 2017) and social emotional learning (Michalec & Wilson, 2020) are moves in the right direction toward teacher wholeness and agency. But more is needed, as most modalities pertaining to SEL and mindfulness center on the response of the individual in times of stress or challenge. This personalized/individualized approach towards teacher support can be effective in the immediate moment, but, because it fails to encompass the entire system of dominant educational structures, it is simply a band-aid for a much larger issue.

In many ways, mindfulness and SEL, as they are currently conceptualized, simply provide tools for educators to stave off burnout in untenable situations. They may allow the educator to survive another day, but to truly create thriving in our educational system, we need to widen our perspective enough to confront the system as a whole. This is where Kierkegaard is most helpful. His philosophy of existentialism offers a framework for clearly locating individual autonomy within a system that is designed to control. Specifically, this framework allows us to position teacher doubt in a positive light and return the power of agency and choice to individual teachers in response to the lived challenges of classroom teaching on a day-to-day basis, so that the individual response is one of freedom as opposed to reactive and designed simply to perpetuate survival.

The Temporal and Eternal Nature of Humanness and Teaching

Like Kierkegaard, we begin normalizing teacher existential doubt by affirming the temporal and eternal nature of the calling to teach. Teachers, like all humans, exist in time. For teachers, time can be a precious commodity. There never seems to be enough of it when it comes to grading, lesson planning, or guiding students through a learning moment. Teachers often feel on the edge of losing control of the classroom as time spirals out and away from them. This emphasis on the efficient use of time as the metric of one's life can lead to a sense of "intensification" (Hargreaves, 1994). It seems that every action and every choice carry the feeling of finality around which there is no turning back or even taking a moment to strike a reflective stance before acting. The current emphasis on testing, account-ability, and the mastery of performance indicators can trap a teacher in the temporal space; and yet even in this cocoon of standards, doubt still exists. Scientific objectivity, the rational mind, is no match for the emotions and the subjective understandings of truth lived out (Haidt, 2006).

Kierkegaard (1941) notes that one quality that separates humans from the rest of the animal kingdom is our capacity to envision an "overarch-ing unity that [the temporal] events can have just for humans. This unity has the potential of providing the separate moments of our lives with the kind of meaning and significance they lack without this unity" (Guignon & Pereboom, 1995, p. 4). For Kierkegaard, this overarching unity is God or what he sometimes calls the "Absolute" (Moore, 2002).

For teachers, the eternal, the overarching unity, goes by the names of calling (Cranton, 2016; Hansen, 1975); the inner-life (Palmer, 2007); or that which is greater than self (Huebner, 1999; Rohr, 2011). As Dwayne Huebner (1999) attests,

> The otherness that informs and accompanies education is the absolute
> Otherness, the transcendent Other, however we name that which goes
> beyond all appearances and all conditions. Education is the openness to a
> future that is beyond all futures. Education is the protest against present
> forms that they may be reformed and transformed. (p. 360)

He adds that "To speak of the 'spirit' and the 'spiritual' is not to speak of something 'other' than humankind, merely 'more' than humankind as it is lived and known" (p. 343).

Just as in Kierkegaard's case where one can never really escape the ever searching and loving presence of the Divine, a teacher can never outrun their inner calling to teach (Hansen, 2021). Because it is an innate part of the teacher, it can be put off or sidetracked but never abandoned. As teacher educators we know numerous stories of teachers who have success-ful careers in other professions, but who one day realize how unhappy they are with their temporal existence. They find the only way to peace is by surrendering to their long-buried passion for teaching; "Yes, I have tried to escape teaching many times. But there is no escaping my divine calling. Teaching had me" (Alston, 2008).

To be a teacher is to embody the temporal and eternal, but at a cost which we will explore in greater detail through the lenses of Kierkegaard's categories of the "aesthetic," "ethical," and "religious." The three stages were proposed by Kierkegaard as a developmental sequence guiding a person through existential uncertainty "to become a genuine self, an indi-vidual in the truest sense" (Moore, 2002, p. xxi). The first response to the disorienting nature of life is to adopt an aesthetic lens, to focus life choices on what immediately brings satisfaction (physical, emotional, and psychological). Individuals expressing an aesthetic lifestyle, according to Kierkegaard (1941), "have no real inner life, no real self to offer to others" (p. xxi). Choices and satisfaction are too narrowly focused on the temporal to the exclusion of the eternal.

In the field of teaching professional development, an aesthetic educator grounds their identity and sense of joy in receiving high marks on a coaching framework. Furthermore, because the self is dependent on compliance to external features that the teacher often has little control over (class makeup, subjectivity of the observer, or the validity of the assessment instrument), "one will always be gripped by the anxiety that some misfortune will result in failure" (Guignon & Pereboom, 1995, p. 6). Fear at the personal level, the imposter syndrome, often robs an aesthetically minded teacher of a sense of well-being and the resolution of existential doubt.

Kierkegaard (1941) calls the next stage the "ethical," which rejects the sense of drifting, characteristic of the "aesthetic" and instead attends to the moral significance of choices. Freedom, the resolution of the existential crisis, is achieved through the "enjoyment and fulfillment of doing one's duty" (Moore, 2002, p. xxii). The ethical moves the individual beyond immediate needs and desires and offers a unifying structure for one's life" (Guignon & Pereboom, 1995, p. 7). It includes elements of reflection and attentiveness to universal values and inner notions of truth. An ethical person lives a life of intentional choices informed by a relationship to something greater than self, as such it is more active than the passive acceptance of desires characteristic of the aesthetic frame (Sacks, 2020).

An ethical teacher is an educator who is committed to moral truths (Hansen, 2021) or dedicated to effective teaching defined by external authorities, for instance the list of best practices, accrediting agencies, district mandated curriculum or the rubrics in evaluation tools. An ethical teacher who follows the instructional rules is a good teacher but "the ethical life is insufficient for solving life's riddles and choices. The ethical life fails to adequately deal with exceptional situations" (Moore, 2002, p. xxiii). Instructional norms and standards are based on what generally works but elements of anxiety and uncertainty still permeate the mind of the teacher because "what ifs" are always a real possibility in teaching.

For Kierkegaard (1941) the limitations of the aesthetic and ethical are resolved in the religious orientation when a person yields to truths that are beyond the individual and social spheres of knowing. By "religious" he means not organized religion but rather, the surrender to that which is greater than self and self-knowing, a spiritual commitment of self-denial. If the aesthetic is about aimless drifting in accordance with passions, and the ethical is about duty to norms, the religious is about the process of transformation, the continual remaking of self in relationship with mystery. While the previous two stages are limited by some reliance on self as a referent point, the fully religious requires a sort of denial of social identity in the search for true meaning: a full release from the social, emotional, and intellectual. In this way, existential doubt is perpetually resolved, folded into fidelity to life-giving forces beyond the narrow parameters of the temporal world. As we will pick up in the next section, this requires what Kierkegaard calls infinite resignation, suffering, and guilt (Moore, 2002).

We argue that a teacher who has entered the religious phase of identity formation is aware of and continuously refines their pedagogical relationship with their calling; a commitment to serve the needs of all learners. They surrender external notions of self and rewards associated with the role of teacher and embrace the mysterious energy that pulled them into the profession in the first place; "Yes, I have tried to escape teaching many times. But there is no escaping my divine calling. Teaching had me" (Alston, 2008). The religious frame ultimately works in coaching because it includes both the temporal and eternal elements of teaching by abandoning perfection as determined by self or others and instead values process and change. As we argue, key to the process of transformation is doubt, Kierkegaard's despair, which constantly invites the teacher to affirm choices that are fully authentic to their gifts. A religious stance invites a conversation and continual exploration around the why of practice. The vignette below serves as an example of a teacher who has acknowledged doubt and now has an opportunity for transformation. At this juncture, an instructional coach could provide her with pivotal support to help her harness the power of doubt.

VIGNETTE: HARNESSING DOUBT

Amaya, a middle school science teacher, feels the pangs of doubt emerge after teaching for a couple of months. While she has experienced moments of confidence and joy, she is mostly weighed down by stress and apprehension. She relates this feeling in an audio journal: "I just feel like I am having to fly by the seat of my pants. And it makes me super stressed and anxious … it always comes from not knowing. It's the uncertainty that really stresses me out." She attempts to navigate this uncertainty by relying on lesson plans designed by the previous teacher. The lessons leave little room for Amaya to infuse her preferred approach to teaching or to take instructional risks. She begins to question her effectiveness in another audio journal,

I've noticed that I haven't been as I think enthusiastic about what I'm teaching, probably because I really don't know if the kids are going to be excited about it or I don't know I have anxiety that it's not going to go right.

Amaya's feelings of uncertainty and self-critique of her instruction are the manifestation of her doubt and beckon an instructional coach or mentor to offer guidance and support.

With the information we have about Amaya's situation, we can begin to craft an instructional coach's response. Taking the lead from the framework shared in this chapter, we can start by acknowledging Amaya's feelings of doubt, uncertainty, and shaken confidence. Moving forward, an instructional coach rooted in educational structures would likely leap to addressing Amaya's lesson plans and engagement strategies. We suggest taking a different tact where growth and transformation are honored. Taking cues from Kierkegaard, an existentialist instructional coach could ask questions such as: *When have you felt the most joy in teaching this year? What about the uncertainty makes you nervous or upset? Who owns your success, you or your students? Tell me about your reason for pursuing teaching. What about that vision is exciting and engaging? What roles might suffering and failure play in refining this calling to teach?*

When teachers embrace doubt, and therefore accept it as a key part of the process of being a teacher, they are able to liberate themselves from the artificial constraints imposed on them by the System of Education. Key to this process is the role of instructional coaches who, embodied by a framework that seeks to harness doubt, can move novice teachers to think beyond technical components (e.g., lesson plans, assessments, etc.) to see where doubt influences their practice. For Kierkegaard, embracing doubt empowers notions of self through choice or what he termed "self-expressions" (Guignon & Pereboom, 1995, p. 11). He saw the self-expressions of *infinite resignation*, *suffering*, and *guilt*—despite their seemingly negative connotations - as modes for an individual's movement away from the temporal and into the realm of the eternal. Kierkegaard viewed these modes as hierarchical with guilt as the highest possible expression of selfhood. These "self-expressions" provide a framework to help instructional coaches and mentors to understand how best to aid novice teachers who are experiencing doubt.

As teacher educators and instructional coaches, we play a critical role in whether novice teachers frame doubt as debilitating or liberating. When it is cast as debilitating, doubt becomes feared, undesirable, and a sign of incompetence. However, when doubt/despair is viewed as liberating, teachers open themselves up to reimagining the possibilities of their teaching practice. In this next section, we demonstrate how these modes of self-expressions, when applied to teacher development, show the essential nature of doubt as a universal vehicle for growth.

For Kierkegaard, *resignation* requires a willingness to renounce the temporal and finite in order to move towards a relationship with the eternal and infinite (Guignon & Pereboom, 1995). Psychological detachment must occur so that one does not need finite things (testing or competencies) to lead a fulfilling life. This does not necessitate a rejection of the temporal and finite, rather Kierkegaard (1941) says, "finite satisfactions are voluntarily relegated to the status of what may have to be renounced in favor of an eternal happiness" (p. 350). For teachers, resignation provides an awakening to the constraints of strict adherence to best practices. Through an acknowledgement of doubt, a willingness to examine one's own views critically emerges (Roberts, 2017). A choice is then made by teachers to move towards wholeness. Palmer (2007) views this as choosing integrity over efficiency: "It means becoming more real by acknowledging the whole of who I am" (p. 14). Resignation is a statement of agency for teachers. They stake claim to their teaching practice and wrest it from the temporal—the accountability mandates and unquestioned allegiance to best practices.

Suffering moves a person into a more intense form of psychological discomfort. Kierkegaard views suffering as the dying away of the temporal and the finite. In this mode, genuine detachment from the temporal requires a continual and renewed commitment that causes intense suffering (Guignon & Pereboom, 1995). For teachers, suffering entails letting go of the familiar and preparing for uncertainty. Novice teachers tend to defer to observed practices or adopt best practices to guide them through their initial years in the profession (Tabacbnick & Zeichner, 1984). Suffering opens a path that has not been charted before, but one that feels more authentic as deep practices replace best practices (Michalec & Newburgh, 2019).

Guilt is a constant awareness that one's own powers are insufficient (Guignon & Pereboom, 1995). Kierkegaard (1941) sees guilt not as the familiar moral attitude of false or insufficient action, rather as an acceptance of the powerlessness of humans to fully understand the infinite and eternal. When applied to teachers, guilt can best be conceptualized as an awakened state. It is the acceptance that teaching is a messy endeavor that will always include ambiguity and uncertainty. Guilt is gaining power through letting go of control. In this mode, teachers can shed the shackles of educational structures and teach with greater self-awareness and be more attuned to what the moment requires of them.

CONCLUSION

To move towards strategies that instructional coaches and mentors can apply to the existential reframing of doubt, we shared vignettes from our experiences as teachers and coaches. In keeping with the epistemology of existentialism, we relied on story, more than analytic argumentation, to bring a sense of lived truthfulness to our argument. The educational philosopher and proponent of care theory, Nel Noddings (2012), notes that "life is not the unfolding of a logical plan.... Rather, meaning is created as we live our lives reflectively. Stories give us accounts of the human struggle for meaning" (pp. 65–66). In our work, as both teacher educators and classroom teachers, we have experienced and observed doubt. We have witnessed and experienced the power of momentarily setting aside the technical aspect of teaching to lean into candid discussions related to the ineffable components of teaching.

In this chapter, we offered a new paradigm: one where teachers are not expected to thrive in untenable circumstances, but they are allowed to confront, address, and harness their own experience of doubt, Kierkegaard's (1941) "despair," as a way to uncover deep and trustworthy truths about their values and identity. The words of a veteran teacher provide us with a stark warning for the consequences of not attending to doubt: "All the joy has been tested and legislated away. All that is left is sand and dust." In the language of existentialism, this teacher is deeply in the throes of existential doubt: questioning where to go next, how to live the teacher's life, and what it means to thrive in the classroom. The teacher's once flourishing and vibrant relationship with teaching has become dry and lifeless.

Two apparent choices loom ever present: yield to the desertification of their love for teaching, to watch it slowly shrivel and turn to dust, or pack up and search for a new oasis. That is, give up and stay, or give up and go. It is the third choice, however, that has inspired us to write this chapter. This option views existential doubt and uncertainty as a gateway to a deeper well of nourishing water, water of the soul and heart of education—water that brings life to the "sand and dust" of legislation, reform, and bureaucracy.

This chapter both acknowledges and responds to the imperfect states of today's educational system. The current environment is an outgrowth of the objectification and commodification of education. In this climate, teacher fullness is frequently dismissed and diminished. The reframing of doubt as an invitation for teachers to reflect and ultimately grow in their practice moves teachers and education back to the essence of teaching. This path has been paved by Kierkegaard as he pushed back against the herd mentality of religious allegiance and challenged individuals to choose a path of agency and self-empowerment. And as we noted earlier in the paper, we like Kierkegaard are not opposed to form and structure, but we are concerned about the ways that systems of power (Danish Church and the modern System of Education) can deform the fullness of human flourishing. For novice teachers, a path to liberated teaching is challenging and nearly untenable without the support and guidance of coaches and mentors. Moving beyond just acknowledging doubt, to seeing doubt as a catalyst for growth can reshape a teacher's developmental path. We see this reframing of doubt as changing the narrative of fear and denial to one of love and open-mindedness.

REFERENCES

Alston, L. (2008). *Why we teach: Learning, laughter, love, and the power to transform lives.* Scholastic Teaching Resources.

Chödrön, P. (2012). *Living beautifully with uncertainty and change.* Shambhala Publications.

Cranton, P. (2016). *Understanding and promoting transformative learning: A guide to theory and practice.* Stylus.

Dillard, A. (2013). *Teaching a stone to talk: Expeditions and encounters.* Harper Perennial.

Elreda, L. M., Jennings, P. A., DeMauro, A. A., Mischenko, P. P., Brown, J. L. (2019). Protective effects of interpersonal mindfulness for teachers' emotional supportiveness in the classroom. *Mindfulness, 10*(3), 537—546.

Gallagher, S. (2019). Professional identity and imposter syndrome. *The clinical teacher, 16*(4), 426–427.

Giroux, H. A. (2013). The disimagination machine and the pathologies of power. *Symploke, 21*(1–2), 257–269.

Guignon, C., & Pereboom, D. (Eds.). (1995). *Existentialism: Basic writings.* Hackett.

Haidt, J. (2006). The happiness hypothesis: Finding modern truth in ancient wisdom. Basic books.

Hansen, D. (1995). *The call to teach.* Teachers College Press.

Hansen, D. T. (2021). *Reimagining the call to teach: A witness to teachers and teaching.* Teachers College Press.

Hargreaves, A. (1994). *Changing teachers, changing times: Teachers' work and culture in the postmodern age.* Teachers College Press.

Hargreaves, A. (2005). Educational change takes ages: Life, career and generational factors in teachers' emotional responses to educational change. *Teaching and Teacher Education, 21*(8), 967–983.

Holloway, J. (2019). Teacher evaluation as an onto-epistemic framework. *British Journal of Sociology of Education, 40*(2), 174–189.

Huebner, D. E. (1999). *The lure of the transcendent: Collected essays by Dwayne E. Huebner.* Psychology Press.

Ingersoll, R., & Merrill, E. (2013). *Seven trends: The transformation of the teaching force, updated October 2013.* CPRE Report (#RR-79). Consortium for Policy Research in Education, University of Pennsylvania.

Kierkegaard, S. (1941). *Concluding unscientific postscript* (D. F. Swenson & W. Lowrie, Trans.) Princeton University Press.

Lemov, D. (2010). *Teach like a champion: 49 techniques that put students on the path to college.* Jossey-Bass.

Michaeli, I. (2017). Self-care: An act of political warfare or a neoliberal trap? *Development (Society for International Development), 60*(1–2), 50–56.

Michalec, P. (2002). A calling to teach: Faith and the spiritual dimensions of teaching. *Encounter: Education for Meaning and Social Justice,* 5–14.

Michalec, P., & Wilson, J. L. (2021). Truth hidden in plain sight: How social-emotional learning empowers novice teachers' culturally responsive pedagogy in Title I Schools. *Journal of Education,* 1–11.

Moore, C. E. (2002). *Provocations: Spiritual writings of Kierkegaard.* The Plough Publishing House of The Bruderhof Foundation.

Newburgh, K. (2019). Teaching in good faith: Towards a framework for defining the deep supports that growth and retains first-year teachers. *Educational Philosophy and Theory, 51*(12), 1237–1251.

Noddings, N. (2012). *Philosophy of education.* Westview Press.

Palmer, P. (2007). *The courage to teach: Exploring the inner landscape of a teacher's life* (10th edition). Jossey-Bass.

Roberts, P. (2017). Learning to live with doubt: Kierkegaard, Freire, and critical pedagogy. *Policy Futures in Education, 15*(17), 834–848.

Rohr, R. (2011). *Falling upward: A spirituality for the two halves of life.* John Wiley & Sons.

Sacks, J. (2020). *Morality: Restoring the common good in divided times.* Basic Books.

Tabacbnick, B. R., & Zeichner, K. M. (1984). The impact of the student teaching experience on the development of teacher perspectives. *Journal of Teacher Education, 35*(6), 28–36.

Zimmerman, A. S. (2019). Recognizing Kierkegaard's existential despair within the lives of early-career teachers. *Curriculum and Teaching Dialogue, 21*(1), 7–20.

CHAPTER 7

RATIONAL COMMUNICATION IN UNIVERSITY EDUCATION

A Jaspersian Theory

Daniel Adsett
American University in Bulgaria

ABSTRACT

In his writings on university education, Karl Jaspers emphasizes the role of freedom and the pursuit of truth. The "Socratic education" he advances sees students and professors working together to investigate ultimate questions in a way that is unconstrained by prior ideological or authoritative commitments. In this chapter, after examining several basic features of the university education Jaspers endorses, I ask how such a free university learning environment can be structured in order to discourage students from adopting anti-liberal and/or conspiratorial ways of thinking. I describe the case of Mike Cernovich, a key figure on the political far right, and argue that by emphasizing the collaborative character of dialogue as an essential element in rational communication, educators can discourage ways of thinking and behaving that see dialogue and communication as a zero-sum game where interlocutors are seen as threatening, even dangerous opponents. Ultimately, I suggest, in Jaspersian education, we need, in addition to promoting free inquiry, to train students to engage empathically with each other such that they come to see one other as collaborators cooperating together in the investigation of the world.

Problematizing the Profession of Teaching From an Existential Perspective, pp. 131–150
Copyright © 2022 by Information Age Publishing
www.infoagepub.com
131

Throughout his career as a psychiatrist and existentialist philosopher, Karl Jaspers published several contributions to the study of university education. The three main works (Jaspers, 1923/2016a, 1946/2016b; Jaspers & Rossmann, 1961/2016)—all titled *The Idea of the University*, though each differs to some degree from the others—offer snapshots of Jaspers's theory of education at different moments in his career, while his occasional lectures and articles expand on themes briefly touched on in the larger works.[1] The first edition of *The Idea of the University* was released in 1923, just one year after Jaspers acquired the chair of philosophy at the University of Heidelberg. The second edition appeared just after the Second World War, in 1946, while the third edition, cowritten with Kurt Rossmann, was published in 1961, just eight years before Jaspers's death. In each of these texts, Jaspers shows how themes essential to his existentialist thought can be related to higher education—the freedom of the individual, the incompleteness of knowledge, the unifying role of philosophy, and the importance of rational communication. Common to each of these works is Jaspers's conviction that the German university ought to be a center for free inquiry and teaching, a realm where professors and students are able to pursue open-ended lines of inquiries into truth without subordinating their investigations to comprehensive and allegedly complete ideologies, plans, or determinate goals.

Within the philosophy of education, Jaspers's views broadly align with those promoted by nineteenth-century German Idealism. For both Jaspers and German Idealism, "[a]n institution remains functional only so long as it vitally embodies its inherent idea," as Jürgen Habermas states in an essay on the topic (Habermas & Blazek, 1987, p. 3). This idea of the university includes not only the freedom to pursue various lines of investigation but also the notion that the university is tasked with cultivating future participants in an "aristocracy of the intellect" (*Geistesaristokratie*) through *Bildung*. This *Bildung* denotes an "inner growth," or development acquired through an elite education and an immersion in classical writings that, in turn, separates what Fritz Ringer (1990) calls the "German Mandarins" from regular citizens (p. 87). The idea of the university, then, includes the educational formation and cultivation of individuals who, on Jaspers' view, will be able to actively contribute to a democratic society (Jaspers, 2016e, pp. 220, 223).

United with both *Bildung* and free inquiry is Jaspers's rejection of totalizing ways of thinking. Human beings have a lamentable tendency to apply specific insights to *all* domains of inquiry. As Jaspers forcefully argues in *Man in the Modern Age*, this totalizing impulse can manifest itself in a variety of disciplines—in sociology, when we are tempted to use sociological categories such as economic classes to comprehensively explain away human freedom and existence; in psychology when we are encouraged to explain all behavior in terms of unconscious mechanisms; and in anthropology, when we are led to say that heritability and physiognomy explain every aspect of an individual's personality and behavior (Jaspers, 2010, pp. 173–181). In each case, we err drastically once we believe we have discovered a final explanatory key. Instead, on Jaspers's view—a view reinforced by his experience with National Socialism—we need to hold these theories in a balance, admitting that they can offer insights in particular situations without believing they offer irrefutable and final explanations of all that is.

Jaspers's conception of the university incorporates these three elements—freedom of inquiry, educational formation (*Bildung*), and anti-totalization. But with the promotion of these qualities in the university there arises the risk that, with no determinate educational plans or goals and with the radical freedom to pursue any lines of thought, students might turn against or reject democratic ideas of freedom, truthfulness, and equality. Despite Jaspers's (2016c) claim that such a university education is an integral part of a democratic society, it is not always clear that this is true. To illustrate my point, I will examine the case of Mike Cernovich, a contemporary conspiracy-theorist, self-help guru, and male chauvinist who, far from emerging outside of the university, became who he is today in large part with the aid of his university education. And while Jaspers admitted that his idea of the university entails a fundamental risk, I suggest, in this chapter, that by emphasizing the importance of Jaspers's theory of rational communication, we can go some way towards reducing the likelihood of educating students who will turn against democracy and towards anti-liberal forms of thinking and behaving.

THE PROBLEM WITH TOTALIZATIONS

Fundamental to the freedom of the individual and the free pursuit of truth, on Jaspers's view, is the rejection of *a priori* totalizations—theories, world-views, or ideologies that are allegedly able to explain, in advance, all future observations. Jaspers's anti-totalizing commitments, evidenced in his already-mentioned criticisms of sociology, psychology, and anthropology, developed into an anti-totalizing theory of philosophy—a "periechontology"[2]—that tries to balance the interests of competing perspectives against the prioritization and absolutization of any single method or worldview (Jaspers, 1947). For Jaspers (1947), the different strands of philosophy that have historically appeared have, in many cases, each tried to unify all phenomena as instances of a single understanding of being and, in so doing, presupposed some foundational unity. In theology, for example, we find theologians claiming that God or Transcendence is ultimate, the explanation for all that is. Materialist philosophers have, in their own way, posited and searched for some fundamental material entity to be the building block upon which all else is constructed. Solipsists or subjectivists, moreover, have posited the individual "I" or "ego" to be the truest reality while idealists claim that the fundamental explanatory principle is an abstract idea or principle. In *On Truth*, the first volume of his incomplete *Logic*, Jaspers tries to hold each of these theories together by both recognizing the insights they offer while rejecting their claims to finality. In each case, these theories, when taken to be ultimately explanatory, err, on Jaspers's view, in absolutizing or totalizing one mode of being to the exclusion of the other modes (Jaspers, 1947).

To counteract these totalizations, Jaspers theorizes the Encompassing (*das Umgreifende*) as what holds each of these modes in a balance. The world is held as just one mode of the Encompassing, for example, and stands in contrast with *Dasein*, the individual considered objectively, *Existenz*, the individual considered subjectively, and Transcendence, what goes beyond the phenomenal realm.[3] By holding each of these modes together in an Encompassing domain that is neither objective nor subjective, Jaspers hopes to balance different ways of seeing the world. In some cases, it is worthwhile to view the human being as a strictly biological entity; in other cases, it is preferable to view the human being as an irreducibly experiencing subject; in still other instances, it is preferable to view the world in terms of its relation to Transcendence or what exceeds all that appears. In all, Jaspers offers seven different modes of the Encompassing—ways of considering Being—while denying that any single mode provides the full truth.

While the articulation of each of these modes and their relations to each other occupies much of *On Truth*, the details of which need not concern us here, Jaspers' anti-totalizing and anti-dogmatic stance, metaphysically expounded in his *periechontology*, also underlies his educational theory. Frequently, dogmatic reductionisms remain alive in large part through institutional and professorial pressure to think and train students in a particular way. In many disciplines, students are taught to think within the boundaries of a particular worldview and find it difficult to publish or express ideas that challenge it.

Even though such totalizations might seem, at first glance, largely benign, Jaspers experienced their nefarious potential with the rise of National Socialism. In his short work, *Nietzsche and Christianity*, a book based on lectures given in Hannover in 1938, Jaspers deviates, in the third chapter, from a strict reading of Nietzsche to elaborate on the dangers of adopting a totalizing view of history. Without mentioning the National Socialists by name, Jaspers claims that "[t]here can be no total knowledge of world history, because we always know only *within* the whole, never *the whole* itself " (Jaspers, 1938/1961, p. 55). Any total views of history are only, at best, hypotheses to be tested by future events. As such, "any self-assured scheme of total knowledge is not only always untrue but also paralyzes the ability to know. It provides only a false unity which satisfies the eye and the mind insofar as they come to rest within it" (Jaspers, 1938/1961, p. 56). In line with our structural inability to have a totalizing knowledge of history is the complementary point that, due to our unknowing, we cannot act on our supposed total knowledge: "[t]here can be no action based upon a *total planning*," Jaspers (1938/1961) writes, "because this would require the whole to be first an object of knowledge" (p. 58). Instead, we are left with only partial knowledge, and this enables only particular actions. We must remain attentive to the structural uncertainty that undergirds, in the form of Transcendence, our empirical encounters and ideal constructions: "[o]nly for finite purposes," Jaspers explains, "can I definitely and real-istically know" (Jaspers, 1938/1961, p. 58). And yet, we are continually tempted, after the loss of the guiding framework once given to us by theol-ogy, to seek after some new guiding framework that claims to explain not only why we are where we are, but also what we must do.[4] Nevertheless, we must resist such totalizing temptations, which can easily generate political totalitarianisms, ideological educational planning, and social ostracism for those unwilling to conform.

FREEDOM IN EDUCATION

To combat the dangerous potential of such totalizations, whether in total views of history or in reductionisms to individual modes of the Encom-passing, two of Jaspers' recommended reforms are especially relevant: the restructuring of the student-instructor relationship and the reestablish-ment of a certain unity among the diverse university faculties.

The Student-Professor Relationship

In all three editions of *The Idea of the University*, Jaspers identifies three kinds of student-professor relationship and endorses that relationship which remains most free of indoctrination and dogmatism. The first student-professor relationship Jaspers describes is that of *scholastic education* (*Scholastische Erziehung*). In this relationship, the purpose of the instructor or professor is to reproduce statements and to transmit them to the next generation, without allowing space for questioning or novel research: "The educational material is system," Jaspers writes. "There are influential authoritative writers and books. The instructor functions impersonally, only as a representative who is replaceable by anyone else. The material is compressed into formulae and definitions" (Jaspers, 2016d, pp. 21, 138,

323). In this setting, the boundaries of knowledge are already determined. All that matters is the rote memorization and transmission of preestablished and authoritative claims.

The second relationship is that of *authoritative education* (*Meistererziehung*). On this model, the instructor or professor is qualitatively different from the students who are encouraged to admire, adhere to, and follow the master. Those who follow a master are then part of a community that deflects responsibility from the student-disciples. The student-disciples then find their personal value in being related to the master and they look to the master and community for support. However, in submitting themselves to the teachings of a master, such student-disciples relinquish their own independence (Jaspers, 2016d, pp. 21, 138, 323).

In both scholastic and authoritative forms of education, students must be obedient to authority, whether this authority is traditional, textual or rests in a charismatic teacher (Jaspers, 1923/2016a). In each case, "scholastic and authoritative education possess a more or less developed doctrine, a vivid, ultimately complete world-image. In each case the spirit is frozen" (Jaspers, 1923/2016a, p. 22). The task, then, is to free students and instructors from the constraints of such restricting authorities.

Jaspers seeks to overcome the dominance of authority with his theory of *Socratic education* (*Sokratische Erziehung*). With Socratic education, there is no foreordained final plan or authority. Instruction does not consist in perfectly transmitting a body of knowledge or a set of beliefs to a new generation: "[t]here is no absolutely certain doctrine," Jaspers writes, "but limitless questioning and unknowing reign in the absolute" (Jaspers, 2016d, pp. 21, 139, 323). Rather, the instructor and the students stand on the same plane, in the way that Socrates engaged with his interlocutors as a fellow truth-seeker and not as an authoritative master. Just as Socrates acted as a midwife, ready to help others give birth to the truth, in Socratic education, the instructors and students "maieutically" assist each other in a common pursuit of truth in what Jaspers calls a "loving struggle" (*kämpfende Liebe* / *liebender Kampf*) (Jaspers, 2016d, pp. 34, 134; Jaspers, 1970, p. 65). It is in this maieutic loving struggle that instructors and students together try to answer pressing questions, develop new lines of thought, and explain themselves to others.

In each of the three kinds of education, there exists a certain awe, reverence, or fear (*Ehrfurcht*). In the scholastic tradition, this reverence is directed towards a long-standing tradition, passed down through generations. In authoritative education, this reverence is directed towards the leader or master, the source of wisdom, while in Socratic education, this reverence is for "the idea of the infinite spirit, in which one must exist on one's own responsibility (reverence before the other and oneself as bearers of spirit)" (Jaspers, 1923/2016a, p. 22). It is only in the third kind of education, however, that this reverence accommodates an absence of totalizations and dogmatisms and an awareness, instead, that we have not discovered a final explanatory principle or developed a total knowledge of what to think or how to act. In the first two forms of education, moreover, truth is thought to reside in something tangible, whether this is the tradition itself in scholastic education or in the master in authoritative education. This leads, in turn, to the conviction that ultimate solutions are present and available, that the truth can be fully and finally known. Consequently, for these first two approaches, the university and instructors can demand memorization, use exams to grade progress, and teach as if knowledge of the ultimate truth is preserved in these practices. Because Socratic education has a reverence for the total truth as what can never be fully captured or known, it recognizes that we cannot predict in advance what will be discovered, learned, or discussed. Nor ought we to teach and evaluate students as if we have a full grasp of this truth. Instead, we can only open a space where instructors and students are free to pursue their own lines of inquiry in a common commitment to uncovering aspects of the truth. This is not to say that, on Jaspers's view, universities must eliminate all exams or no longer expect students to acquire well-tested knowledge; it is, rather, to say that such examinations and expectations do not define what we ought to expect from students at a university, nor must they limit the questions asked and solutions pursued.[5]

Relationships Between the Faculties

In addition to theorizing a student-instructor relationship that allows for free investigation and a culture of wonder in the face of truth, Jaspers describes how the various faculties in a university ought to be related and unified in order to, at the institutional level, create conditions for educating (*ausbilden*) well-rounded students. At the intersection of our inability to have total knowledge and our commitment to ultimate coherence stands the unity of truth as an ideal. We must posit a certain unity of truth and the correlative unity of the university faculties in order to avoid the complete fragmentation of various pursuits of truth into unrelated and isolated domains. Otherwise, Jaspers writes, truth and the diverse university faculties concerned with it could only exist as mere aggregates presenting diverse subjects or domains side-by-side without any justification or unifying idea. Because total knowledge and a final grasp of truth is impossible, we need to accept this unity as only an ideal—something posited and assumed nondogmatically—such that the different approaches to truth must be seen as relating to a more comprehensive ideal unity (Jaspers, 1946/2016b, p. 161).

Drawing from the medieval university tradition, Jaspers suggests that we reestablish philosophy, considered broadly, as the unifying force in the university, the faculty that brings harmony to the higher schools of theology, jurisprudence, medicine, and, possibly, a department of technology. But philosophy, understood in this broad sense, does not denote strictly or narrowly what we, today, consider a philosophy department; instead, Jaspers appeals to an older notion of philosophy that unites the humanities and the natural sciences into one department. This unity of the human and natural sciences, *Geisteswissenschaften* and *Naturwissenschaften*, as philosophy, broadly understood, would enable students to acquire a wide-ranging foundation and awareness of not only different topics, but also of different methods, before moving on to training in more specialized disciplines, whether medicine, law, theology, or technology.

Training in both the sciences and the humanities would provide, Jaspers claims, a familiarity with different approaches to truth. On Jaspers's view, the sciences, as distinct from certain non-scientific disciplines like philosophy, understood in the narrow sense, are concerned with methods. They use particular methods to arrive at "compellingly certain and universal" knowledge for it is only through particular, well-defined methods that researchers can place confidence in results that can be shared, duplicated, and considered true for all (Jaspers, 2016d, pp. 111–112, 292–293). In the natural sciences, this involves observation and experimentation. For the human sciences, this requires partaking "in the human past [and] the knowledge of the breadth of human possibilities" by means of "the filling of the soul with the contents of myths, images, works, [and] human reality" (Jaspers & Rossmann, 2016, p. 321). But learning scientific methods produces more than just an ability to generate results. Jaspers claims that familiarity with science and its methods produces a certain integrity and truthfulness: "Science arises from integrity and produces it," he writes. "No truthfulness is possible that has not incorporated the *scientific attitude and way of thinking*" (Jaspers, 1946/2016b, 123). In the sciences, students are forced to distinguish between the compellingly certain (*zwingend Gewußten*) and its opposite (*nicht zwingend Gewußten*). And it is this training in distinguishing these two that requires students to grow comfortable with defending their conclusions and with generating criticisms of the results of their instructors and peers.

The sciences, however, with their methods for achieving compelling and universally valid results, have certain limitations. Most significantly, they are unable to direct themselves insofar as the results the sciences obtain do not give us insight into the ultimate questions: "scientific *knowledge of a subject*," Jaspers writes, "is not *knowledge of being*" (Jaspers, 2016d, pp. 116, 295). By this, he means that the particular results reached about particular beings or domains of being cannot be applied to the whole, to being as such. We cannot use scientific results or even scientific methods to make claims about ultimate questions, such as the meaning of life, the direction our society must take, what topics ought to be researched, what values ought to motive scientific research, or the goals for which research is conducted. Science, Jaspers writes, must not be guided by either utility or by taking itself as an end in itself. Rather, it is guided by a *will to know* (*Wissenwollen*) (Jaspers, 2016d). And it is philosophy, considered narrowly, and guided by an orientation towards Transcendence and ultimate truth, that can help guide scientific research while operating within the realm of values and the limits of knowledge.[6] In short, then, science, as the practice of generating universally valid and compelling results, is guided by philosophy in the narrow sense, which does not concern itself, on Jaspers' view, with knowledge claims, but, instead, maintains a commitment to unknowing—a kind of Socratic ignorance (Jaspers, 2016d, p. 303). Hence, science is guided by the will to know *and* by the admission of ignorance.

Such a university education demands the creation and facilitation of an "aristocracy of the intellect" (*Geistesaristokratie*).[7] Like many of the other mandarins of his own and prior generations, Jaspers believed that a certain aristocracy must be preserved, that certain individuals are more suited for intellectual work than others, and that we must not encourage a glorification of the average or the masses (Jaspers, 2010). Though we cannot discuss in detail the merits or demerits of such an aristocracy here, it is important to note that Jaspers believed, drawing from Abraham Flexner, that democratic societies require an intellectual aristocracy, not in order to fill political positions, as Jaspers makes clear, or to be leaders (*Führer*) of the people, but in order to allow individuals to challenge each other to be the best possible versions of themselves and to pursue various lines of thought to the furthest extents possible (Jaspers, 2016d, pp. 45, 191, 345). In essence, then, universities should offer a space where students from every social strata are able to be educated into an intellectual elite, where students share a common *Bildung* and, together, possess an appreciation for free inquiry unobstructed by ideological constraints.

THE RISK OF FREEDOM

Given Jaspers's vision of university education, however, a problem arises: in Jaspers's effort to eliminate totalizations, absolutizations, and reductionisms from university education and in his effort to level the field between professors or instructors and students, does not the envisioned university risk assisting in the formation of malicious individuals' intent on sowing, not totalizing systems, but chaotic nihilisms? In short, does not Jaspers's emphasis on freedom create room for those who would promote disorder, antagonisms, and controversies in the name of freedom? In what follows, I will describe the case of Mike Cernovich, a male chauvinist and blogger of the political far right who draws inspiration from his education in philosophy to disseminate anti-liberal, empirically false, and anti-democratic ideas. I will ultimately argue, in the section following this one, that a Jaspersian university can reduce the chances of producing still more Cernoviches by cultivating an atmosphere of rational communication—an environment where students are encouraged to see their own flourishing and investigations as achieved *alongside* and not *in competition with* fellow students and professors.

Born in 1977 to a working-class, conservative Pentecostal family in Kewanee, Illinois, Cernovich began his postsecondary education at a local college where, according to journalist and profiler Andrew Marantz, "[t]he professors let him criticize any text, including the Bible and the Constitution. You were allowed, even encouraged," Marantz (2019) explains, "to make extreme arguments: that logic or truth or beauty were meaningless concepts, or that studying the words of dead white slaveholders was a waste of time" (p. 137). Fascinated by the life of the mind, Cernovich went on to study philosophy at the University of Illinois, Springfield, where he found himself attracted to Nietzsche's anti-Christian ideas that "traditional morality was a form of spiritual enslavement, a way for the ruling classes to keep the rest of society fearful and weak" (Marantz, 2019, p. 137). The ideas of Nietzsche and the other thinkers Cernovich read allowed him to abandon the traditional constraints of his upbringing. Nevertheless, he found the apparent freedom permitted in college and university classrooms somewhat inconsistent and insufficient: "[t]he professors claimed that they wanted their students to be as open minded as possible," Marantz writes, "but of course that wasn't really true. There were limits, and you learned pretty quickly what they were" (Marantz, 2019, p. 137).

After completing his undergraduate degree, Cernovich studied law at Pepperdine University but then, prevented by a rape charge from practicing law, he focused on internet blogging. Though his charges would eventually be dismissed, and his record expunged, Cernovich achieved prominence within men's rights and conspiracy-theory circles for his online provocations. His masculinist blog, *Danger and Play*, outlined a philosophy of independence and male dominance (Cernovich, 2015).[8] It was also during this time that Cernovich freely accused whomever he disliked of practicing pedophilia (Singal, 2016).

At first glance, it might seem that Cernovich's (2015) ideas are just the superficial ravings of a provocateur. Afterall, how can we attribute a consistent philosophical position to someone who, on the one hand, freely disseminates conspiratorial claims, while, on the other hand, produces a film, *Hoaxed*, meant to critically examine and expose "fake news?" How can someone so unconcerned with truth suddenly express worry about the unreliability of the media? We could easily and with good reason conclude that Cernovich is narcissistic and his concern with "fake news" is just a case of projection. Or we could conclude that Cernovich has no position other than that of complete nihilism. I want to suggest, however, that while these insights might have merit, there is something more unsettling going on.

One hint of Cernovich's worldview appears in the opening lines of *Hoaxed*: "All media is narrative," he states, "and we are in a war of narratives" (Downey & du Toit, 2019). Cernovich then compares himself to a professional wrestler, a comparison he expands on in his interviews with Dave Rubin. In the first, 2016, interview, Cernovich admits, "I'm just the heel, I'm the bad guy. I might as well be Ric Flair, the million-dollar man, you know" (The Rubin Report [TRR], 2016). And because politics is all a scam, where even the apparently virtuous are thoroughgoing liars, "well then you just go with the best showman. And that's where we are now in life." After all, "What do people love? ... Drama. People love drama, people love conflict. Conflict is attention" (TRR, 2016). Ultimately, given that everyone is an actor in a vast drama composed of nothing more than competing narratives, on Cernovich's view, the winners are simply those with the better narratives which, in his case, is determined by the "head count," or the numbers of the dead (Downey & du Toit, 2019). Because, for example, Marxism is responsible for many millions of deaths, its narrative is of a lower quality than Capitalism. Truth is not about getting things right or achieving accuracy, whether through coherence or correspondence; it is, rather, about getting certain results. And while Cernovich, more recently, has tried to tame his public image, having replaced his *Danger and Play* blog with the more benign *Cernovich.com*, it is unclear that this taming of an "Internet Troll" into an "Internet Dad" is not itself just one more way to acquire some measure of power: in his most recent interview with Rubin, Cernovich admits that "[j]ust being a nice person makes people so angry" (TRR, 2019).[9]

It is tempting to write off Cernovich as just another troll and internet conspiracy theorist, someone to be dismissed as an adult bully. While it is true that his presence online has been largely noxious, to just blame Cernovich's actions and claims on, for example, a deficiency in reasoning or thoughtfulness would be to ignore the intellectual and philosophical motivations for his conduct. Though Cernovich has written no systematic work of philosophy, three central tenets can be identified.

First, there is Cernovich's advice to reject long-term goals and to live for the moment in a way that would embrace Nietzsche's theory of the eternal return (Cernovich, 2015, p. 155). The future is built out of decisions in the present, so the task is to "take personal responsibility for your life" and no longer look to the future for gratification (Cernovich, 2015,

p. 154). Living in the moment and taking personal responsibility are, for Cernovich, directly related: to blame one's failures on external structures is to fail to take ownership: "Are you going to sit around and rant about the unfairness of the world, like some Tumblr dork?" Cernovich asks, "Play some video games? Maybe you're getting over a hang over? … Are you going to cry yourself to sleep like some lovesick teenager? Or are you going to make the decision to take ownership of your life?" (Cernovich, 2015, p. 157). One can either act now or continue nurturing a Sartrean "bad faith."

Second, there is Cernovich's (2015) promotion of narcissism and egoism. If you want to be liked, you must act like a narcissist. Those who think narcissism is morally wrong "haven't gone beyond good and evil," he writes (p. 47). You can either be envious of others who have relationships you wish you had or, he advises, "you can make people like you" (p. 47). Influencing others with initial impressions requires that you promote yourself by wearing the right clothing, comporting yourself confidently, and knowing when to use humor (pp. 48–49). For Cernovich, these are not just innocuous ways to boost confidence or achieve better interactions with others; they are methods for getting what you want, for controlling the situation, and for subtly manipulating others, if only for the short term and for instantaneous gains.

Finally, there is Cernovich's (2015) radical distain for the weak. When providing advice on how to relate to one's family and their potentially negative opinions, Cernovich writes:

> Unless someone is living the life you want to live, why are you even listening to them? People don't like how you are living? What have they accomplished? What qualifies them to tell you anything about life? Oh, because they are family? So what? My brother is a loser who just got out of prison for shooting his meth dealer. I haven't talked to him in a decade. Why would I associate with such a scumbag? Because he's family? (p. 72)

Later on, Cernovich (2015) writes that "[y]ou don't owe your parents anything. Your parents were motivated by evolutionary forces to procreate. They selfishly choose to have you. You can selfishly decide whether or not to keep them. If you want to become a man, you will need to reject the losers. That includes your family" (p. 73). Though Cernovich goes on to state that he has a good relationship with some members of his family, the central point is the radical individualism, egoism, and anti-egalitarianism at issue. Fundamentally, for Cernovich, one has to reject the weak and forge one's own path.

Taken together, Cernovich describes a kind of Nietzschean *Übermensch*, a Superman or Overman, who promotes himself[10] above the interests of others, who incarnates the will to power—both physically and socially—a will that not only strives to overcome all burdens, but takes total responsibility for himself and lives in the moment, willing to risk an eternal return of the same.

REASON AND COMMUNICATION IN EDUCATION

Given Cernovich's philosophical education, conducted in an environment where the questioning of traditional positions was, in large part, permitted and the elaboration and defense of one's own views was encouraged, what can we say about Jaspers' own educational project? Is there not a risk contained within the freedom Jaspers promotes? Jaspers himself admits such a risk when he writes that "the freedom of life in this idea [of the university] has, however, 'dangerous' results.... The student has the freedom to degenerate" (Jaspers & Rossmann, 2016, p. 324). Must we settle with a bare awareness that the freedom to learn and investigate the world risks producing internet trolls, male chauvinists, and conspiracy theorists?

Initially, it might seem that Cernovich's advice could mesh well with Jaspers's own ideas. In each case, there is a certain aristocratic impulse, a rejection of total planning, and an admiration for the "great." This is not surprising given that both are indebted to Nietzsche. But, even given these superficial commonalities, Jaspers would reject Cernovich's *modus operandi*. In what follows, I offer three reasons Jaspers would both reject Cernovich's views and deny that Cernovich is the kind of person universities should hope to nurture.

First, and least convincing in my view, Jaspers might claim that Cernovich has misinterpreted Nietzsche. On Jaspers's view, the *Übermensch* Nietzsche describes does not clearly refer to something we can turn ourselves into. It is, rather, something that we wish to produce—a future being that will transcend human limitations. On Jaspers's view, instead of seeing the *Übermensch* as something one can become in this life, we must see it as a goal pursued through self-sacrifice: "[t]he truly basic attitude," Jaspers writes, "calls for self-sacrifice so that a greater being may emerge: our humanity has value only as a transition and a decline. It is required of us that we 'dance beyond our own selves' " (Jaspers, 1936/1965, p. 168). But this critique is not fully convincing. For one, Cernovich offers no sustained interpretation of Nietzsche. Though it is very clear he is influenced by his reading of Nietzsche, there is no requirement that we read Cernovich's advice back into Nietzsche's texts, or that we see Cernovich's writings as strictly Nietzschean. Furthermore, there are numerous readings of Nietzsche and Nietzsche's own writings lend themselves to a very diverse range of interpretations, each one often claiming superiority over the others. And finally, Jaspers's vision for the university is not one of total devotion to the teachings of earlier thinkers—that would entail a degeneration into a form of authoritative or scholastic education. Rather, on Jaspers's view, in reading and thinking through the texts of earlier thinkers, we are called not to unquestioning devotion, but to dialogue and communication.

Second, Jaspers might blame Cernovich's approach on the absence of any scientific training. As we have seen, Jaspers holds that natural scientific training should be united with training in the humanities in order to produce well-rounded individuals. While the humanities teach students to engage thoughtfully with the works of tradition, the sciences teach students to apply a specific method and to produce results that are defensible and repeatable. And whereas the natural sciences proceed by trying to understand phenomena in terms of their constitutive parts (*Erklären*), the humanities strive to understand phenomena in terms of how they fit within a broader whole (*Verstehen*). Thus, Cernovich would not have acquired an appreciation for the kinds of methods and approaches to truth that lead to scientific results. While this might explain, in part, Cernovich's attraction to conspiratorial thinking and the ease with which he found himself accusing others, sometimes correctly sometimes falsely, of misconduct, there is little doubt that Cernovich's approach is something that is only confined to those with strictly humanities educations. While scientific training might have done Cernovich some good, I am skeptical that it really solves the problem.

This brings us to the third critique Jaspers might level against Cernovich's approach, the critique I find the most convincing. For Jaspers, what is missing in Cernovich's approach is rational and genuine communication. In Jaspers's periechontology, six modes of the Encompassing are united by Reason, the seventh mode, and it is the role of Reason to find links, community, and dialogue between the other six modes. For example, Reason is tasked with helping those devoted to *Dasein*—to understanding the biological and psychological drives of human beings—to engage in conversations with those investigating Spirit—the unifying ideas and ways of thinking of a culture or civilization. Reason strives for unity between these six modes but, knowing that the modes cannot be reduced to each other or to Reason, it also knows that this unity is unattainable. Nevertheless, it forges ahead (Jaspers, 1947).

Jaspers's claim that Reason is a drive for unity and not, for example, a bare thinking according to logical laws or an algorithmic deduction of conclusions from available evidence derives from Kant's description of Reason in his first critique. After identifying the structures of Sensation and the Understanding, Kant goes on to explain the freedom of Reason: whereas Sensation is passive and receives impressions and whereas the Understanding spontaneously and automatically synthesizes the products of Sensation according to rules, Reason freely generates unifying ideas from the products of the Understanding. Reason is, fundamentally, a free drive for unity and the unconditioned. However, as Kant forcefully argues throughout his first critique, the unconditioned and a complete unity are never fully attainable. Hence, Reason is on a never-ending quest for what we cannot ultimately achieve (Kant, 1998).

Basing his theory of Reason firmly on Kant's, Jaspers takes Kant's conclusions about the unconditioned and the impossibility of complete unity to mean that a total view of things, a total worldview, or a final theory of everything is impossible and it is from this insight that his critique of totalizations draws much of its force. However, there is another aspect to Reason: in Reason's quest for unity, it seeks to bring everything into conversation with everything else. Being rational, then, or conducting oneself in accord with Reason is to both recognize the impossibility of attaining complete unity *and* to desire wide-ranging communication.

In the second volume of his three-volume *Philosophy*, Jaspers explains in more detail what genuine communication involves. Existential or genuine communication begins, he writes, with the recognition that we are not sufficient on our own. It is only those who are not self-sufficient and entirely self-contained monads (an impossibility) who then enter into communication: "[a]s a single isolated consciousness I would not communicate anything, would ask no questions and give no answers, and would accordingly not be self-conscious—the very word indicates a distinction of the self from something else" (Jaspers, 1970, p. 51). Those who falsely believe themselves to be self-sufficient and isolated individuals see genuine communication to be a weakness, a way of admitting their incompleteness. But, as Jaspers makes it clear, the very being of self-consciousness is based on incompleteness. Becoming self-aware requires the inputs of others who, for example, help us learn a language, help us identify ourselves, and help us learn the concepts we use to understand ourselves. Thus, even our most basic self-understanding is grounded on incompleteness and communication with others.

The kind of communication Jaspers espouses does not end with the mere exchange of facts and statements, as if communication corresponds with the mere transfer of information and with each interlocutor replaceable, as in the case of scholastic education, by any other. Nor is it the case that such communication involves a competition whereby each interlocutor tries to "one-up," "shame," or "own" the other, as if communication is a zero-sum game. We see such deficient forms of communication on display today, even among those calling for more dialogue or conversation, whether these are moderated by news anchors or take place through Twitter battles or YouTube videos. Jaspers characterizes these incomplete forms of communication as follows:

> The trick is to compel sophistically what can no longer be refuted with
> ease. If I fail in controversy to entrap the other in my arguments and thus
> to achieve a false conviction, I can effectively tire him out by endless delay,
> by bringing up new possibilities, by referring to other authorities as deci-
> sive. The question, then, is simply who will hold out longer. (Jaspers, 1970,
> p. 91)

Such forms of communication differ radically from what should be encouraged in Socratic education.

In contrast with the kind of deficient communication carried out as a
kind of will to have power over one's opponents, existential or genuine
communication, on Jaspers' view, is a loving struggle, an encounter where
each participant tries to understand the views of the other as thoroughly
as possible, and where each participant is engaged in an immediate and
unrepeatable relationship with the other. Existential or genuine communication is concerned "with utter candor" Jaspers (1970) writes,

> with the elimination of all kinds of power and superiority, with the other's
> self-being as well as with my own. It is a struggle in which both combat-
> ants dare to show themselves without reserve and to allow themselves to be
> thrown into question. (p. 60)

In such instances, participants understand that their own well-being is
not separate from the well-being of their interlocutors, that each is united
in the investigation of truth, that each wills the best for the other, and
has empathy for the other. It is this kind of communication, and not the
pathological kind found in the writings and videos of Cernovich and those
like him that must characterize the free exchange of ideas in Socratic education, and it is, I suggest, the promotion of empathic communication
that, when coupled with free inquiry, can go a long way towards nurturing
inquisitive, thoughtful, *and* compassionate citizens.

TACTICS FOR PROMOTING RATIONAL COMMUNICATION
IN THE CLASSROOM

Given these observations, how might instructors advance an atmosphere
of rational communication within their own classrooms? Is there a way to
prevent non-dogmatic instruction from devolving into relativism and from
there into a bare play of powers? Can an educational environment remain
committed to truth while recognizing that this ultimate truth—the truth
of the Encompassing—is not fully contained within any of the different
modes of the Encompassing? In what follows I offer two recommendations
for developing truth-seeking rational communication in the classroom.

First, in my own teaching, I have found it very helpful to encourage students to think about and defend views they might not hold or accept. Suppose a classroom is predominantly inclined to embrace a Rawlsian theory of distribution (Rawls, 1999). The students generally believe that the just distribution of resources is inextricably tied up with fairness. Initially, these students might see proponents of Marxism, Utilitarianism, or Libertarianism as irrational, as espousing incoherent views that need to be refuted or that are even dangerous to society. However, even if a Rawlsian theory of distribution is the best among the alternatives, instructors, in this situation, might be wise to ask the students to imagine they are Libertarians, for example, or Marxists and then ask these students to justify their adopted view. In doing so, students would need to place themselves in the shoes, so to speak, of a Libertarian or Marxist or Utilitarian and view the world, even if for a short time, from that perspective. They could then identify the reasons motivating their adopted view and see why some might find it compelling. Additionally, they could also begin to see their own views from the perspective of the adopted view and, in doing so, identify some weaknesses in it. Though students might never change their minds (and this is not the intent), by carrying out this exercise, they can begin to see their own views through the lens of another and, as a result, grow to empathize with those with whom they fundamentally disagree.

Closely tied to the first tactic, the second recommendation is to assign compelling fiction. Several studies have shown that those who read literary fiction are better able to see the world from the perspectives of others (Kidd & Castano, 2013; Oatley, 2016). Being able to feel the pain of others, whether real or fictional, can help one overcome the tendency to want to destroy or demolish one's opponents for the views they hold. Readers of literary fiction can begin to identify goals common to themselves and those about whom they read, and this skill can manifest itself in the classroom and persist outside of it. Classmates and instructors with different religious, social, and political beliefs can become less threatening once one has imagined, with the assistance of fiction, how it feels to inhabit their world. Once one finds others less threatening, one can more easily work with them towards shared goals.

With these two closely related tactics, educators, I believe, can not only help students freely express divergent points of view, but they can cultivate an atmosphere where students come to see themselves not as isolated individuals in a constant struggle with their rivals, but as co-collaborators engaged in the common project of unraveling truth in time.

CONCLUSION

To provide an answer to the question asked at the beginning of this chapter of whether an education that emphasizes free inquiry risks educating anti-liberal individuals, it appears we can identify an answer. University education must not be reduced to the bare memorization and transmission of facts, as in scholastic education, or to a devotion to specific authorities, masters, or leaders, as in authoritative education. Nor should university education be a free-for-all where students and instructors are left to fight over various theories and experiments in an effort to out-compete their peers, as if education should be a fight to the death. Rather, essential to university education and free inquiry is a Jaspersian "loving struggle" where interlocutors are trained and encouraged to see their instructors and peers as collaborators and fellow participants in the pursuit of learning and truth. It is this loving struggle which prioritizes empathy over aggression and honesty over wily tactics that, I believe, separates adversarial and deleterious ways of living from dispositions cultivated through cooperation, partnership, and good faith. Thus, in the educational environment for which Jaspers advocated, collaborative, empathic, and loving forms of dialogue must be taught in the very atmosphere that also inspires the free and unconstrained pursuit of truth.

REFERENCES

Cernovich, M. (2015). *Danger & play: Essays on embracing masculinity*. CreateSpace Independent Publishing.

Downey, S., & du Toit, J. (Directors). (2019). *Hoaxed: Everything they told you was a lie* [Film]. El Ride Productions.

Habermas, J., & Blazek, J. (1987). The idea of the university: Learning processes. *New German Critique*, *41*, 3–22. https://doi.org/10.2307/488273

Jaspers, K. (1947). *Von der wahrheit*. R. Piper & Co. Verlag.

Jaspers, K. (1961). *Nietzsche and Christianity* (E. B. Ashton, Trans.). Henry Regnery Company. (Original work published 1938)

Jaspers, K. (1965). *Nietzsche: An introduction to the understanding of his philosophical activity* (C. F. Wallraff & F. J. Schmitz, Trans.). Henry Regnery Company. (Original work published 1936)

Jaspers, K. (1970). *Philosophy: Existential elucidation* (Vol. 2). The University of Chicago Press.

Jaspers, K. (2010). *Man in the modern age* (E. Paul & C. Paul, Trans.). Routledge Revivals. https://doi.org/10.4324/9781315823690 (Original work published 1931)

Jaspers, K. (2016a). *Die idee der universität [1923]*. In K. Jaspers, *Schriften zur universitätsidee* (pp. 1–68). Schwabe Verlag. (Origina work published 1923)

Jaspers, K. (2016b). *Die idee der universität [1946]*. In K. Jaspers, *Schriften zur universitätsidee* (pp. 103–202). Schwabe Verlag. (Origina work published 1946)

Jaspers, K. (2016c). Die verantwortlichkeit der universitäten. In K. Jaspers, *Schriften zur universitätsidee* (pp. 213–217). Schwabe Verlag.

Jaspers, K. (2016d). *Schriften zur universitätsidee* (O. Immel, Ed.). Schwabe Verlag. https://doi.org/10.24894/978-3-7965-3533-8

Jaspers, K. (2016e). Universities in danger: The coherence of knowledge. In K. Jaspers, *Schriften zur universitätsidee* (pp. 219–221). Schwabe Verlag.

Jaspers, K. (2021). *The origin and goal of history* (M. Bullock, Trans.). Routledge Classics. https://doi.org/10.4324/9781003133674 (Original work publihsed 1949).

Jaspers, K. & Rossmann, K. (2016). *Die idee der universität: Für die gegenwärtige situation entworfen.* In K. Jaspers, *Schriften zur universitätsidee* (pp. 255-443). Schwabe Verlag. (Original work published 1961)

Kafka, P. (2019, August 29). What happened to the formerly fearsome right-wing media troll? *Vox.* Retrieved June 25, 2021, from https://www.vox.com/recode/2019/8/29/20839601/milo-cernovich-loomer-alex-jones-cnn-olivery-darcy-recode-media-peter-kafka

Kant, I. (1998). Critique of pure reason (A. Wood & P. Guyer, Trans.). Cambridge University Press. (Original works published 1781/1787)

Kidd, D. & Castano, E. (2013). Reading literary fiction improves theory of mind. *Science, 342*(6156), 377–380. https://doi.org/10.1126/science.1239918

Marantz, A. (2019). *Antisocial: Online extremists, techno-utopians, and the hijacking of the American conversation.* Viking.

Markovits, D. (2019). *The meritocracy trap: How America's foundational myth feeds inequality, dismantles the middle class, and devours the elite.* Penguin Books.

Miron, R. (2012). *Karl jaspers: From selfhood to being.* Brill. https://doi.org/10.1163/9789401208062.

Oatley, K. (2016). Fiction: Simulation of social worlds. *Trends in Cognitive Science, 20*(8), 618–628. https://doi.org/10.1016/j.tics.2016.06.002

Rawls, J. (1999). *A theory of justice* (Revised edition). Belknap Press.

Ringer, F. (1990). *The decline of the German mandarins: The German academic community, 1890–1933.* Wesleyan University Press.

Sandel, M. (2020). *The tyranny of merit: What's become of the common good?* Farrar, Straus and Giroux.

Singal, J. (2016, December 21). How Mike Cernovich is pizzagating his latest victim. *New York Magazine.* Retrieved June 25, 2021, from https://nymag.com/intelligencer/2016/12/how-mike-cernovich-is-pizzagating-his-latest-victim.html

Southern Poverty Law Center. (n.d.). *Mike Cernovich.* https://www.splcenter.org/fighting-hate/extremist-files/individual/mike-cernovich

The Rubin Report. (2016, March 18). *Donald trump and the war on free speech* [Video]. Youtube. https://youtu.be/K03gRy6qjKY

The Rubin Report. (2019, May 14). *Trump, censorship, and trolls* [Video]. Youtube. https://youtu.be/Ogx1XjogSkY

NOTES

1. Karl Jaspers's (2016d) writings on university education have been edited and published together. All translations from this volume are my own.
2. Jaspers's neologism "periechontology" derives from *periechō* (meaning to encompass) and *ontology* (meaning the study of Being) (Miron, 2012).
3. In total, there are seven modes of the Encompassing: Spirit, Dasein, Consciousness-as-Such, *Existenz*, the World, Transcendence, and Reason.
4. In *The Origin and Goal of History*, first published in 1949, Jaspers (1949/2021) expands on his critique of "total planning." Here, he levels his critique against all forms of totalitarianisms and, in particular, communism (pp. 172–193). In a footnote, Jaspers expresses his support for and indebtedness to the ideas of Walter Lippmann and Friedrich Hayek (pp. 279–283).
5. Jaspers himself makes it clear that "exams are sociologically inevitable," (Jaspers, 1923/2016a, p. 32).
6. Here, Jaspers means philosophy as a narrow discipline, not philosophy as what encompasses both the human and natural sciences.
7. Due to the constraints of space and the focus of this chapter, I cannot evaluate the value of such an "aristocracy of the intellect" here. But two recent and influential criticisms of a related meritocracy are (Sandel, 2020) and (Markovits, 2019).
8. The extent of Cernovich's viciousness is on display at the Southern Poverty Law Center's profile on him at (Southern Poverty Law Center, n.d.).
9. Given Cernovich's past, there is little reason to think his current persona is nothing more than another ploy, another mask, put on after he found himself losing influence (Kafka, 2019).
10. For Cernovich, the *Übermensch* is most certainly male.

CHAPTER 8

FOUNDATIONS OF EDUCATION

Absurdity and Ambiguity

Stephanie Schneider
State University of New York College at Old Westbury

ABSTRACT

This chapter explores the manner in which Existentialism is able to illuminate the central tensions in a Foundations of Education class. This chapter
will use the construct of ambiguity (a term used by Simone De Beauvoir)
and absurdity (a term developed by Camus) to explore whether or not a
Foundations of Education course should even exist within teacher education
programs. The course itself is dialogic and looks hard at the "self" and the
"other" using this dialectic. Using the work of existentialists, phenomenologists, and education theorists, this chapter explores how Existentialism can
provide a rationale for the Foundations of Education course.

A Foundations of Education course is often the first course in the sequence
of any teacher preparation program. Students in the course are there, presumably, because they want to become teachers. No matter the curriculum
taught in foundations, they start to shift their thinking from a student view
to a teacher view. They begin the journey of identifying as teachers and
start realizing that teaching (and schooling) is under constant scrutiny from
outside reformers, taking away the free will that they thought they may
have in the profession.

Problematizing the Profession of Teaching From an Existential Perspective, pp. 151–165
Copyright © 2022 by Information Age Publishing
www.infoagepub.com
151

The foundations of education are taught in a myriad of ways, within different contexts, using different texts. How should one interpret the term "foundations of education" and have a sense of where to begin? Should foundations be a mechanistic or technical view of how schooling works or a blend of social sciences to understand the theoretical lens of schooling? In this chapter, the author will explore the existential nature of the foundations of education. Why does such a class need to exist in teacher preparation programs? What is the purpose of such courses? Perhaps, most importantly, what do teacher candidates learn from such courses?

Using the work of existentialists, phenomenologists, and education theorists, this chapter try to figure out what the important takeaway is for the Foundations of Education course as well as see whether or not existentialism can provide an answer.

FOUNDATIONS OF EDUCATION: THE COURSE

I'm currently sitting and planning my seventh semester of teaching a Foundations of Education course. The texts I am planning to use have changed again (for the fifth time), the focus of the class shifted for the sixth time, and I am actually wondering what the objectives of this course are. Sure, the course description says something about the history, sociological nature, and philosophy of education are in there, but there is one burning question is in the back of my mind: What do the students, these preservice teachers, need to know in a Foundations of Education course? Is it a technical, mechanical course where they should be introduced to schooling and pedagogy? Is it for the theory, of which I am unsure anyone remembers after the course is over? I was joking with a colleague one day and said that planning for this course is absurd. Which, of course, made me think of Albert Camus's *Myth of Sisyphus*. Am I rolling a boulder up a mountain just to see it roll down every semester?

The second, and more pressing issue deals with the ambiguity of the course wrapped up in what we teach, and how we teach it. Elliot Eisner (1979) wrote of the three kinds of curricula that we teach. The explicit (what "the curriculum" is made of, the implicit (things we teach without saying it is a part of "the curriculum," like raising hands), and the null or hidden curriculum (what we do not teach). Simone De Beauvoir (1994) provides a clue how to navigate the self/other dualism, that we can use for foundations of education courses.

Presumably, the course is for preservice teachers, many of whom are learning about the entire system of education in the country. But what exactly does this entail? Does a preservice teacher care about the history of education? Why teachers are not well-respected (salaries for the number of years educated)? What philosophies were used in creating schools and pedagogy? Alternatively, do preservice teachers need to know about the minutia of schools? The roles of the various adults in a school building? The ways schools and school districts are organized? The various safety measures and drills?

In some ways, one needs to break down what the technical is. I think it comes down to the following: Content knowledge, content pedagogical knowledge, classroom management, lesson planning, and how to engage students. Additionally, what texts are considered to be foundational texts in education and why is philosophy so important to the foundations of education are questions that engage me the most as a professor.

I realize that most practicing teachers would say yes to the practical, and no to the theoretical. As a teacher, I seldom reflected to the point where I was making a lesson plan "Deweian" or "Freireian." Rather, I was just concerned about if students met the learning objectives on that particular day.

So, I had to take stock of why this course is necessary in the first place. As a professional program, students need to make a shift from thinking as students to thinking like teachers. Students need to have a personal paradigm shift to learning and then need to be able to put the new knowledge to use for them in their future. The content of the course is important, but more important than this is the pedagogy students see in the course. In response to this epiphany, I threw out the textbook that purported to contain what a Foundations of Education course "should" include and rewrote the curriculum. What I saw throughout my foundations courses was that the most important thing in the class was dialogue.

Dialogue itself can be broken down into the existential divide of self and other. The opinions and positions that we all have are subjective. To anticipate De Beauvoir's work, *The Ethics of Ambiguity* (1994), one must think about the ambiguity between our individual freedom with the recognition that we are all part of the class. Some of the topics in the course deal directly with questions of politics, race, gender, sexual orientation, gender identity, religion, and class. The discussions need to be productive, so, as an introduction to dialogue, Paulo Freire's seminal work *Pedagogy of the Oppressed* (2007) along with the Michael Apple's work *Ideology and Curriculum* (2004) were used. The point is not to make my students struggle through two difficult texts but to teach them how to think about the educational system as a whole and their place within this context as students and as future educators. The theories we discuss in class are places where students can get a new language that they can use to talk about what is going on in the system in which they belong. And yet, there is the constant pull of the "more practical" world of education that I rarely talk about.

The pedagogy used in the course, however, is one that is dialogic. The students and I are constantly engaged in discussions that are about the texts and wider applications. The discussions usually surround my students' experiences. Since my students are diverse, they have a variety of experiences that help to open the eyes of the others in the class. This chapter will explain why a Foundations of Education course is existential in nature, why we need to use dialogue or the dialectic form of pedagogy, how hermeneutics plays out in how students start to think like teachers, and how ambiguity, and absurdity play big roles in the Foundations of Education.

EXISTENTIALISM

Existentialism is a philosophy developed in the 20th century that put freedom at the center of existence. Existentialism came to be prominent in the United States in the 1950s and 1960s but developed in Europe earlier in the 20th century. Webber (2018) states, "Existentialism originally defined by Simone de Beauvoir and Jean-Paul Sartre is the ethical theory that we ought to treat the freedom at the core of human existence as intrinsically valuable and the foundation of all other values" For example, if we do not have the freedom to exist, then we cannot even begin to ask questions about ethics or epistemology. Freedom gives humans the ability to act in an authentic way, a way that is true to themselves. Being inauthentic, or fake, is acting in bad faith. In education, we are taught things that sometimes connect with us, and other times do not. The subjects taught in school, math, science, history, English languish arts, foreign languages, and so forth, are ways that require cognitive understanding, and do not necessarily step into the realm of existentialism. However, according to Morris (1966, p. 123), it is the attitude of the student where existentialist education begins. Morris (1966, p. 123) quotes Kneller (1958): "The existentialist attitude towards knowledge radically affects the teaching of those subjects which are dependent upon systems of thought or frames of reference: it states that the school subjects are only tools for the realization of subjectivity." Learning, at least from an existential standpoint, is something that is subjective. We turn now to the work of Martin Buber, who puts the frame of self and other at the center of pedagogy.

Martin Buber (1970), in his work *I Thou*, sets up a dialectical kind of education. The meaning of the word "dialectic" come from the Greek meaning of the art of conversation (Adkins, 1999). I and Thou are two authentic beings that must be in the conversation wholly and honestly, for the dialectic takes place only with two (or more) beings who recognize freedom in another:

> You do not need moral genius for educating character, you do not need someone who is wholly alive and able to communicate himself directly to

his fellow beings. His aliveness streams out to them and affects them most strongly and purely when he has no thought of affecting them. (Semel, 2010, p. 195)

Buber envisions the spirit of a teacher who is free. He envisions a teacher who knows that he must let go of the idea that students should simply follow in a teacher's path and, rather, that students must carve out their own path. To start to have students do this in class, there is constant dialogue. I also tend to give readings that are diametrically opposed to one another with no commentary from me. Students then feel free to decide what they think is right, and as long as they are able to from reasonable arguments with textual details, they are "correct." For me, one of the hardest things to do is to allow students to be free to do this. For example, one semester I had students read a *New York Times* column by Roger Cohen on the "Suffering Olympics." I was using this as a way to talk to my future social studies teachers to think about the multiple ways that history is presented. In 2008, the Czech Republic issued the *Prague Declaration on European Conscience and Communism*. This document came to my attention while reading Roger Cohen's op-ed piece in the *New York Times* entitled "The Suffering Olympics" (Cohen, 2012). In this piece, Cohen (2012) explains the "double genocide" that went on in the Bloodlands, and the plight of Eastern Europeans to get the same recognition as the Holocaust victims of Nazi Germany. In Lithuania, where Cohen interviewed Prime Minister Andrius Kubilius, the question of whether or not Lithuanians were primarily perpetrators or victims of the Holocaust came up. Kubilius stated that it was "a very painful and shameful thing" and "some Lithuanians took part in that." He continued "It's obvious that Stalinist crimes were also very terrible and painful, although you cannot compare them" (para. 10-11U). The *Prague Declaration on European Conscience and Communism* has several key points that need elucidation. One point in the *Declaration* is the call for "recognition that many crimes committed in the name of Communism should be assessed as crimes against humanity serving as a warning for future generations, in the same way Nazi crimes were assessed by the Nuremberg Tribunal." Another is the call for "recognition of Communism as an integral and horrific part of Europe's common history" and "acceptance of pan-European responsibility for crimes committed by Communism." These are a siren call to get similar recognition that Nazi victims do. In fact, as Roger Cohen points out, a possible reason for the lack of recognition was, in the end, Stalin did help to defeat the Nazis. In reading the document, I found that, aside from recognition, there is a call for education that acknowledges the perils of Communism alongside the perils of fascism. My students were given the opportunity to argue about the representation of the violence of Communism should be given the same attention as the Holocaust. For this, they were able to argue about morality, ethics, and what should be included in the curriculum. Moreover, they were taught about what is included in the curriculum, and why.

The teacher must be aware that students may not respond in ways that the teacher is used to, so the teacher must be aware and actually listen to fulfil his or her professional obligation. Listening is one way for us not dominate conversation and to "fully embrace the other" (Gordon, 2011). As Gordon (2011) stated,

> For Buber, to truly listen entails being present to the other, that is, responding to the other as a whole person and creating a space in which the other can speak his or her own words and meaning. When one is open to the other's being, one does not try to speak for the other or to impose one's own language, concepts, and interpretive schemes on others. (p. 207)

In the above example on the "Suffering Olympics", students responded in ways that I never thought they would. One student claimed Stalin was worse than Hitler, another said violence in the beginning of a revolution was necessary, just like the American Revolution. I had to be nimble to continue the dialogue. This scenario made me realize that ambiguity was a huge part of this course.

THE ETHICS OF AMBIGUITY

Ambiguity, along with the absurd, nihilism, angst, is based off of the problem of freedom and arises out of experiencing the inevitable tensions of the world. If freedom is at the core of human existence, freedom must be tempered because we live with others. We don't have complete freedom to do as we choose if we live amongst others. Simone De Beauvoir's work, *The Ethics of Ambiguity* makes the case that ethical, individual freedom can only come with the freedom of others. To De Beauvoir, ethics come not from any external justification but from internal motivation. To this end, she rejects other philosophies which do not advance this view such as Utilitarianism or Marxism. Both of these philosophies take the collective unit as the starting point and do not include individual freedom (De Beauvoir, 1994, p. 22).

Sartre (2003), from his work, *Being and Nothingness*, states, "Man is condemned to be free." Sartre implies that we have freedom, and yet, do not always know what to do with that freedom. If we are free to act, we have unlimited choices, and so many choices may paralyze us before we act. If our actions do not impact others, no ethical discussions need to happen. However, humans are constantly engaged in the tension between the "self" and the "other." De Beauvoir makes this tension clear in when she is talking about the ambiguity of self and other, subject and object. There is an ethical responsibility to consider the "other" when acting. For Sartre, the freedom of existence is a punishment. If the self is truly free, it has no moral responsibility to the other, the self exists for itself. De Beauvoir makes this the center of her moral argument that we must give attention to the other.

For example, at any given moment, I am simultaneously both a subject navigating the world and an object within other people's subjective view of the world. So, what am I? Am I a subject or an object? What if I am both of them simultaneously and that existing within that duality creates a certain level of tension for me? To that point, at any given moment, I am both an individual person and a member of a collective group, family, nation-state, class, and so forth. So, what am I? Am I an individual or a part of a larger group? What if I'm both simultaneously and that existing within that duality creates a certain level of tension for me? Mind and matter. Self and other.

Buber (1972) in *I and Thou,* makes the distinction between I and Thou between the attitude of objectification, "Ich-Es" ("I-it") and the attitude of dialogue "Ich-Du" ("I-thou"). "The external "objective" assumes a single correct perspective where everything can be situated or located" (Wegerif, 2019). The internal view, or view of the self that the other, or external "objective" that takes the other seriously is "dialogic" because from this perspective meaning always assumes at least two perspectives at once and, the moment there are at least two perspectives then the gap between them opens up the possibility of an infinite number of possible new perspectives and new insights" (Wegerif, 2019). It is from the multiple new insights that we can overcome the strict duality of self/other that existentialists, including De Beauvoir, cling to.

When it comes to teaching, the dualities are the main point of contention for Paulo Freire. Freire (2007), in *Pedagogy of the Oppressed,* it is clear that the banking system of education highlights the duality, and harms both the teachers and the learners. The banking system is as follows:

> [A] fundamentally *narrative* character. This relationship involves a narrating Subject (the teacher) and patient, listening objects (the students).…
> His [the teacher's] task is to "fill" the students with the contents of his narration- contents which are detached from reality, disconnected from the totality that engendered them and could give them significance. Words are emptied of their concreteness and become a hollow, alienated, and alienating verbosity. (p. 71)

In other words, the narrative, which is usually to enforce the status quo and not challenge or invite questions, is not an ethical way of teaching, because it does not invite interpretation or acknowledge ambiguity in the first place.

For De Beauvoir, to escape this ambivalence is to escape this duality. The ethical part of existing is existing with others. In this case, dialogue is one ethical practice. In the classroom, Freire (2007) offers a pedagogy of problem-posing. Problem-posing education takes humans historicity as the starting point. Freire, much like other existentialists, realizes that we are in a constant state of becoming. In order for education to happen, there is an awareness of incompletion, and this is where education can begin (p. 84). To compare banking and problem-posing pedagogies, Freire states,

> Banking education resists dialogue; problem-posing education regards dialogue as indispensable to the act of cognition which unveils reality. Banking education treats students as objects of assistance; problem-posting education makes them critical thinkers. Banking education inhibits creativity and domesticates (although it cannot completely destroy) the *intentionality* of consciousness by isolating consciousness from the world, thereby denying people the ontological and historical vocation of becoming more fully human. (pp. 83–84)

Problem-posing education has dialogue at the center of the practice. Simply put, Problem-posing is developing a *Teacher-Student or Student-Teacher* model, where teachers learn from the students, just as much as students learn from teachers. Here, the typical oppressor (teacher) works in conjunction with the oppressed (student) to create a dialogue using everyone's fonts of knowledge to create an education of equality. Using the ethics of De Beauvoir, where we must all acknowledge an other's humanity, the Problem-posing works much better to create an ethical space.

However, dialogue also presents problems. As Elizabeth Ellsworth (1989), asks, "Why doesn't this feel empowering?" What if critical pedagogy only gives voice to the already privileged? Ellsworth explains that teachers are constrained by their own privilege. For example, I am a White-skinned, middle class, cis woman. This is already a huge privilege when I speak to my Black and Brown students, my students who are economically disadvantaged, my students who grew up under different circumstances. I simply do not have the language to speak about the experiences of my students. Ellsworth also goes into the fact that professors and teachers have institutional power (p. 308). We have more formalized education and can play the game of formal schooling. In most literature and history taught, the "self" is seen from a cis, Christian, white skinned, middle or upper class, thin, heterosexual man. The "other" is everyone else. My class, overall, accepts that problem-posing education is emancipatory, in a way that the baking system could never be. Although dialogue is imperfect, for most of my classes at least, there is room to explore the self and other, especially related to education.

Ambiguity lies in the space between self and other. In a foundations of education course, there is this tension between the ways in which we learned, and how we are learning to teach. The ways that we communicate to our students, however clearly, can lead to confusion. The things that we teach in Foundations of Education may not relate to our students' futures, but they can help them think about problem of ambiguity as it relates to pedagogy.

The coursework of Foundations of Education aims to get at this ambiguity. We talk about the three kinds of curricula (Eisner, 1979, p. 97) all schools have. They are: Explicit—what we teach/the curriculum as written, local, state, and national standards. Implicit—the culture or values that schools teach, without stating those values in any obvious way. Hidden or Null- what is explicitly not taught in schools. Eisner (1979) writes,

> It is my thesis that what schools do not teach may be as important as what they do teach. I argue this position because ignorance is not simply a neutral void; it has important effects on the kinds of options one is able to consider, the alternatives one can examine, and the perspectives from which one can view a situation or problems. The absence of a set of considerations or perspectives or the inability to use certain processes for appraising a context biases the evidence one is able to take into account. A parochial perspective or simplistic analysis is the inevitable progeny of ignorance. (p. 97)

To get at this point, students analyze the following quote and connect it to the three kinds of curricula, using the social studies curriculum as an example.

> The paradox of mapmaking, however, is that as soon as you begin shrinking a geography down to usable size, you necessarily are forced to misrepresent it. By making choices about what to include and what to leave out, you change the map from a document faithfully documenting an area to one furthering a particular point of view. Writing contains the same paradox. As soon as we start picking and choosing relevant details to "propel the story forward" (literally or figuratively), we change the story to fit the narrative. (Blanding, 2014, p. 3)

The social studies curriculum does much of the same. Think about what children learn in about social studies. Think about what you learned in social studies. This semester, we will focus on what is not in the curriculum. We will focus on the spaces that do not get attention. Your first assignment is to think about the above quotes and your own experiences in school. What didn't you learn in social studies but want to? Who got left out? What events are left out? Why is this an issue? Conversely, why do historians leave events and people out? Create a thread between these quotes and your experience. Write your answers on a separate sheet of paper to be handed in and discussed next class.

- "Why do we just know a few influential Black leaders in American history?"
- "There is almost no mention of the Latino/a movement."
- "LGBT issues are too controversial to bring up." "Why do we not talk about the feminist movements?"
- "Why are some mass atrocities worse than others?"

One student of mine said the following during a recorded interview:

> When you brought up the subject of the paper, the hidden curriculum, I immediately thought of my mother. She's not from here, she's from Jamaica. She's always saying how they don't teach us our history. I'm like what? Yes they do ... she's like no they don't teach us about our history ... you're not going to find everything about African-Americans in your textbook. And I used to go back and forth with her cause at the end of the day, I'm learning what they're teaching me...and my mind's not going outside of that ... I'm just going based on what my teachers are telling me. That's most important.... And then growing up, at the end of the day, my teachers still aren't pushing that issues saying "Oh guys, do more research on African-American history, they aren't pushing that ... so therefore, once you (the researcher) mentioned the hidden curriculum, that's the first thing I thought about."

Another student said the following:

> I'm a gay guy. I'm White, Christian, look straight or whatever. And, although I see me in the curriculum, I don't see me. I know sexual orientation isn't an outward feature, but if we don't tell our students, don't talk about the fact that families look different, and don't recognize that looking like the most powerful people in the room isn't the same as being one, then we are only hurting ourselves.

The three kinds of curricula show the ambiguity in what we are explicitly teaching our students, and what they need to figure out on their own. Their identities, their *selves*, are necessary for them to learn and understand before they can move onto treating others ethically. By learning about the three kinds of curricula as future teachers, they can make explicit what is hidden or implicitly taught.

ABSURDITY

To borrow from "To Posterity" a poem by Bertold Brecht (1940), we truly live in absurd times! Foundations of education as a class in most teacher preparation programs is absurd. We go through the motions of teaching the historical, social, economic, philosophical, and so forth, of education at the state, national, and global levels for what? What edification can students get from a course that does not address pedagogy or content for the subjects they are teaching?

Seemingly everything has taken a turn to the political, we don't have the same truths let alone a desire to behave ethically for the common good. While De Beauvoir (1994) wrote extensively on ambiguity, she could not ignore absurdity. She writes:

> The notion of ambiguity must not be confused with that of absurdity. To declare that existence is absurd is to deny that it can ever be given a meaning; to say that it is ambiguous is to assert that its meaning is never fixed, that it must be constantly won. Absurdity challenges every ethics; but also the finished rationalization of the real would leave no room for ethics. (p. 129)

In as much as humanity's existence is ambiguous, it cannot be summed as absurd.

> Human beings are continuously seeking to disentangle the ambiguity which governs their existence. Absurdity enables human beings to point out the inconsistencies which govern ethics. If the world were utterly perfect, there would be no need for ethics because all human beings would automatically uphold morality. (De Beauvoir, 1994, p. 129)

However, because there is perpetual absurdity, there must be ambiguity. "I have never seen anyone die for the ontological argument" (Camus, 1955, p. 3). We abandon truth as soon as the truth is a threat. This is how false beliefs and bad faith become the norm. The primary issue then becomes existence itself. Indeed, Camus (1955) starts his essay on the absurd, "There is but one truly serious philosophical problem, and that is suicide. Judging whether to life is or is not worth living amounts to answering fundamental question of philosophy" (p. 3). He goes on to say that every other question one can ask is secondary to this primary concern.

The essential paradox arising in Camus's philosophy concerns his central notion of absurdity. Accepting the Aristotelian idea that philosophy begins in wonder, Camus (1955) argues that human beings cannot escape asking the question, "What is the meaning of existence?" Camus, however, denies that there is an answer to this question, and rejects every scientific, teleological, metaphysical, or human-created end that would provide an adequate answer.

> Thus, while accepting that human beings inevitably seek to understand life's purpose, Camus takes the skeptical position that the natural world, the universe, and the human enterprise remain silent about any such purpose. Since existence itself has no meaning, we must learn to bear an irresolvable emptiness. This paradoxical situation, then, between our impulse to ask ultimate questions and the impossibility of achieving any adequate answer, is what Camus calls *the absurd*. Camus's philosophy of the absurd explores the consequences arising from this basic paradox. (Aronson, 2017, para. 2)

> Camus's understanding of absurdity is best captured in an image, not an argument: of Sisyphus straining to push his rock up the mountain, watching it roll down, then descending after the rock to begin all over, in an endless cycle. Like Sisyphus, humans cannot help but continue to ask after the meaning of life, only to see our answers tumble back down. If we accept this thesis about life's essential absurdity, and Camus's anti-philosophical approach to philosophical questions, we cannot help but ask: What role is left for rational analysis and argument. (Aronson, 2017, para. 3)

In trying to understand the absurd in Foundations of Education, I found myself looking at the content of the course. There are generally really wonderful topics to discuss and are necessary for anyone wanting to go into education. However, not much of it is useful when it comes to actual teaching. The topics in a typical Foundations of Education class deal with social, economic, historic, and philosophic issues. In the heat of teaching in front of a class, I doubt anyone with any sense will suddenly stop and ponder the spending per pupil of their school district. Yet, educators need to internalize the structural and institutional boundaries of schools. They need to understand how power works, who has it, who can use it, and why power begets power. They may come to realize that their school has less supplies than a neighboring one, or their schools have twice as many Advance Placement courses.

In my first teaching job, my Honda Civic, at that point about 10 years old, was sharing space with my students' BMWs. Many parents brought lawyers to IEP meetings and demanded things that I thought were inconceivable. Privilege works in many ways. Part of the absurdity that teachers live through is how the system works to keep the status quo. Critical race theory, a legal theory first developed by Kimberly Crenshaw (1989) and her work on intersectionality, recognizes the intersection where some groups need more protections than others. Critical race theory asks us to pay attention to the world, especially the 13th and 14th Amendments of the United States Constitution (Then and Now Podcast). Critical race theory has its critics, mainly from the Conservatives, that says teaching critical race theory is anti-American and promotes the idea that the United States was built on White supremacy. It is very tricky to incorporate new ideas into the mainstream, like the pushback from Nikole Hannah-Jones's (2019) 1619 Project, including the Trump administration's 1776 Commission. To me, the important things are to read the text, to understand the point of view, and to be able to talk about the text in a measured, critical way. The inability to have the same facts about a subject is absurd. An assignment that I love to give is to have my students watch, for one week, the Tucker Carlson on Fox, and then watch Rachel Maddow on MSNBC for another week. Students must then write down what the main stories and what was said about them. Perhaps unsurprisingly, we must be living in two different worlds for all they have in common. This plays out in the classroom as having no central grounding in truth. My class loves to say one side is closer to the truth than the other, but the lack of knowing what the truth is, is absurd.

Another absurdity of the Foundations of Education is teaching pre-service teachers that they have pedagogical freedom. Districts are choosing sets of prescribed curricula that dictates almost every question a teacher must ask. If the curricula is so prescribed, really anyone can teach. Why should our pre-service teachers bother going to school for teaching when the publishers are creating curricula for teachers to use. If absurdity is the rejection of any sort of meaning for existence, then is there even a meaning to what we do in teacher preparation programs?

The big question then, is do we simply go with the absurd, or do we find ways to fight it? If we are metaphorically rolling a boulder up a hill, should we, as teacher educators just walk away? Let the politicians, policy makers, and those who have never taught make decisions on curriculum? I think the answer here is no. In the Phantom Tollbooth, a story about a little boy named Milo, is the picture of the absurd, "When he was in school he longed to be out, and when he was out, he longed to be in. On the way he thought about coming home, and coming home he thought about going" (Juster, 1961, p. 9). As teachers, we certainly have found ourselves in this mood and there is no doubt students have felt like this.

> It seems to me that almost everything is a waste of time," he remarked one day as he walked dejectedly home from school. "I can't see the point in learning to solve useless problems, or subtracting turnips from turnips, or knowing where Ethiopia is or how to spell February." And, since no one bothered to explain otherwise, he regarded the process of seeking knowledge as the greatest waste of time of all. (Juster, 1961, p. 9)

It is this quote that leads me to believe that we must continue on in spite of the absurdity. It is true that absurdity will always be here, but there has to be some logical and rational debate about education.

CONCLUDING THOUGHTS

Foundations of Education is a course that I struggle to plan for every single semester. I switch up texts and adapt modalities to teaching in a global pandemic. Existentialism puts freedom first, and through freedom, we are able to truly decide what is important for us to teach. By using a dialectic pedagogy, Freire and Buber offer ways to connect with our students to help shift the ways we think about education for both the teacher and student. We can honor the duality of self and other by fully listening and trying to understand the subjective nature of interpretations of texts and conversations. The ethics of ambiguity that de Beauvoir introduces makes us aware that we need to remember that freedom, especially in the classroom needs to remember that there is a fully autonomous other. The absurd lies in the content of the course: What is actually needed, and will our students remember anything? To get around the despair of the absurdity and to become happy to roll that boulder up the mountain, we must think about the larger happiness of teaching future teachers and the impact that they will have. Demonstrating the dialectic form of pedagogy can make us free to make choices that include our students in the process of teaching, so they may at least learn how to think like one.

REFERENCES

Adkins, V. K. (1999). Buber and the dialectic of teaching. *The Journal of Educational Thought, 33*(2), 175-181.

Apple, M. (2004). *Ideology and curriculum* (3rd ed.). Routledge.

Aronson, R. (2017). Camus. *The Stanford Encyclopedia of Philosophy.* https://plato.stanford.edu/entries/camus/

Blanding, M. (2014). *The map thief.* Gotham Books.

Buber, M. (1972). *I and thou.* Scribner's.

Bertold Brecht. (1940). *An die Nachgeborenen* [To those who follow in our wake] (Scott Horton, Trans.). https://harpers.org/2008/01/brecht-to-those-who-follow-in-our-wake/

Camus, A. (1955). *The myth of Sisyphus and other essays.* Vintage International.

Cohen, R. (2012, January 31). The suffering Olympics. *New York Times.* http://www.nytimes.com/2012/01/31/opinion/the-suffering-olympics.html

Crenshaw, K. (1989). Demarginalizing the intersection of race and sex: A black feminist critique of antidiscrimination doctrine, feminist theory, and antiracist politics. *University of Chicago Legal Forum, 1*(8), 139–167.

De Beauvoir, S. (1994). *Ethics of ambiguity.* Carol Publishing Group.

Eisner, E. (1979). *The educational imagination.* Macmillan.

Ellsworth, E. (1989). Why doesn't this feel empowering? Working through the repressive myths of critical pedagogy. *Harvard Educational Review, 59*(3), 297–324.

Freire, P. (2007). *Pedagogy of the oppressed* (30th Anniversary Edition). Continuum.

Gordon, M. (2011). Listening as embracing the other: Martin Buber's philosophy of dialogue. *Educational Theory 61*(2), 207–219.

Hannah-Jones, N., Desmond, M., Villarosa, L., Boule, J., Morris, W., Interlandi, J., Stevenson, B., Muhammad, K. G., Lee, T., Elliot, M., Hughes, J., & Stewart, N (Ed.). (2019). The 1619 Project. *New York Times Magazine*. https://www.nytimes.com/interactive/2019/08/14/magazine/1619-america-slavery.html

Juster, N. (1961). *The phantom tollbooth*. Alfred Knopf.

Morris, V. C. (1966). *Existentialism in education: What it means*. Harper and Row.

Sartre, J. (2003). *Being and nothingness* (2nd ed.). Routledge Classics.

Semel, S. F. (2010). *Foundations of education: Essential texts*. Routledge.

Webber, J. (2018). *Rethinking existentialism*. Oxford University Press.

Wegerif, R. (2019). Dialogic education. In *Oxford Research Encyclopaedia of Education*. http://education.oxfordre.co

SECTION IV

THE TEACHING OF EXISTENTIALISM

CHAPTER 9

AGENCY PRECEDES ESSENCE

Existentialism, Ecology, and the New Materialisms

Daniel O'Dea Bradley
Gonzaga University

ABSTRACT

Over the last century, existentialism has often worked to reinforce and inten-
sify the anthropocentric and voluntaristic aspects of Western Modernity. It
thereby contributes to our alienation from material nature and our separation of philosophy from the natural sciences. These separations, in turn, may
enable our ecologically catastrophic treatment of the nonhuman world. Thus,
one may be inclined to think that the rising interest in materiality and the
growing concern for ecological ethics ought to motivate a rejection of existentialism. In this chapter, I argue that this is not the case. I argue that certain
versions of existentialism can help to cultivate an axiology that includes the
more-than-human and a philosophical sensibility closely attuned to materiality. To achieve this, however, one must first elucidate more pluralistic versions
of existentialism that recover some of the deep historical promise opened by
a sustained reflection on the distinction between *existence* and *essence*. This
promise has, to date, gone partially unfulfilled due to the exclusive emphasis
on consciousness that recent forms of existentialism have inherited from the
Cartesian tradition. This chapter will show that one plausible route to the
goal of a renewed existentialism is opened by the shift of focus from *autonomy*
to *agency* in Bruno Latour's philosophy of science and technology.

Problematizing the Profession of Teaching From an Existential Perspective, pp. 169–188
Copyright © 2022 by Information Age Publishing
www.infoagepub.com

"Existence Precedes Essence.... *Man* exists only in so far as *he* realises himself, he is therefore nothing else but the sum of his actions, nothing else but what his life is."

—Jean-Paul Sartre[1]

"Essence is Existence, and Existence is Action.... There is no other way to define an *actor* except through *its* actions.... As soon as freedom of movement is granted back to non-humans, the range of agents able to participate in the course of action extends prodigiously."

—Bruno Latour[2]

Intellectual curiosity is among the most attractive of human traits, as we see when the joy of discovery lights up the face of a mentor, colleague, or student. And from our own practice of the intellectual life, we know that participating in the search for truth is among the most delightful of human experiences. In philosophy over the last century, however, our naïve enjoyment of the beauty of knowing has been qualified by our recognition of the troubling and even repulsive tendencies that can work within it. At its worst, the act of discovery can degrade into processes of prediction and calculation that serve our desire to manipulate and control the resources around us. This is a perennial danger for the intellectual life, as signaled by the etymology of our word *comprehend*, from the Latin *prehendere*: "to lay hold of, seize, grab, snatch, take, catch, accost."

Although the philosophy of existentialism, too, can be coopted by these forces, existentialism arose precisely to combat the dangers inherent in an unrestrained intellectualism. By claiming that one's existence precedes one's essence, existentialism challenges the tendency to reduce all things to an abstract intelligible principle or essence. In particular, this attention to existence reveals three aspects of things that limit a complete assimilation of them into our conceptual frameworks by which we "comprehend" reality. These three are: haecceity, contingency, and finitude.[3] They will be discussed further in light of their theological origin later in this chapter, but, as a first approximation, we can say that *haecceitas* teaches us to regard that which calls forth our interest not only as a universal kind to be categorized, but also as something that has come into being in this particular way. For example, an attunement to haecceity teaches me to see an animal that I am tracking though the snow not only as a bobcat of the species *Lynx rufus* but also as *this* individual bobcat with its own characteristic ways of being. Second, an emphasis on existence teaches me to see this animal not only as a transient type of an enduring kind but also as a concrete being that has come into existence at some point in the recent past and that will die in the not so distant future, thus focusing my attention on the animal's *finitude*.

Third, existentialism teaches me that the fact of this bobcat's existence as this particular thing is *contingent*; this bobcat could have been different than it is or, potentially, could not have existed at all.

The relation between finitude and historicity means that existentialism will always remain closely attuned to the ways that things come into being. In Sartre's philosophy, however, existentialism tends to fall back into the pernicious modern dualism in which genesis can be understood as the result of either efficient cause or conscious choice. This means that there are only two alternatives: any change is the result of either (1) blind mechanistic forces (i.e., nature), or (2) autonomous action, a goal chosen by a consciously self-determining subject (i.e., a human individual). Methodologically, this emphasis on autonomy allows reflections on *haecceitas* and contingency to mutually enlighten each other. For my individuation comes about through the choices I make, and I could have chosen a different path. The emphasis on autonomy, however, also puts an existential approach in opposition to a reflection on the full meaning of finitude. Thus, substantively, existentialism is able to call on all the resources of Kantian ethics, the discourse of human rights, and the politics of liberalism, for all of these strands of thought seek to eliminate as many restrictions on human autonomy as possible so that the individual is able to choose his or her own path as fully as possible. The price to be paid for these alliances, however, is a formalism in which the material conditions of existence tend to be seen only as impediments to the expression of the will of the individual, and the meaning of historicity tends to be reduced to a reflection on our ultimate death. In other words, what matters is not the content of one's choices but merely that the choice itself was not constrained by outside forces.

Further, in populist versions, such as (Sartre, 1946/1956) "Existentialism is a Humanism" and the "Objectivism" of Ayn Rand (Rand 1943 and 1957), the philosophical movement of existentialism exhibits an unappealing disregard for the different levels of responsibility that are attributable to different members of a society based on the concrete realities of unequally distributed socioeconomic and cultural resources. As a result of this failure to fully engage in the consideration of a thing's material conditions, existentialism becomes vulnerable to the older criticisms of Kantianism which claim that ethics of autonomy serve to defend an unjust bourgeois political order and that such ethics lead to the alienation of the person from the material world, from any broader community, and even from their own embodiment.[4] Thus we see that there are dangers inherent in *haecceitas*, contingency, and finitude," for these concepts can lead us into individualism, libertarianism, and alienation.

To the extent that this is the result, existentialism is at risk of becoming subsumed into the worst aspects of Western modernity. Thus, for students motivated by the contemporary critiques of anthropocentrism (in ecological ethics), alienation (in social ethics), and postcolonialism (in political ethics),[5] existentialism may appear to be an outdated 20th century movement that is unhelpful for younger generations. In this chapter, however, I use this critique as a foil to point to a more compelling version of existentialism that may be more plausible to these contemporary students. A brief historical survey shows that existentialism is, indeed, fundamentally tied to modernity; however, by developing a new version of existentialism in the context of Bruno Latour's actor network theory (ANT),[6] we can expand our thinking beyond the narrowed versions of modernity that recognize value only in human beings. Following Latour, we may be able to overcome the axiological dualism of Cartesian-Sartrean thought by shifting the locus of value from *autonomy* to *agency* and by recognizing agency in the non-human and even nonliving world. Using Latour's sociology of science and technology, we can see agency as not reducible to conscious acts of will and, rather, as something that extends far beyond the human. This gives us a theoretical grounding for Sartre's emphasis on how the material conditions produced by our economic and political systems have implications for a human ethics, and this new framing of agency also helps us move towards overcoming the alienation of the human being from the rest of the natural world.

THE DEEPER HISTORICAL ORIGINS OF A LESS MONOLITHIC (AND LESS ANTHROPOCENTRIC) MODERNITY

Existentialism is the result of a centuries long meditation on how to think about the truth of a thing's existence in its own right, in a way that cannot be immediately collapsed into an account of the thing's essence. In other words, existentialism wants to know what can be learned from the fact *that* a thing is apart from all that can be learned about *what* it is. For example, as we saw above, a traditional scientific inquiry will respond to the question, "What is it?" with the answer, "It is a bobcat," but in late modernity we have become accustomed to dissatisfaction with this answer, particularly with regard to human beings. We do not accept that a complete account will tell us that this is a "human being" or "a woman." Instead, we want to know about the ways she has developed her own existence in this or that particular way. There is a deep history to this tendency. The original impetus for definitively separating existence and essence came from theistic philosophers, particularly those in the Islamic tradition, such as Ibn Sina, who wanted to adopt the legacy of Greek philosophy but also to incorporate the notion of creation central to the Abrahamic religions.[7] Greek philosophy had differentiated finite beings from the infinite divine ground of being and thus already had an ontology that could be called theological. The distinctive contribution of the Abrahamic religions is to claim that creation is the free and loving act of a personal God. This means that each being comes into existence (1) not as compulsory or automatic emanation but as a free gift (contingency), (2) not only as the token of an intelligible kind but loved as an individual (*haecceitas*), and (3) not only as the instantiation of a universal essence, but as irreducibly constituted in its individuality by the material and historical act of creation (finitude).

Significantly, even when translated out of their original religious setting, these orientations toward contingency, *haecceitas*, and finitude make ontological questions more meaningful and more personal. They do this in an ambiguous way, however, exhibiting both a gloomy, even nauseating character that points to the precariousness and groundlessness of each individual life but also to an uplifting moment that reveals the ways that each individual life is charged with adventure and personal significance. With this ambiguity in mind, we can expand on our preliminary formulation of these three central concepts (*haecceitas*, contingency, and finitude) to highlight the way they lead us towards a more clearly existentialist philosophy. To say that my life is contingent means that it has no necessary grounding, thus suspending my existence over the abyss of nothingness but also making it something for which to be grateful. *haecceitas* means that despite all its great successes, the search for intelligible universal concepts and patterns succumbs before the particular thing as it exists in its opaque individual reality, but this also opens room for the cultivation of an interior life and an ethics of the individual that mark the expansive "inscapes"[8] of modernity. Historicity points to our finitude and necessary demise, but it also means that the concrete, material, and temporal conditions that give rise to something's existence are to be valued for producing this particular individual in all its uniqueness and are thus to be given due consideration in the pursuit of truth.

For these reasons it is now commonplace to assign the proximate intellectual beginnings of modernity not to Hobbes, Descartes, and Locke in the 17th century, but to the later Medieval period as Jewish, Christian, and Muslim thinkers attempted to engage Greek philosophy while reasserting the characteristic insights of their religious traditions.[9] Linking modernity to the Abrahamic reception of the Greeks provides a deeper historical horizon for modernity,[10] but also a broader geographical horizon as well. In its original development, modernity may still be called Western, but "Western" now refers not only to the parts of northwestern Europe controlled by the colonial powers (England, France, and Germany), but, rather, to everything west of India, including the Arabic and Persian cultures of West Asia and North Africa (Greater Middle East) as well as the traditionally Christian or Muslim cultures of Sub-Saharan Africa, such as Axum and Mali. This broadening of modernity provides a more pluralistic geographical and historical framework that allows us to rethink contingency, haecceity, and finitude outside the narrow confines of western Europe's response to the rise of Galilean science and the Christian wars of religion.

THE EXISTENTIALISM OF
"EXISTENTIALISM IS A HUMANISM"

It is now widely understood that Sartre's 1946 essay, "Existentialism is a Humanism," should not be taken as the definitive statement on existentialist philosophy. It was written as a defense of the movement for a popular audience, and most existentialists, including Sartre himself, have repudiated at least some of the claims in the essay. Nonetheless, it clearly articulates a great deal of the popular appeal that has animated existentialism over the last three quarters of a century, and it succinctly poses the dangers that a more adequate account of existentialism will have to address.

It is in this essay that Sartre gives us the famous slogan, "Existence precedes essence." Significantly, he formulates this as what is held in common between theist and atheist versions of existentialism. Even more importantly, he explains the meaning of this slogan by way of contrast with technological devices produced by human artifice. For example, Sartre tells us (1989, p. 4) that the manufacturer who makes a paper knife must pay attention to both

> the conception of a paper-knife and to the *pre-existent* technique of production which is a part of that conception.... The paper-knife is at the same time an article producible in a certain manner and one which serves a definite purpose, for one cannot suppose that a man would produce a paper-knife without knowing what it was for. Let us say, then, of the paperknife that its *essence*—that is to say the sum of the formulae and the qualities which made its production and its definition possible—*precedes its existence*.

Thus, an artifact is (supposedly) subsumed without remainder into its universal intelligibility, which is exactly reducible to its function. on this view, all the creative and meaningful activity that goes into the production of the knife is accomplished in the design, which Sartre (1946/1956, p. 289) calls "a formula," and any individual knife can only come to attention through defects that deviate from that formula and thereby limit its usefulness. Luckily, Sartre (1946/1956, p. 291) continues by showing us that this is not an exhaustive ontology, for

> there is at least one being whose existence comes before its essence, a being which exists before it can be defined by any conception of it. That being is

man.... Man is nothing else but that which he makes of himself. That is the first principle of existentialism.

For Sartre, unlike that of the knife, the existence of each particular human being is charged with meaning. These human lives are full of creative activity and narrative interest that only emerge through the unfolding of time. In light of this temporal character, the elements of existence that are irreducible to essence remain burdensome and troubling, for their meaning is neither transparent nor guaranteed. Nonetheless, every moment is also a participation in the openness of a truly momentous adventure.

The problem is that Sartre pays for this purposiveness by radically separating the creative activity of the human being from the merely inert and passive causal determinism of everything else. In doing so, Sartre self-consciously models his philosophy on the dramatic plotline that Descartes presents in Chapter 5 of the *Discourse on Method*. That is, in the face of an onslaught of inhuman reductivism that would degrade the human being to the status of a machine, the brave philosopher of daring and nerve will come to save the day with his novel and creative thinking (as an exemplar of the very faculty that gives humans their meaning). As Sartre (1946/1956 p. 18) puts it,

> This theory [existentialism] alone is compatible with the dignity of the human person. All kinds of materialism lead one to treat every person including oneself as an object—that is, as a set of *pre-determined reactions,* in no way different from the patterns of qualities and phenomena which constitute a table, or a chair or a stone. Our aim is precisely to establish the human kingdom as a pattern of values *in distinction from the material world* (emphasis added).

Unfortunately, saving the human and its realm of values by pitting the human *against* the material is untenable, for it identifies value with consciousness in a way that alienates the human from nature. As Sartre completes his famous formula for what unites all existentialists: "they believe that existence precedes essence—or, if you will, that we must begin from the subjective" (p. 4). Later in the essay he returns to defend this notion of subjectivity from its critics by asking, "What do we mean to say by this, but that man is of a greater dignity than a stone or a table? For we mean to say that man primarily exists—that man is, before all else, something which propels itself towards a future *and is aware that it is doing so*" (emphasis added, p. 5)

In *Nausea* (Sartre, 1969) and *Being and Nothingness* (Sartre, 1946/1956), Sartre conducts serious philosophy by putting the phenomenological method to work to reveal extremely important and lasting insights about the relation between intentionality and existence as the correlation between noesis and noema is pushed beyond its ordinary limits. In a famous scene in *Nausea* (Sartre, 1969) he protagonist of the novel, Roquentin, links his disturbing experiences of nausea to the key component of existential philosophy: an encounter with the existence of things in ways that exceed an account of their intelligibility as essences. As Roquentin (Sartre, 1969, p. 131) puts his discovery,

> No necessary being can explain existence: contingency is not a delusion, a probability which can be dissipated; it is the absolute, consequently, the perfect free gift. All is free, this park, this city and myself. When you realize that, it turns your heart upside down and everything begins to float ... here is Nausea.

This phenomenological description of the contingency of beings reveals the relation between the abyssal and the gifted nature of things; this, thereby, points to the claim that these things are free. This freedom of things, however, remains disconnected both from their causal function and from their differentiated singularity. Roquentin tells us (Sartre, 1969, p. 129), "the diversity of things, their individuality, was only an appearance, a veneer. This veneer had melted, leaving soft, monstrous masses, all in disorder—naked, in a frightful, obscene nakedness." Again, he explains,

> The world of explanations and reasons is not the world of existence. A circle is not absurd, it is clearly explained by the rotation of a straight segment around one of its extremities. But neither does a circle exist. This root, on the other hand, existed in such a way that I could not explain it. Knotty, *inert, nameless*, it fascinated me, filled my eyes, brought me back unceasingly to its own existence. In vain to repeat: "This is a root"—it didn't work anymore. I saw clearly that you could not pass from its function as a root, as a breathing pump, *to that*, to this hard and compact skin of a sea lion, to this oily, callous, headstrong look. The function explained nothing: it allowed you to understand generally that it was a root, but not *that one* at all.

The problem with this dominant strand of modern existentialism is that it tends to think that only willful human activity is able to provide the transition from bare existence to intelligible and *meaningful* reality. Thus, the quotes above should give us a rudimentary foil against which to develop an account of existentialism that provides for more integrated relations between materiality and meaning. Giving existence its due must not be allowed to divide reality ontologically into two kinds: on the one hand, conscious embodied persons—active, individuated, and function-generating—and, on the other hand, non-humans—inert, undifferentiated, and without function.

LATOUR'S ACTOR NETWORK THEORY

Latour is as adamant as Sartre or any other existentialist that we not reduce a thing to its intelligible essence. Latour rose to prominence in the 1980s as a sociologist of science pointing out the ways that scientific truths are "constructed" over time through the technologically and culturally mediated practices of science. He was equally adamant, however, that we not limit creative and generative activity to human beings thereby reducing the non-human to inert causally-determined passivity. Playing on Sartre's famous slogan, Latour (2007, p. 77) posits, "Essence is existence." Like Sartre, he goes on to immediately define existence in terms of generative activity. But there is a crucial difference, for Sartre links this generativity to the willful activity of consciousness. Latour breaks this link with consciousness and instead defines action, *first*, by its effect. Latour (1999a, p. 122), writes, "Essence is existence and existence is action," but he continues:

> There is no other way to define an *actor* except through *its* actions, and there is no other way to define an action but by asking what other actors are modified, transformed, perturbed, or created by the character that is the focus of attention.

Most significantly of all, he understands this as explicitly recognizing the generative creativity of the nonhuman material world. As he put it, "as soon as freedom of movement is granted back to non-humans, the range of agents able to participate in the course of action extends prodigiously" (Latour, 2007, p. 77).

If this generative activity is defined first in terms of its effects, this activity also reverberates back onto the ontological status of the actor, establishing it as a center of activity and thus providing it the ground for a differentiated identity that allows it to stand out from the rest of the reality. As beginning students of philosophy learn early in their study of the subject, the question of unity (differentiation, individuation, genesis, identity through time, etc.) seems obvious before they begin to think philosophically, but it soon becomes one of the most fascinating and intricate of all puzzles. Latour's answer to this great question is to claim that the unity of a being is not grounded in an eternal intelligible essence, but neither is it grounded in the unity of apperception that marks consciousness. Both of these are included in Latour's notion of an *actant,* but the relative unity of an actant is ontologically and onto-genetically more primordial than consciousness or essential substance. This is because essence is derived from action. However, it is important to note that, because action is always defined in terms of relations with other beings, this is not an absolute individuation but rather a relational one. To capture this, Latour speaks of beings as *intermediaries* in ongoing exchanges and transformations (1998 p. 437; Latour, 1999b, 2005) or as *nodes* in a network in which action cannot be derived from inputs such that the future is determined by the past but is instead the result of creative action. This action is not the sole result of any individual; the action, instead, is distributed among the variously engaged nodes (Latour, 2007).

On this basis Latour's theory provides the outline of a very plausible variant of existentialism. It develops many of the promises held open by the commitment to an examination of existence prior to essence. However, far from establishing an impoverished ontological dualism of human versus nature and cultivating an anxiety-ridden and self-absorbed reflective philosophy that alienates consciousness from the material world, Latour's theory recognizes a profusion of creative agents across the various faculties of nature, including the physical, chemical, and biological, as well as the self-reflective and voluntaristic realm of persons. Values affirmed by conscious acts of the will are included in this account but are certainly not exhaustive; furthermore, when we execute these conscious acts, we are participating in a much broader context by which we are intimately interwoven with the social, biological, chemical, and physical world. Equally important, because we are responsible for our actions but in a distributed way, this version of Existentialism does a much better job of recognizing the different levels of responsibility that can be attributed to different members of a society as well as opening a more expansive discussion about the positive and negative contributions our technologies make to the moral life of our communities.

As attractive as this mission may be, our culture is so immersed in an ontological dualism that sees the non-human as nothing more than inert, value-free, matter (and all purpose and value as a product of human consciousness) that it will take significant work even to begin to make it convincing. Latour's long career has been spent developing the tools to do just this. I find four main claims that are central to establishing this agency-based existentialism by which the precedence of existence over essence intimately interweaves us with (rather than alienating us from) our biological nature and the material world around us: (1) Technology studies show that technologies are truly agents that creatively shape the world—including the moral world—around us. (2) Global Warming and the geosciences have discovered that the earth systems themselves exhibit agency. (3) Science studies reveal that the things discovered by science, such as stars, atoms, and bacteria, are not just theoretical models, but ontological entities whose natures (essences) are real but are established by the relatively stable interactions that emerge from their activity. Finally, (4) even the discovery of all these diverse forms of agency is not enough to set us free from our cultural blinders without a genetic account of why we are so wedded to our Human/Nature dualism.

To establish this last point, Latour (e.g., 1998, pp. 422, 426) argues that we are still suffering under the doubly reinforcing legacy of iconoclasm (in both science and religion) that dominated western Europe in the 17th century. It is widely argued that the Reformation was driven in large part by the desire for a direct access to God that would reject all forms of mediation: the *social mediation* of saints, priests, and nuns, the *artifactual mediation* of statues, stained glass, incense, holy wells, and so forth, and (in its more extreme tendencies) the *material mediation* of divine grace through water, fire, smoke, bread, wine, and other elemental forms. To this religious critique Latour (1998 p. 425; Latour 1999b, p. 222; Latour 2005, p. 35) adds the less widely-discussed claim that the science of the time was also marked by a deep iconoclasm that rejected the mediation of any instruments, technologies, or social organization between the scientist and nature. Latour argues that this was the result not only of Protestant iconoclasm seeping into science but also the traumatic effect of the wars of religion which resulted in the desire to separate our beliefs about reality into two very different kinds: On the one hand, private and subjective value-claims (metaphysics and religion) would henceforth be shared only with our friends; and, on the other, indubitable and objective fact-claims (science and science-based ethics) to which all rational people of good will must assent would henceforth govern the public sphere. This genealogical account is helpful for my argument, for it points to a specific legacy that when undermined could allow for alternative forms of modernity.[11] However, most directly important for this chapter are Latour's claims about nonhuman agency and its existentialist character (points 1–3 above), and it is to these that we will now turn.

TECHNOLOGIES AS AGENTS:
THE EXISTENTIAL ANGST OF THE MOBILE "PHONE"

Philosophy is a discipline that is unusually interested in its own history. When we practice philosophy, and even more when we teach it, most practitioners show at least some interest not only in the truth claims that philosophers make, but in the history of the development of those claims. This is rather unusual, because, by contrast, when we try to understand science and technology, we are generally only interested in the final result. Since the 1970s, however, sociologists have spent a great deal of time looking at the ways technology and scientific knowledge are generated, and they have convincingly shown that when we look at the details of how these disciplines operate, many of our assumptions turn out to be based on erroneous philosophical presuppositions rather than actual practice. Foremost among these illusions is the belief that the form and purpose of our technologies are determined prior to their production. A favorite example in Science and Technology Studies (STS) is the form of a bicycle. We take for granted that a bike is composed of a triangular frame and two equal sized wheels. But a look back at the wide variety of early designs, such as the Penny Farthing and the Boneshaker, reveal that it took decades of negotiation between the competing values of safety and speed and the introduction of new materials such as rubber for tires, before the form was "black-boxed" into what we know as a bicycle today (Bijker & Pinch, 1984). Equally important, what a technology is *for* is just as much a matter of historical negotiation as form. This is easily forgotten in our familiarity with our devices, but, as in so many other areas, our words often carry linguistic traces of a less settled past: For example, we call the portal to the internet that we carry in our pockets a "phone," while we call the one on our desk a "computer."

Thus, when Sartre says, "one cannot suppose that a man would produce a paper-knife without knowing what it was for," we may recognize the rhetorical force with which it calls us to feel the forlornness of our indeterminacy *in comparison with that for which a purpose is always already guaranteed*. But if this is good pedagogy, it is bad philosophy of technology, for it does not describe the actual history of the genesis of our devices. The recognition of the socially constructed nature of our technologies has had a salutary effect on the politics of technology by making us explicitly aware that the right to determine the nature of our technologies does not lie within the purview of the designer and manufacturers alone but should rather be constituted by a fully democratic process and should be guided by a reflection on the common good.[12]

Latour, however, goes even further. He agrees that designers, manufactures, shareholders, users, and anyone else involved in the production and use of a technology should be recognized as actants in a network that is collectively responsible for the nature of our technologically constituted world. However, Latour also argues that the technologies themselves are actants. As he writes in the essay, "A Collective of Humans and Nonhumans" (1999a, p. 198), "Yes, society is constructed, but not socially constructed." One of Latour's favorite examples for explaining the agency exhibited by things is that of the traffic calming device that is called a "speed-bump" in the United States and a "sleeping policeman" in the United Kingdom (a term analogous to the French *gendarme couché*). Without a doubt, the speed bump has agency: It slows down cars. Equally without doubt, this activity is the result of a function for which it was designed and built by the city's infrastructure engineers. Crucially for Latour, however, this is not an exhaustive account of its agency, and we can see this by comparing it to other techniques for slowing traffic. For example, we could hire a traffic cop to stand on the corner and waive a flag. This police officer would also slow traffic, but his agency exceeds this function in very different ways. He would demand lunch and bathroom breaks, extra pay for holidays, and a retirement pension. He would also make the neighborhood feel more heavily policed (with all the variable effects that has in different contexts).

Our asphalt speedbump would have none of those surplus agencies, but it would have different ones rooted in its own nature. In some ways it is correct to say that this agency is more physical and less social than the presence of the human cop. Traffic is slowed not with the threat of fines that would deplete the accumulation of capital in the driver's bank account, but by the threat of a jolt that would jar his or her body and wear out the shocks and struts on their car. The transition to a speed bump, however, might also have social effects, such as encouraging the cultivation of skateboarding culture. Partially this is because of the looser social restraints effected by the removal of the watchful eyes of a police officer, but, crucially, it is also because the very materiality of the asphalt bump provides a resistance that the skater can creatively engage (launching off its sides, ollieing over the top, etc.). We can now see a multiplicity of agencies at work in the speed bump. It, like the human police officer it replaces, (partially) *calls for* the cars to slow down—along with the neighbors who complained, the city council members who decided to ask the Roads Department to devise a solution, the civil engineers who designed it, the construction crew that built it, the limitation of suspension springs to absorb a shock, and so forth. But it also (partially) *calls for* the cultivation of skater culture—along with the smooth pavement, skate-board manufacturers, MTV documentaries that make skating cool, the youth culture in which MTV is possible, and so forth.

In no case does the technology act on its own, but it does have agency as we can see by comparing a world in which it does exist to one in which it does not. The result is the recognition that

> technologies incite around them a whirlwind of new worlds. Far from primarily fulfilling a purpose [by which they will legitimately be assigned an essence *later*], they *start* by exploring heterogenous universes that nothing, up to that point, could have foreseen and behind which trail new functions." (Latour, 2002, p. 250)

Far from pitting us against our technologies in a zero-sum battle for agency the way the law of autonomy does (i.e., either you generate the principle of your action from yourself alone *or* you become determined by external forces), Latour's network theory integrates us into a richer non-human world *of which* we are neither (completely) masters nor (completely) victims, but, rather, *with which* we are participants. This helps us to see the mistaken view of time common to both modernist progressives (who want us to escape the subjectifying tendencies and "anthropomorphic" illusions of "primitive" cultures by rushing toward the future) and romantic retrogressives (who want us to escape the objectifying tendencies of "technological" society by rushing toward the past). As Latour (1999a, p. 196) writes, those who attribute " 'objectivity" and 'efficiency' to modern technology and 'humanity' to low tech *poiesis* have been deeply mistaken." This is because "the adjective modern does not describe an *increased distance* between society and technology or their alienation, but a deepened *intimacy*, a more intricate mesh between the two."

CLIMATE CHANGE

I hope that this chapter will encourage those interested in existentialism to read more about the philosophy of technology with an open mind about the claim that technologies exhibit their own agency, an activity which is the ground of their essence in a manner resonant with existentialist views of humanity. For most people in our culture, however, the idea of design is so closely tied to causal determinism about identity as to be unbreakable. For this reason, it may be helpful to look away from the technological toward a case where materiality more clearly escapes human will and even opposes it. Unfortunately, we have the perfect example of this in *climate change*. What is so morally horrifying is that the destruction of living beings and ecosystems occasioned by climactic disruption (changes in land and ocean temperatures, sea level rises, reduced snowfall, increased storm intensities, changed rainfall patterns, etc.) is that they are anthropogenic. It is our fault. But what is so philosophically disorienting is that we are realizing human beings are only triggering *reactions* from a whole host of actors, systems, and relationships that are together responsible for effecting planetary climate conditions.

The term *Anthropocene* is helpful in certain ways. It focuses our attention on the fact that the climate effects we are now experiencing are brought about by human activity and that they are so massive as can only be described at the epochal level of geology—changes on the scale of millions of years and visible in the rock itself. On the other hand, however, *Anthropocene* is a misleading designation, for the nature of the climate is not *solely* a matter of human activity. We are not the only actors, and we do not know how the other actors will themselves respond. As Latour puts it (2018, p. 41), "the current disorientation derives entirely from the emergence of an actor that reacts and will continue to react to human actions." This puts everything into question; "how are we to act if the territory itself begins to participate in history, to fight back, in short to concern itself with us?"

This way of speaking would have once immediately been accused of regressing back into a prescientific, anthropomorphic way of thinking. Latour (2018) often notes that climate change plays an important role in undermining the rhetorical force at the heart of this modernist charge. As he caustically puts it, "we used to deride primitive peoples who imagined that a disorder in society, a pollution, could threaten the natural order. We no longer laugh so heartily" (p. 40). The strength of his case, however, is unrelated to the genealogical claim that the rigid dichotomy between objective facts and subjective values has always been a myth and that really (Latour, 1993, p. 46) "we have never been modern." This genealogical deconstruction of modernity is an important part of Latour's contribution, as we have seen briefly above. But here we want to focus on climate change as the result of the contemporary scientific discipline of atmospheric chemistry, which on the Earth (and this is the point) is always a subdiscipline of geobiology.

To elucidate this claim, Latour uses his formidable story-telling abilities to compare the scientist/inventors Galileo Galilei and James Lovelock and to contrast the visions of the natural world metonymically evoked by these proper names. Lovelock is one of the founders of Earth Systems Science. In particular, he was the first scientist to reveal the ways that interactions between biological, chemical, and physical processes on Earth maintain conditions hospitable to life. His path to these insights was a circuitous one. He was a part of early attempts to create apparatus for measuring the components of the atmosphere, and in 1957 he invented the first electron capture device. For his expertise in this field, he was invited by NASA in the early 1960s to be a part of the search for life on Mars. An obvious difficulty for this project is that no matter how much of the planet one searches and finds to be empty of organisms, there remains the possibility that life exists somewhere else that you have not yet looked. Lovelock, however, came to realize that one does not need to search every nook and cranny of the Red Planet to know if it harbors life, for if there are living beings on Mars, they should leave a telltale imprint on the chemical composition of its atmosphere. In particular, a global chemical equilibrium would indicate the absence of life. Thus, with spectroscopy techniques to determine the chemical composition of the planetary atmosphere, we could determine whether life exists anywhere on the planet. In the later 1970s, measurements of the Martian atmosphere made by Viking I revealed chemical processes near equilibrium, and from this lack of dynamism we learned that Mars is most likely a lifeless place.

In turn this led Lovelock to the realization of how odd the Earth is compared to the Moon, Mars, Venus, or any other of the thousands of exoplanets we have discovered. As Latour puts it, once we realize how different our atmosphere is, "the terrestrial astronomer concludes in a flash of intuition, something must maintain this situation in place, some agency that has not yet been made visible."[13] This agency is life, which on planet Earth acts on the atmosphere in complicated feedback loops that keep its chemistry from a linear path towards equilibrium—an agency that has been at work since long before humans evolved. This is the basis for what Lovelock would go on to call "Gaia Theory." Many scientists still do not like the mythical name, but the truth that living beings affect the chemistry of the atmosphere in ways that maintain harmonious conditions for living beings (in homeostatic chemical disequilibria) has now become the central organizing principle of the new discipline of Earth Systems Science.

When Galileo raised his telescope to the moon in 1609, he saw the similarity between the Earth and the superlunary world and for the first time conceived of a homogeneous universe, the Earth and the planets and the stars all being acted upon in the same way—as bodies in motion—by the same universal forces of physics. Far from the humiliating "narcissistic wound" that was postulated by Freud, this set humanity free from its provincial sublunary habitation to soar toward the limitless reaches of the universe through technoscientific control of a dead, objective reality. Galileo's discoveries were published the next year in *The Starry Messenger*, the same year that the earth reached a local CO_2 trough effected by the regrowth of New World forests (and their function as a carbon sink) that occurred due to the genocidal effects of European colonization on Indigenous Americans who had been managing the landscape with fire and other techniques for thousands of years. The year 1610 thus marks the conjunction of a mercantilist political economy and a philosophical outlook rooted in the orientation toward the world as material to be exploited.[14]

Perhaps Lovelock's trip to Pasadena in 1961 and the turn in the philosophy of science it occasioned, along with the rising ecological consciousness and postcolonialism of that decade, will mark a turn of similar epochal significance. In this new register (Latour, 2015, pp. 78–79),

> The blue planet suddenly looks like a long string of historical *events*, random, specific, and contingent events, as though it were the temporary … *result* of geohistory. It is as though, three and a half centuries later, Lovelock had taken into account certain features of that same Earth that Galileo *could* not take into account if he were going to consider it simply as a body in free fall amidst all the others: its color, its odor, its surface, its texture, its genesis, its aging, perhaps its death, this thin film within which we live, in short, its behavior, in addition to its movement.

This returns us to the central aspects of reality with which we began, contingency, finitude/historicity, and *haecceitas*, applied now to the living ecosystems of Earth. This is not a coincidence, for Latour shares the commitment to thinking existence prior to essence that marks the existentialist project. Returning to this point helps complete my thesis by showing how Latour has given us an alternative to 20th century existentialism, and it also helps avoid a misunderstanding that has made Lovelock's "Gaia theory" so hard for many to accept. When Latour attributes agency to things, he includes the existentialist emphasis on the adventure of temporality, but he does not link this to consciousness or will. He is not suggesting some sort of panpsychism by which the planet Earth is self-conscious or chooses its own path, but we should not think that these are the only forms of agency.

Like for Sartre and other recent existentialists, this commitment to existence is rooted in the conviction that for a thing to have meaning it must have agency, and that there is no agency when the thing's being is strictly determined by the causes that gave rise to it. For an existentialist, this is why a reductive account of efficient causation, or an account rooted in an appeal to a universal essence is equally unsatisfactory. Latour argues that either of these forms of reductivism fall prey to the same rationalist mistake. The mistake is to believe that

> the concatenation of causes and effects ... must not lead to any dramatic effects, precisely because—and herein lies its beauty—the consequences are *already there* in the *cause* [whether efficient or formal]: there is no suspense, nothing to wait for, no sudden transformations, no metamorphosis, no ambiguity. Time passes *from the past toward the present*. In these stories (which are in fact *not* stories), then, nothing happens, in any case no *adventure*. (Latour, 2001, p. 53 [emphasis original])

Contrary to Sartre and others, however, Latour wants to overcome this atemporal rationalism not by abandoning the sciences. In fact, Latour (2015) argues that it is by giving a proper account of the actual practice of the acquisition of scientific knowledge that we can overcome this rationalist tendency in our philosophy of science and, indeed, in the humanities as well. As he argues, "what makes scientific reports so propitious for studying the *multiple character of agency* is that the character of agents mobilized cannot be described except through the *actions* by means of which they have been pinned down." For a character in a novel, he says (p. 56), "you can act as though you started from the essence to infer the properties." This is because through familiarization "we invert the order of things, and we get in the habit of starting from the name to deduce or summarize what it does." Going back to the process of discovery, however, we recover the proper order of knowing: specifically, "the competences of these agents— that is what they are—are defined only through their performances."

In a work of this length, I do not have the space to articulate more fully Latour's philosophy of science by which he supports this claim that ontology and epistemology are so much more closely intertwined than modern philosophy allows.[15] However, following Latour's philosophy as described in this chapter, the connections between Latour's philosophy and existential philosophy should already be emerging. Like all existentialists, Latour suggests that the meaning of the world is not pre-given, but emerges from creative agency, for what things *are* is the result of what they have *become* through what they *do*. There are significant differences as well, however, by which Latour expands our understanding of existentialism. Most importantly, rather than disconnecting us from the natural world, existentialism can reveal our interrelation with all the myriad forms of agency in the physical universe and, in particular, within the web of life on Earth.

Further, *haecceitas* remains a central category, but it will no longer so easily fall into individualism and even atomism. Each being is unique, based on its particular history, but this oneness is not an absolute unity. Rather, each thing is a gathering of characteristic ways of relating to other sources of agency. Thus, this form of existentialism will be less concerned with authenticity, and this form of existentialism's understanding of agency will not be so quickly reduced to political categories of autonomy.

The intention of this chapter has been to introduce Latour as a way of teaching existentialism to students motivated by ecological concerns and the desire for a more intimate connection to materiality. It is now the task of these students, themselves, to cultivate the more substantive implications for the political and personal, and also the social, technological, ecological, and material realms that we inhabit and share with all the others.

REFERENCES

Bijker, T., & Pinch, W. (1984). The social construction of facts and artefacts. *Social Studies of Science, 14*(3), 399–441.

Bradley, D. (2021). The fruit of the vine. In *Satya Nilayam: Chennai Journal of Intercultural Philosophy, 32*. https://religioustech.org/wp-content/uploads/2021/05/Bradley-The-Fruit-of-the-Vine-2.pdf

Latour, B. (1993). *We have never been modern* (Catherine Porter, Trans.). Harvard Press.

Latour, B. (1998). How to be iconophilic in art, science, and religion? In C. Jones & P. Galison (Eds.), *Picturing science producing art* (pp. 418–440). Routledge.

Latour, B. (1999). *Pandora's hope*. Harvard Press.

Latour, B. (1999). Thou shall not take the Lord's name in vain: Being a sort of sermon in sociology of religion. *Res, 39*, 215–234. https://spire.sciencespo.fr/hdl:/2441/5l6uh8ogmqildh09h61i5ishk/resources/79-res-sermon.pdf

Latour, B. (2002). Morality and technology: The end of the means. *Theory, Culture & Society, 19*(5/6), 247–260.

Latour, B. (2005). Thou shalt not freeze frame. In J. D. Proctor (Ed), *Science, religion, and the human experience*. Oxford University Press.

Latour, B. (2007). *Reassembling the social: An introduction to actor-network-theory.* Oxford Press.

Latour, B. (2015). *Facing Gaia.* Polity Press

Latour, B. (2018). *Down to earth.* Polity Press.

Rand, A. (1943). *The fountainhead.* Bobbs Merrill.

Rand, A. (1957). *Atlas shrugged.* Random House.

Sartre. J. (1956). Existentialism is a humanism. In W. Kaufman (Ed.), *Existentialism from Dostoyevsky to Sartre* (pp. 1–27). Meridian. (Original work published 1946)

Sartre, J. (1969). *Nausea* (Lloyd Alexander, Trans.). New Directions Paperbook.

Sartre, J. (2022). *Critique of dialectical reason: The complete edition* (Quintin Hoare & Alan Sheridan-Smith, Trans.). Verso.

NOTES

1. Sartre, "Existentialism is a Humanism" p. 300.
2. *Reassembling the Social*, p. 77.
3. *Haecceitas* is a Latin term made famous by Duns Scotus to refer not only to a thing's individuality, but to that which individuates it as an individual. Thus, *haecceity* has an ontological and not only epistemological significance. Further, Aristotle understood intelligibility to require concepts that differentiate between different *kinds* of things. Thus, a philosophy inclined towards *haecceitas* will be attuned to the limits of conceptual forms of understanding. For an example of the way this late medieval philosophical orientation was taken up into existentialism, see the opening lines of Nietzsche's *Ecce Homo* (p. 1), *"Seeing that before long I must confront humanity with the most difficult demand ever made of it, it seems indispensable to me to say who I am.... Hear me! For I am such and such a person. Above all, do not mistake me for someone else."* "Contingency" refers to the claim that things are not necessary, but could always have been different. "Finitude" is a related term that refers to the character of things as situated within a temporal and finite horizon of meaning that will, sooner or later, collapse. Thus, finitude means that things will never be able to show themselves in an absolute way or a fully intelligible way. There is perhaps no more evocative account of these realities than the experiences Sartre recounts in *Nausea.*
4. Sartre, himself, sees these problems and moves toward a more Marxian philosophy later in life. See (Sartre 2004, 2022) *Critique of Dialectical Reason* (Vols. I and II).
5. For a characteristic example of each of these three movements, see (I) Arne Næss, (1973). "The shallow and the deep, long-range ecology movement: a summary." *Inquiry: An Interdisciplinary Journal of Philosophy.* 16(1–4): 95–100; (II) Fredric Jameson, *Postmodernism, or, the Cultural Logic of Late Capitalism. Duke University Press. 1991; (III)* Julia Kristeva, *Desire in Language: A Semiotic Approach to Literature and Art*, Columbia University Press, 1980.
6. See Latour (2005) *Reassembling the social: An introduction to actor-network-theory.* Oxford University Press. See also the way this has been developed for example in literary criticism: Rita Felski (2015). *The Limits of Critique.* University of Chicago Press and in studies of design: Albena Yaneva (2009).

Making the social hold: Towards an actor-network theory of design. *Design and Culture*, *1*(3), 273–288.

7. For Ibn Sina's distinction between essence and existence, see Ibn Sina, *Book of Healing*, I, 5, 31, 1–9. For a hermeneutic reading of the theological motivation for this philosophical claim, see Etin Anwar, "Ibn Sīnā's Philosophical Theology of Love: A Study of the Risālah fī al-'Ishq (2003)." *Islamic Studies*, *42(2)*, 331–345.
8. See for example, G. M. Hopkins (1985), "As Kingfishers Catch Fire," and Thomas Merton (2007), *New Seeds of Contemplation*.
9. As an example of radically different thinkers who nonetheless share this common view of the origin of modernity in the Abrahamic tradition see Gilles Deleuze (1994), *Difference and repetition*, Trans. by Paul Patton, p. 39 and Catherine Pickstock (2005) "Duns Scotus: His historical and contemporary significance." *Modern Theology*, *21*(4).
10. Certainly, this means to the Duns Scotus and the Franciscans of the 14th century, but also to the earlier Muslim philosophers that made their work possible.
11. Due to space constraints and the fact that I have developed the potential of this genealogy for intercultural dialogue more fully in a companion article (Bradley, 2021) this fourth important element of Latour's thought will not be developed more fully here.
12. For example see Andrew Feenberg (1991), *Critical theory of technology*. Oxford University Press.
13. *Gaia*, 78.
14. See Antonio (1613), *A short treatise on the wealth and poverty of nations* and Kyle Whyte (2017). "Our Ancestors' Dystopia Now: Indigenous conservation and the Anthropocene" In Ursula K. Heise, Jon Christensen, & Michelle Niemann (Eds.), *The routledge companion to the environmental humanities*. Taylor and Francis. pp. 206–215.
15. Latour's *Pandora's Hope* (1999), Chapters 4 and 5 are a good place to start.

CHAPTER 10

TEACHING IS ... OTHER PEOPLE

Existential Reflections on Coteaching Phenomenology With Undergraduate Students

Lauren Manton, Brigid Flaherty, Cecelia Little, and Peter Costello
Providence College

ABSTRACT

In this chapter, we create an account of coteaching an upper-level philosophy course (phenomenology) that also works to illustrate what we think are existential revisions to the practice of pedagogy. We connect phenomenological concepts such as pairing, intersubjectivity, and intercorporeality found in canonical authors such as Edmund Husserl, Maurice Merleau-Ponty, and Jacques Derrida with a rich description of student and professorial lived experience. We do so in order to argue that the classroom ought to be (and is) its own laboratory, that students teach the teacher as much as the teacher does the students, and that far from "watering down" education by means of coteaching, education is enriched and made more significant and elegant by having undergraduates take on pedagogical responsibilities. Our experience of coteaching has lead overall to increased mediation of pedagogical structures and thereby to a deeper understanding and more equitable opportunities for all involved. The point, in short, of this chapter is that coteaching allows greater room for learning to become a communally-centered continuum of reflection.

Problematizing the Profession of Teaching From an Existential Perspective, pp. 189–206
Copyright © 2022 by Information Age Publishing
www.infoagepub.com

What follows is a piece cowritten by Peter Costello, a Professor of philosophy, and three of our senior undergraduate philosophy majors, Lauren M., Brigid F., and Cecelia L. Each of these students took our phenomenology course (PHL 430) with me during the prior academic year. The following year (Brigid and Lauren in Spring 2015, Cecelia in Spring 2021) I invited them to coteach the course with me while taking an independent study focused on the pedagogy that we would develop for that course. After they accepted my invitation, we worked together on revising the syllabus, on implementing techniques for leading small group discussions, on writing and delivering some large-group presentations, and on developing principles and goals for the practice of commenting on student drafts and papers.

As part of her independent study, each student agreed to write a final reflection on the course texts and her own experience. After sharing their own final reflections, we compiled the following account together. We believe this account to be both a defense of the practice of teaching philosophy together and a meditation on certain themes in phenomenology and existentialism—most notably, the themes of community and self-perception. We hope that this reflection on form and substance, or method and content, can persuade others to adopt similar pedagogical practices.

SITUATING THE ARGUMENT WITHIN
EDUCATION BROADLY CONSTRUED

Implicit in this descriptive, qualitative account of our experience is this twofold assumption: namely, that coteaching philosophy courses with undergraduates *works* and that it works in two ways: first, to increase each undergraduate student's engagement (both he who takes the course and she who coteaches it); and, second, to shift philosophy as a discipline, specifically, from a process of an undergraduate's submission to an expert to a process of democratic cocreation with the instructor(s).

Such a twofold assumption is new, perhaps, to the discipline and practice of philosophy in the contemporary academy. We would like to note, however, that coteaching is rooted in the earliest practice of philosophy, namely, in the Socratic gathering of other people, including those deemed least likely to contribute, as in the Plato's *Meno* (2002), in the pursuit of truth. Even the slave in the *Meno*, even the priestess of Apollo in her one word answer to Chairephon in Plato's *Apology* (2002), and even Thrasymachus (perhaps especially Thrasymachus, we might say) in Plato's *Republic* (1992) are indispensable to the movement toward the Good that each Platonic dialogue recounts and solicits.[1]

Furthermore, coteaching is not at all new to disciplines that border on philosophy, such as education or global studies. In recent scholarship on education theory, colleagues such as W. Corry Larson and Abigail J. Goebel in "Putting Theory Into Practice: A Professional Development School/University Co-Teaching Project" (2008) detail how coteaching with undergraduate education majors allows for those students to develop "a greater confidence in their ability to handle classroom management situations over the course of the course" (p. 57) and to realize an increase in their "overall sense of efficacy" (p. 58). We grant that coteaching *in the primary or secondary schools* with undergraduates is different from coteaching with undergraduates in higher education courses. However, it is important to note with Larson and Goebel, and others such as Carol A. Woodburn, who in "Students as Coteachers in an Urban High School Mathematics Class" (2010), discusses the practice of coteaching in high school math classes, how efficacy increases when undergraduate students are allowed to occupy an equal space with professors.

In addition, in Global Studies, Nicholas Longo advocates in "Deliberative Pedagogy in the Community: Connecting Deliberative Dialogue, Community Engagement, and Democratic Education" (2013) for what he calls "deliberative pedagogy," a way of teaching that can "go beyond a simple teacher–learner dichotomy by fully incorporating the ecology of educational opportunities available to students" (p. 13). Our experience in coteaching the phenomenology course therefore seems to us the next logical step in what Longo argues is a movement toward "a new framework for teaching and learning, what might be termed 'collaborative engagement'" (p. 14).

However, even given the placement of our practice within a certain set of conversations regarding teaching and learning, there are doubtless many people who will view undergraduate philosophy courses as a "bridge too far" to take coteaching. What can an undergraduate really learn in one course that would allow her to function in a parallel, collaborative way with a professor who has studied this very difficult material for longer than she has been alive? This, it would seem, is the challenge our research faces: not that it is novel but that it upsets a discipline that has largely been critical of such theories as those laid out by Paolo Freire in *Pedagogy of the Oppressed* (1972) concerning a pedagogy that is, if not deliberative, then surely liberating. There is just too much at stake, some might argue, to allow philosophy to be replaced by a community of interested amateurs.

It is this last prejudice that we would most like to surmount. And this will be no easy task. Even the practice of coteaching *with another professor* encounters many obstacles, as Beach, Henderson, and Famiano observe in "Co-Teaching as a Faculty Development Model" (2007): "a major obstacle to faculty development aimed at bringing about fundamental change is that instructors attempting to change traditional practices are acculturated into and surrounded by a culture that reflects their current practices" (p. 200). And even advocates of coteaching as a faculty practice, such as Beach, Henderson, and Famiano are, themselves are not yet at the point of collaboration with undergraduates. Rather, students are often a worry, not a resource—"students often pose another barrier to teaching change by resisting new instructional strategies" (p. 200).

In what follows, however, we stand united together in our advocacy for this practice. We argue not only for the practice of coteaching with undergraduates but for the way the very *content* of phenomenology (and its related area, existentialism) seems to require that we fashion our methodology for pedagogy as collaborative.

But let us assume that our experience was meaningful, and that it was rooted in the texts themselves. Even if our readers concede the point and smile at us condescendingly—that is, even if we are successful in this content-based argument, we are bound to be assailed by this content-based conclusion: that is, coteaching may well work in phenomenology or existentialism courses, but not in other branches or courses in philosophy. Particularly by colleagues who teach Analytic philosophy, we may hear it said that only something so careless and vague as poetry could ever be taught communally. Perhaps Continental thought, but surely not Popper or Searle. Maybe Heidegger but never Quine.

If the argument reaches this point, however, I think that all we can offer to challenge this last claim are two things: First, we have demonstrated quite well, we think, that in at least one branch of philosophy not only is the method of coteaching with undergraduates successful anecdotally, but it also seems to be sanctioned within the content of that branch itself. And second, the ones who inaugurate some new, successful practice are not responsible for its development in other areas. Those who are specialists in Quine, therefore, have their own work to do to teach with undergraduates in helpful ways. Our method and experiences are accounted for below and, in addition, within the results of our classroom evaluation forms. We stand by them.

EXISTENTIAL REDEFINITION OF TEACHING AND LEARNING

One of Jean-Paul Sartre's most famous lines comes from his play *No Exit* in which one of three characters trapped in a hellish room proclaims that "Hell is—other people" (1989, p. 45) It is not hell because of heat or guilt. It is hell because, even in guilt, we seek to justify ourselves to, to dominate, to fascinate, or to hide behind others. Our lives, Sartre seems to imply, whether in this world or the next, are a struggle for mutual recognition.

And our failure to achieve that mutual recognition is what prevents forgiveness of one another, what subverts the alleviation of guilt, and what curtails the education of our perceptions.

For Sartre, it may seem that the impossibility of mutual recognition situates us within hell both now and forever. However, we take the play to emphasize that it is only with an always imperfect, always-out-of-reach mutual recognition that we can come to see the situation of human existence as embedded within a shared, finite world. An imperfect recognition is still hopeful, still a reckoning with a shared world that our freedom can always take up and remake. We could leave hell with more educated perceptions of each other, Sartre seems to say. And so, the play has a moral—the embrace of coteaching as the motor toward mutual recognition here and now.

This chapter, although about coteaching a phenomenology course, involves an existential redefinition of teaching in a way that resonates with Sartre's play. Teaching is not just *for* others. It is not just *about* others and their learning. Teaching is *made up of* others. Teaching is the attempt to make together the fabric of mutual recognition within which we attempt to clothe ourselves. Teaching is, thus, not hell. Teaching is possibility, but it is a possibility that must be taken up together and lived actively and responsively, or else teaching may very well transform itself and those who learn within it into a hellish period within a system of force and punishment.

Paolo Freire in *Pedagogy of the Oppressed* (1972) leads one to see both the existential and phenomenological roots and potential of such a redefinition of teaching and learning. Giving up the "banking model" of education for a "problem-posing" method, Freire insists that the way teaching and learning is usually performed is an existential contradiction. As teachers and students, we contradict ourselves, we live *against* ourselves. We alienate each other: "the students, alienated like the slave in the Hegelian dialectic, accept their ignorance as justifying the teacher's existence—but, unlike the slave, they never discover that they educate the teacher" (p. 59). In a sense, then, students are worse off than slaves, because even slaves can see that the master depends on them. The student? She may "never discover" her role. What then can we do?

Education can have a liberating effect, Freire (1972) says, if it is focused on students as learners and on the reconciliation of learning with teaching. Instead of living against one another, we can connect and live *with* one another in learning as a shared process: "education must begin with the solution of the teacher-student contradiction, by reconciling the poles of the contradiction so that both are simultaneously teachers *and* students" (p. 59).

This reconciliation allows education to become "the practice of freedom" (Freire, 1972, p. 69), a dialogue about how life is and can be lived in relationship to the world and to one another. This dialogue is a creation, an act of naming and describing experience that is not complete if some simply take in what others say. Instead,

> to exist, humanly, is to *name* the world, to change it. Once named, the world in turn reappears to the namers as a problem and requires of them a new *naming*. Men are not built in silence, but in word, in work, in action-reflection. (p. 76)

Teaching and learning, then, involve ongoing, productive descriptions of experience. It is a phenomenology that orients itself toward teachers and students together who take their experience as something that matters to them and shifts it toward the world where that experience can be further taken up, shaped, surpassed, and remembered.

Freire's vision implies that what occurs in a book, or in a classroom, is not a static given. There is no first or final account of a work of philosophy or of a classroom project. Restating or explaining a claim of Husserl or Heidegger must itself be placed along a continuum of responses, within a dialogue that makes room for new acts of discussion and naming. There may be formalist structures discovered, but these, too, are dependent on all of us in order to make them matter to us and to the world.

Since Freire (1972), a number of other scholars have also tied existentialism and phenomenological discussions of mutual recognition to higher education. Notably absent, I find, however, is Freire's emphasis on the shared overcoming of the contradiction between teacher and students. Here are three examples:

Alison Phipps and Ronald Barnett, in "Academic Hospitality" (2007), engage in a post-existential and post-phenomenological discussion of hospitality in the writings of Derrida and Ricoeur. They take the charge of higher education to be a welcoming, one that is complex and requiring dialogue. However, Phipps and Barnett still presuppose hospitality as mainly occurring mainly between colleagues in the corridor. Less present for them is the idea that college professors need to promote a hospitality toward students and to challenge the hierarchical presentation of education.

Ada S. Jaarsma, Kyle Kinaschuck and Lin Xing, in "Kierkegaard, Despair, and the Possibility of Education: Teaching Existentialism Existentially" (2016), go further and coauthor an intriguing paper together on the teaching of existentialism courses. As a professor and as undergraduates reflecting together, they are able to describe teaching in a rich, complex manner. This is as it should be. After all, who could better describe the successes and failures of teaching than the students who endure it? They successfully articulate what makes the teaching of existentialism different— namely, it prepares undergraduates for resistance. Yet, for all their insights, it does not seem that, for Xing, Kinaschuck, and Jaarsma, students could be thought to move into the role of teachers within the classroom—students, they presume, can only "teach" outside of the class by resisting and challenging the necessity and inevitability of typical pedagogical structures, such as grading, and so forth.

Denise Claire Batchelor, in "Vulnerable Voices" (2006), a paper on existentialism and education which comes close to Freire's view, acknowledges the very problem of alienation and suppression (including self-suppression) among students in higher education. She also posits that it is up to those who teach within the academy to think creatively and to empower students. But she does not advocate coteaching as a way to empower students to speak from and to listen to their peers. She does not clearly and consistently advocate for the professor to become more vulnerable voluntarily in order to promote greater communities of care.

As we continue in this chapter, I would argue that we should take existentialism to its logical conclusion. We engage in coteaching precisely in order to be hospitable to each other and to the texts, to resist the overarching structures of higher education that focus on success and benchmarks, and to recognize and empower the vulnerable. It is, finally, in order to promote the *enactment* of phenomenological description and the pursuit of existential freedom that we engage in this practice.

SUMMARY OF THE SEMESTER

Though their roles in our phenomenology course were obviously similar in structure to the traditional role of teaching assistants or graduate assistants within a graduate program in philosophy, I believe that Brigid's, Lauren,'s and Cecelia's roles were more effective than those graduate-level roles often are. Our regular reflection, our planning, and our discussions about what might work better on a given day worked to ensure that. In addition, I would argue that their roles were certainly more complex, or at least more layered, than my own role as a graduate teaching assistant at a State University was.

On the one hand, Lauren, Brigid, and Cecelia were present (though not enrolled) as undergraduate students in the phenomenology course itself and were enrolled in an independent study course with me during the semester they were coteaching. In the independent study, they were evaluated by me and had to answer to what I saw as the demands of the course we were coteaching. Brigid and Lauren were thus at times in the typical position of the student, able to learn from a professor and responsible for reading and writing reflections on the material as directed by that professor.

On the other hand, Cecelia, Brigid, and Lauren were also teachers. Even though I required that we routinely meet before and after we had taught that day in order to plan and reflect on what happened in the classroom, they were equals in terms of how those conversations went. In fact, outside of the actual act of grading the students in the phenomenology course, an act which I alone performed as the instructor of record for the course, Brigid and Lauren were empowered to alter or shift any of the components of the class as they saw fit. They had read and written on these texts in the previous academic year. As they reread and reconsidered these texts, they were permitted (actually, encouraged) to develop their skills at interpretation and at communicating their interpretations to others.

By them occupying these two roles, student and teacher, I believe that they made the course a resounding success for the other students and for me as well. Cecelia, Lauren, and Brigid managed to connect their role as student and their role as teacher in such a way as to motivate and inspire other students in the course to participate, to read, and to write effectively. In addition, they have inspired me to continue the practice of coteaching with undergraduates at the level of an introductory course.

In what remains of this chapter, we would like to share some reflections on the method and content of our course. In these next sections, we hope to highlight what it means to offer undergraduates this coteaching opportunity and what phenomenological insights might mean when the act of coteaching becomes one of the texts on which all of us can reflect while also reading primary texts by Husserl, Merleau-Ponty, Kant, and Derrida.

METHOD

In this section, Lauren communicates some important takeaways from coteaching. She reflects on her role and on the way the class was a text that taught her phenomenological insights. She primarily focuses on the way in which coteaching can enable the difference, or the gap, between students and instructors to become manageable and even productive for the purposes of reading and writing about the texts we presented.

Lauren M.

Going into coinstructing phenomenology, I thought I needed to demand of myself that I display a mastery of the philosophers uncharacteristic of an undergraduate student—a mastery proper to a philosophy PhD. I knew that I would feel like a failure if I was given the position of "instructor" of a 400-level philosophy course and then I performed at a level far below every professor that I had ever encountered. What I learned from coin-structing an undergraduate course as an undergraduate, though, is that an instructor's presenting herself to the class as really no better than they are, perhaps quite unlike the strategy of the standard professor, is the best way to promote student learning.

A 400-level philosophy course, phenomenology nonetheless, is bound to intimidate the majority of a class of non-majors with little to no expo-sure to philosophy. The instructor of such a course ought to minimize its formidability where she can. In such a course that uses the traditional teaching method—a PhD standing at the front of the room and giving well-constructed lectures packed with the wealth of knowledge that he has attained from years of study—there is a huge gap between teacher and student that establishes the student as inferior.

I am in the minority of students who use this insurmountable gap to push myself to be as close to perfect as I can, as close to the level of the PhD as I can. This is not to say that other students do not push themselves. Rather, many students push themselves when confronted by professors. But a gap so great cannot help but leave most students with the nagging thought that they cannot ever really "get" the material, as a PhD does, so they ought not to try very hard. When the one person in the room who really "gets" the material is someone whom none of the students can see herself becoming, none of the students will think that she could ever really "get" the material.

The best way to structure a course like our phenomenology course is thus to establish a gap between teacher and student great enough to get the student to strive toward her full potential but small enough to allow her to see the teacher as embodying her own potential. Finding the appropriate gap is finding the "sweet spot" between two inappropriate extremes.

The first extreme I have already postulated as problematic and am seek-ing to replace: the traditional lecture from a single PhD, the creator of the huge gap. The second is having undergraduate students take over the entire instructional role of the undergraduate course, almost, if not entirely, closing the gap. Anyone can foresee problems with maintaining academic accuracy and rigor in a college class taught solely by undergraduate stu-dents. Furthermore, without some gap, the students will not be able to push themselves anywhere near their full potential.

Should we have been coinstructors then? My answer is yes. For some students, even empowering words from a PhD who is sensitive to the gap between students and professor are not effective enough to adequately shrink the gap. Some students still cannot manage to see a seasoned PhD as embodying their own potential.

What we did in terms of our coteaching with Dr. Costello was to allow the maximum academic rigor to be preserved (which is in keeping with the traditional model of the PhD serving as the primary instructor of the course), but also to make the gap as manageable as possible with our own empowered copresence. When a student cannot manage to see the PhD as embodying her own potential, she can surely see another undergraduate student as someone whom she herself can become after working hard in this one course.

One student, a nonmajor, from our class explained to us at our office hours how having undergraduate coteachers has empowered her to take on the daunting task of trying to understand works by Husserl, Kant, Derrida, and Merleau-Ponty on her own. Once the undergraduate student-teachers worked with the students in small groups and revealed just how challenging the readings were even for them, she realized that there was nothing wrong with her own struggling. She then saw the undergraduate student-teachers as just like her, as what she could become if she worked hard enough in the course. Only then could she overcome the feeling of being insurmountably inferior and so strive toward her full potential with nothing holding her back.

This student's experience in phenomenology should be every student's experience. Every student should see her potential as a learner and be able to confidently push herself toward it. An upper-division course that is open to students with minimal exposure to philosophy is the type of course with the biggest gap between students and teacher. The very structure of such a course can prevent students from excelling. Such a course thus needs to be strategically structured so as to create the perfect gap: the gap large enough to push students to grow, but small enough to allow students to see in the first place that the instructor(s) are embodying the great potential that they themselves can grow into. The way to achieve this ideal gap is for the instructors to present themselves to the students as just like them—as no better, just more experienced. Only then can a student believe that she can truly "get" the material, and only then will she start trying to.

CONTENT

In this section, Brigid communicates some important takeaways from coteaching in terms of the themes we discussed and the books that we read. Her reflections are specific meditations on material from works by Merleau-Ponty and Derrida in reference to her own placement as a teacher in the classroom. She articulates what teaching means in terms of a network of relationships, of self-perceptions, and of readings.

Brigid F.

In his essay *The Child's Relations with Others* (1964), Merleau-Ponty discusses the development of a child's awareness of herself through her awareness and relationship with others. One topic he discusses that has glued itself to my teaching experience is the idea of placement. A child is able to understand the placement of others in the world before she has fully placed herself. Merleau-Ponty describes the process via the instrumentation of a mirror: it is not until the child sees a person behind her in the mirror who gestures towards her reflection in it as if it were the actual space of her body that she can place herself as the thing which reflects the image into the mirror in front of her.

In my experience, not only could I not understand myself as a teacher until someone else placed me in a classroom full of students willing to participate in this educative experience, but I also could not understand myself until the students gave me the same help that the adult gave to the child in Merleau-Ponty's example. Our students pointed to me as a teacher so that I could know myself as a teacher.

Although the experience of understanding myself as a teacher was a semester-long process (and I hope one that will continue to develop for as long as I teach), a defining moment came when I gave my first short presentation to the class. The topic was Jacques Derrida's discussion of the *parergon* in *Truth in Painting* (1987). Perhaps it was so defining because it forced me to reflect on the dynamics of a classroom. What is the *ergon* in a class? There could be many answers: the subject, the professor, or the collection of students. The more substantive question for me, however, is: what is the *parergon* of a class, and where does it end?

Throughout the semester, the class's ability to extend beyond the confines of the subject matter led me to see the class and its parts (subject-matter, professor, students, location on campus and place in time) as a parergonal structure that enabled me to understand myself as "teacher." In order to explain this, we must discuss Derrida's (1987) *parergon*.

Derrida (1987) defines the *ergon* simply as the "principle subject" (p. 54), which determines the *parergon* to be that which is not the principle subject, or that which "[acts] alongside, right up against the work" (p. 54). Therefore, the *parergon* is, on the one hand, a secondary element in comparison to the subject, and, on the other hand, a necessary accompaniment that enables the *ergon* to be the main subject. The *parergon*, "comes against, beside, and in addition to the *ergon*, the work done [fait], the fact [le fait], the work, but it does not fall to one side, it touches and cooperates within the operation, from a certain outside" (p. 54) so that, through the act of framing, the *parergon* may focus the viewer's attention on the *ergon* itself. Although the *parergon* seems to be a supplementary tool that enables the *ergon* to stand as the premier object, Derrida will continue his argument to prove that one cannot simply draw the boundary that separates *ergon* and *parergon*. The *parergon* is complementary to the *ergon* because the two fuse together to form one object that is capable of focusing and refocusing the observer so that she may be drawn towards the *ergon* through the framing powers of the *parergon*.

So how does the relationship between the *parergon* and the *ergon* relate to the dynamic of a classroom? What is the subject in the classroom that must be framed so that observers are pulled towards it? I argue that the subject is learning itself and that the parergonal structure that surrounds it is the subject matter, the students, the professor, and all other aspects that one can include in a class. The ergon is the act of learning, an active experience that is dynamic by nature so that it may be framed by other types of actions and actors.

Somehow, I was placed as a teacher in this dynamic *ergon* that I call the act of learning. I was placed because of the *parergon* that both framed my experience and forced me to focus on the *ergon*, learning, by pointing (the function of a frame) to the different relationships connected to the act of learning. I came to be placed by recognizing the interplay between *ergon* and *parergon*.

One cannot learn without forming a relationship: with the text, with the students, and with the professor. The relationship between the subject and the *parergon* is indispensable and leads to a relationship with the *ergon* itself. I was pulled towards the texts—each word of Derrida, Husserl, and Merleau-Ponty led me to desire to understand the subject of phenomenology. I was pulled towards the students. In 20 different ways, 20 students reached out to me for support. Whether it was an e-mail at 10:30 P.M. to meet for five minutes to relieve the anxiety of an English major who thought she had never produced the level of analysis necessary for understanding Merleau-Ponty (she had) or a 9:00 A.M. coffee on a Saturday morning with a marketing major who had a talent for relating the experiences described by Husserl to the relationships she had with random people she came across in the library.

Each relationship led me to a new way of understanding. Through the learning of the twenty students in our class, I came to learn new things about the philosophers that we read. I was pulled towards the professor, who took my snarky, self-deprecating humor as a challenge to prove to the class that we all knew things and could bring those small pieces of knowledge into the classroom in order that we may weave them together to create a collaborative learning experience. I was pulled towards Lauren, the other student who was my teaching partner, who challenged me to think in different ways about passages I had read before and whose company I enjoyed over lunch on Thursdays before our weekly class. All of these people and objects pulled me towards themselves, and in doing so, pointed me towards the activity of learning, the *ergon*.

In the action of being pulled towards learning, I was pointed towards my place as "teacher." Through this experience, I was able to come to understand myself in that role. Perhaps the most beautiful part is that I understood myself as a teacher in the act of learning, not in the act of teaching. Yes, I taught twenty students this semester—you can ask them or ask me, and you'll get the same answer. In this act, though, I learned that my placement as a teacher is not a rigid place, it changes dependent on the class, on the students, on the texts. To borrow the language of Derrida (1987) once more, I am grateful that my placement as a teacher is fluid, since "this here, this place is announced as a place deprived of a place" (p. 38). The *ergon* depends on the *parergonal* structure that surrounds it. Learning is not dependent on a geographical location. Learning is experiential. It is phenomenological. It is dependent on the people and on the subject. Learning is given, and the parergonal frame is the source of that givenness, pulling us towards itself and placing us so that we may come to understand it and ourselves.

WORK AS SELF-REFLECTION

In this section, Cecelia responds to the particular tasks she took on as a coteacher. And she uses Husserl and her own reflection to further her own goal to become a college professor. She talks a great deal about her role as commenter and note-taker, which puts her in dialogue with other students.

Cecelia L.

Reading the phenomenology students' first papers ... was a new experience for me, because I was able to not only see where numerous students were struggling with a particular topic but also to see the depth of understanding that most students already had regarding our first few topics. I, too, could more easily see where I may have needed to explain my own points made in class further, and I was able to learn thus from the students' writing.

I was both delighted and surprised, too, to notice a time or two that a student used a phrase or definition that I found rather apt and insightful after only attending a few classes, only to remember that Dr. Costello or even I had offered that exact phrase or particular wording to the students. Along the same lines, I was very excited to see that some students used the phrasing of other students (which I was able to notice by having taken notes for each class) to aid in their understanding, and to improve upon their own past comments.

Regarding the more technical and peripheral parts of class, I appreciated the fairly set model of the class, both as a student and coteacher, and I know that many of the students of the past two semesters did as well. Knowing what to expect from class time, especially in a class that occurs once a week, left out any guessing or negative anticipation, allowing students and professor alike to focus on and work through constructive class time, for which everyone could much more easily have been prepared.

Having a student (myself) write notes for each class seemed to be beneficial, as students (again, like myself!) who are in the habit of writing down everything they can, may have been afforded the opportunity to focus a bit more on the intricacies of our class conversations. The notes and "whiteboard discussions," too, proved beneficial for more visual learners, as the students could see the progression ... visibly through our material, and provided a permanent reference of those movements. I had a few students tell me that they referred to the notes posted several times throughout the semester, to fill in gaps in their understanding, just as some students might by referring to others' electronic posts on our learning platform and class notes.

Regarding the benefits of the weekly summaries the students wrote periodically throughout the semester, I suggested that, before class began, we encourage the students to attempt to answer a question that the readings had raised for them. I have seen this done in other classes, and generally implement the same practice where I can, as I have found it helpful to not only evaluate my own understanding, and helpful in writing valuably and substantively on nearly any subject. Summarizing is crucial to developing a complex and deep understanding of any text, especially those within philosophy, and I found that my own summaries, even of difficult material, gradually become more accurate and intricate throughout that first semester. Similarly, I saw the same benefits in my practice of writing several of the weekly review-introductions, by which I reviewed my own notes from the previous week, using those to refer back to portions of the text.

Each week, I tried to not only summarize the previous, but add to our previous discussions using the knowledge and understanding I already had the advantage of having from the previous semester. I, too, was able to find gaps in my own understanding through this process, and several times dove deeper into the texts than I had last semester, in efforts to prepare myself for further student questions, and to fill in those same gaps potentially riddling these students' understanding as well.

I noticed at one point, almost midway through the semester, that I came into phenomenology the second time with the belief that any holes or gaps in my understanding would equate to similar gaps in other students' understandings. This belief originated from my past experiences of having teachers and professors either laugh off or dismiss questions they could not answer, often failing to recognize that a second pair of eyes (even those of a student) may find a certain passage easier to understand, despite differences in the depth of their philosophical knowledge.

It is phenomenology itself that proved me wrong. It was specifically our discussions of Husserl, combined with that of Dr. Costello's view on the phenomenological lives of children, that unwound this strange misunderstanding in my mind. Phenomenology, philosophy, literature, and life itself carry with them vast complexities, and never in our lives can we approach a new set of beliefs, way of thinking, or a new facet of the world without bringing along the influence of our past experiences. Our course, Husserl asks that we "bracket" those experiences in phenomenological study, in order to get at the crux of that which is perceived, but that practice is difficult and must be done consciously and with purpose. Phenomenology helped me to understand, especially through this semester, that experience itself is as good a teacher as any professor or parent. Experience can allow students with little to no prior philosophical "knowledge" to understand and draw out the intricacies and contours of our phenomenological material.

CONCLUSION

What we hope you can take away from the reflections of Brigid, Cecelia, and Lauren here is that the act of coteaching phenomenology, as a once-a-week, 2½ hour, upper-division philosophy course, produced important insights in both the registered students and in the instructional team. There is good reason for trying to implement this practice more widely, especially at smaller, liberal arts colleges where innovations in teaching are desired and rewarded. In what follows, I will give my own summary reflection on the experience and on the insights that were generated by the practice of coteaching..

Peter C.

For each course, we began the semester with readings by Edmund Husserl (2012). I took the lead in the beginning and focused our attention as a class, and as an instructional team, on themes of intentionality, perception, and intersubjectivity. A good deal of time of our first month, then, was spent unpacking the interaction between noesis and noema from *Ideas I* and the pairing of self and other from the 5th Cartesian Meditation.

As we discussed Husserl (2012) together as an instructional team in our independent study, I could see each coteacher developing a way forward in her role as coteaching. Lauren's insights concerning the "gap" between students and teachers, and the successful deployment of a manageable gap in coteaching, came out of a rich reflection that she did on two themes in Husserl—namely, intentionality and intersubjectivity. First, Lauren noticed, Husserl appears to manage the difference between an activity of lived experience and the object of that activity by means of his discovery of their correlation as noesis and noema. This prevents philosophy from becoming dumbstruck by the "veritable abyss" that opens up "between the meanings of consciousness and reality" (p. 95). Second, Lauren realized, the task that the description of pairing in Husserl's 5th Cartesian Meditation presents us is one of determining further the gap between oneself and the other. The gap between our subjectivities, then, is not simply a requirement to be accepted; it is also an invitation to further work together.

Lauren was not simply indebted to Husserl or to her own acts of explication of his works. Lauren's reflections on teaching, and on the idea of enacting a manageable gap, are also very much her own. Phenomenology showed her how not only to describe but also to enact meaningful limits to her acts of perception such that her perception could proceed further and inform more about the world. Lauren, in a real sense, I think, made headway with Husserl's very difficult notion of the epoche and its role in pedagogy.

As we moved on to Kant and Derrida around the notion of artwork, we began to more intentionally cooperative. Lauren and Brigid established mini-lectures and lead groups. And so together we saw the origins and the supersession of phenomenology. We saw how different the practice of establishing conditions for the possibility of something were from the description of phenomena as they demand to be described. And we also began to understand how phenomena were not just self-showing but rather surrounded by a particular halo of coappearances that needed to be described rigorously. We spent much of the second month then discussing Kant's (1987) description of beauty in the *Critique of Judgment* and of the *ergon* and *parergon* in Derrida's (1987) *Truth in Painting*.

As we moved through these two chunks of material, I noticed Brigid developing an interpretation of how someone like Derrida really was doing phenomenology when he talked about the latent problems or contradictions in Kant's descriptions. We needed to enlarge the epoche, Brigid thought, to allow for more than the noesis and noema in their paired interactions. We needed to bring in elements that only traced themselves within the phenomenological sphere.

Brigid's written reflection thus allows Merleau-Ponty (whom we read last) and Derrida to help situate self-perception within a much more complicated place. Going beyond the binaries of self and other, beyond Husserl's exploration of givenness and cogivenness, Brigid notices that what inspires givenness, the motor at least of most of phenomenology, is what does *not* fully appear, and what even *resists* appearing in its genesis and development—in this case the phenomena of learning and teaching and even self-perception.

What we have done as an instructional team, then, is not only to assist the class of undergraduates in their coming to terms for the first time with rigorous, difficult texts in phenomenology. What we have done is also to teach one another and ourselves about those same texts in the context of reflecting on the demands of coteaching.

With Cecelia, I believe that every student's experience in phenomenology and indeed in philosophy ought to be one of engaging the establishment of a community of inquiry and in the revision of one's assumptions by way of the *epoche* and the method of phenomenology itself. Like her, I believe that constant self-reflection on where I am as a teacher is integral to my capacity to communicate the text under discussion. On my own, and as an original phenomenologist, I believe that such insights as those of these three students, and indeed all our students, are possible by virtue of our ongoing contact, our pairing, with the *texts* of phenomenology. For above all it is these texts themselves (*zu den Sachen selbst*) that encourage coteaching and in front of which students can be guided according to the proper deployment of gap and of (dis)placement.

POSTSCRIPT

The practice of coteaching with undergraduates is now one that I have engaged in four different courses (two philosophy courses and two public service courses). The amount of work involved for the university professor is a good deal more than in an ordinary course. I have found that I need not only to prepare to cede some control and authority but also to be responsible, even without control, simultaneously for the growth and education of two very separate but intersecting groups of students. This practice, to say the least, is not easy and increases professorial vulnerability. Perhaps it needs to be said that I do not think every student is capable of succeeding at coteaching. However, philosophy as a discipline is, in my view, in decline within the halls of higher education. Inaugurating such a strategy or method may, at the least, enable the discipline to grow and flourish and to show students and administrators alike that it can be productive for human beings who want to recapture a sense of the meaningfulness of their own agency and existence.

REFERENCES

Barnett, R., & Phipps, A. (2007). Academic hospitality. *Arts and Humanities in Higher Education, 6*(3), 237–254.

Batchelor, D. (2006). Vulnerable voices: An examination of vulnerability in relation to student voice. *Educational Philosophy and Theory, 38*(6), 787–800.

Beach, A. L., Henderson, C., & Famiano, M. (2007). Co-teaching as faculty development model. In D. R. Robertson and L. B. Nilson (Eds.), *To improve the academy.* Jossey-Bass.

Derrida, J (1987). *The truth in painting.* University of Chicago Press.

Freire, P. (1972). *Pedagogy of the oppressed.* Herder and Herder.

Husserl, E. (2012). *Ideas: General introduction to pure phenomenology.* Routledge.

Jaarsma, A. S., Kinaschuk, K., & Xing, L. (2016). Kierkegaard, despair, and the possibility of education: Teaching existentialism existentially. *Studies in Philosophy and Education, 35*(5), 445–461.

Kant, I. (1987). *Critique of judgment* (Werner S. Pluhar, Trans.). Hackett.

Larson, C. W., & Goebel, A., J. (2008). Putting theory into practice: A professional development school/university co-teaching project. *Journal of the Scholarship of Teaching and Learning, 8*(2), 52–61.

Longo, N. V. (2013). Deliberative pedagogy in the community: Connecting deliberative dialogue, community engagement, and democratic education. *Journal of Public Deliberation, 9*(2), Article 16. http://www.publicdeliberation.net/jpd/vol9/iss2/art16

Merleau-Ponty, M. (1964). The child's relations with others. In *Primacy of perception.* Northwestern University Press.

Plato. (2002). *Five dialogues* (G. M. A. Grube, Trans.). Hackett.

Plato. (1992). *Republic* (G. M. A. Grube, Trans.). Hackett.

Sartre, J.-P (1989). *No exit and three other plays.* Vintage International.

Woodburn, C. A. (2010). Students as coteachers in an urban high school mathematics class. In C. Murhpy & K. Scantlebury (Eds.), *Coteaching in international contexts: Research and practice* (pp. 369–382). Springer.

NOTE

1. The slave's inability to participate in "institutional" learning allows Socrates in *Meno* to show that a purely abstract concept (the number pi) is something anyone can be brought to acknowledge and deploy by means of the right method. The slave thus is essential in showing everyone else in the conversation how ethics, if not teachable, is something that one can be brought to recognize. In *Republic*, Thrasymachus is by all accounts oppositional to Socrates and yet, Socrates says, "I too begged him to stay, and I said to him 'After hurling such a speech at us, Thrasymachus, do you intend to leave before adequately instructing us or finding out whether you were right or not'" (344 d-e, pp. 20–21).

ABOUT THE AUTHORS

Daniel Adsett has a PhD in philosophy from Marquette University and is currently an Assistant Professor at the American University in Bulgaria.

Dan Bradley is a Professor of Philosophy at Gonzaga University. He earned his PhD in Philosophy from the National University of Ireland.

Peter Costello is professor of philosophy and chair of the department of Public and Community Service at Providence College.

Brigid Flaherty is a PhD.student in Political Science.

Steven Fleet is a 30-year educator in education, philosophy, and the arts dedicated to promoting critical and creative thinking.

Christopher J. Kazanjian, PhD, is an Associate Professor of Educational Psychology at El Paso Community College.

Sandra M. Kazanjian, MA, is a Campus Teaching Coach in Literacy/Biliteracy at Western Hills Elementary School.

Cecelia Little is a JD student with a particular interest in jurisprudence.

Tyler Loveless is an editor and researcher in Washington, DC. He received his MA in Philosophy from George Washington University.

James M. Magrini taught philosophy and ethics at College of DuPage for 15 years. He has authored seven books, including *Heidegger After the Turn: Literature, Poetry, and Education* (Routledge), coauthored with Elias Schwieler.

Lauren Manton is a senior business intelligence developer and aspiring thought leader in her field.

Paul Michalec brings to his teaching an affinity for ecological thinking, interdisciplinary knowledge, holistic models of teaching, and transformative learning opportunities.

Katherine Hall Newburgh, PhD, is the founder of Books of Eden Publishing. She is the author of *The New Eden: Paradise Retold*.

Dan Riordan, PhD, is an Assistant Professor at Pacific University. He is passionate about supporting teachers and their well-being.

Stephanie Schneider is an Associate Professor in the School of Education at the State University of New York College at Old Westbury. Her research interests include the philosophy of education, the use of dialogue in pedagogy, teacher education, and assessment.

Elias Schwieler is Associate Professor in the Department of Education at Stockholm University. His recent publications include the monographs *Aporias of Translation: Education, Literature, and Philosophy* (Springer) and *Heidegger After the Turn: Literature, Poetry, and Education* (Routledge), coauthored with James M. Magrini (Routledge).

Glen L. Sherman, Associate Professor and Chair of Psychology, Saint Elizabeth University, earned his doctorate at Duquesne University's existential-phenomenological psychology program.

Aaron S. Zimmerman is an Assistant Professor of Curriculum Studies and Teacher Education in the College of Education at Texas Tech University. He received his PhD in Curriculum, Instruction, and Teacher Education from Michigan State University.

CPSIA information can be obtained
at www.ICGtesting.com
Printed in the USA
BVHW031938150722
641988BV00003B/43